Vietnam Awakening

... you're on earth,
there's no cure for that.
— Samuel Beckett

Vietnam Awakening

*My Journey from Combat to
the Citizens' Commission of Inquiry
on U.S. War Crimes in Vietnam*

MICHAEL UHL

McFarland & Company, Inc., Publishers
Jefferson, North Carolina, and London

LIBRARY OF CONGRESS CATALOGUING-IN-PUBLICATION DATA

Uhl, Michael, 1944–
     Vietnam awakening : my journey from combat to the Citizens'
Commission of Inquiry on U.S. War Crimes in Vietnam /
Michael Uhl.
          p.   cm.
     Includes bibliographical references and index.

     ISBN-13: 978-0-7864-3074-1
     softcover : 50# alkaline paper (∞)

     1. Vietnam War, 1961–1975 — Personal narratives — American.
     2. Vietnam War, 1961–1975 — Protest movements — United States.
     3. Vietnam War, 1961–1975 — Atrocities.   4. Ulh, Michael, 1944–
     I. Title.
     DS559.5.U35   2007
     959.704'3 — dc22   2007015653

British Library cataloguing data are available

Cover photograph: Rocket attack in Duc Pho, March 1969

Manufactured in the United States of America

*McFarland & Company, Inc., Publishers
     Box 611, Jefferson, North Carolina 28640
     www.mcfarlandpub.com*

In memory of Pamela Booth

❖   ❖   ❖

For Susan

Acknowledgments

I would like to acknowledge the readers who commented on my manuscript at various stages of its preparation, beginning with my doctoral committee: Rita Arditti, Elizabeth Kamarck Minnich, David Smith, Norman Rasulis, Joseph Gerson, Diane Phenneger Mikhlin and Georg Fertig. The text as it generally appears here was edited by Steve Fraser from a much longer dissertation under contract from the Veterans Administration, which generously underwrote the cost of my doctoral program. My good friends Dan Rosen, Tom Goulde and Maureen O'Connor read the longest versions of the text, and offered welcome support and encouragement. Thanks is also due to another good friend, Francine Smilen, for her suggestion on the title, and to Mary Susannah Robbins for her comments on the preface. And not least I am grateful to my *cari amici* in Sicily, Pascale Dodin, Salvatore Maniscalco, and Turi Dimino for their support in the compilation of the index. All errors and omissions are the responsibility of the author.

In the words of Noam Chomsky, who has read and commented on this manuscript, this is my *Bildungsroman*, the story of my coming of age.

Michael Uhl
Walpole, Maine

Table of Contents

Preface

Vietnam Awakening: My Journey from Combat to the Citizens' Commission of Inquiry on U.S. War Crimes in Vietnam was written to satisfy, in part, the requirements of a doctoral program at the graduate school of the Union Institute. Within my combined fields, American studies and writing (creative nonfiction), this text serves as a demonstrable synthesis of that eccentric interdisciplinary pairing.

While a memoir narrative threads the entire text, the social and historical contexts for the autobiographical elements are ever widening as the story unfolds. The first chapter of Book One, "Days of Slumber," offers a background sketch of a boy growing up in a materially secure and conformist suburb of Long Island just after World War II. Rather than belabor the internal dynamics of family and psychological development that more closely typify the memoir idiom, I have sought to capture several broader external influences that better explain — at least to myself— how I came to serve in Vietnam, and why my subsequent political and social awakening should not be misconstrued as a "conversion experience" rooted exclusively in the horrors of war.

From the inside out I was always in conflict with my childhood environment. But what I've discovered in this abbreviated retrospective is how the cultural messages I heard most clearly in my youth always pointed toward a non-conventional life as the most authentic path for me. Being analytical by temperament, I may sometimes write with too cold an eye when recalling what I did or how I acted in a given circumstance and thus miss or avoid an opportunity to properly acknowledge — even repent — some particular moral failing or character flaw. But in such a tale as this of innocence, war, and redemption, the facts — frequently unwrapped by my own considered reflections — can and do speak quite revealingly for themselves.

Military training and a stint of stateside duty provide the setting for

1

Chapter II, "Days of Wakening." The deep aversion I felt toward serving in the military had been momentarily disabled when I joined ROTC as an undergraduate senior just as the draft threatened to remove me from college and deny me the bachelor's degree I viewed as the equivalent of a union card. Despite my assignment to the comparatively elite Counterintelligence Corps, where I was exempt from the more robotic rituals of the parade ground and camp discipline, the confining dimensions of garrison life gave palpable and immediate scope to my social alienation. So much so that I volunteered for war to escape the army. In Vietnam I would find both a lifelong subject and, more importantly, an existential *raison d'être*. Chapters III and IV, "Days of War," is my memoir of that experience where I learned, if nothing else, what I would really be willing to fight for — or, in this case — against.

Book Two chronicles through sixteen contiguous episodes my immediate postwar years as a front line activist in the anti–Vietnam War veterans' movement. It is in the recalling of these "Days of Reckoning" that I witness my personality, chronically ambivalent and passive, suddenly explode into action to the point of shameless self-projection upon the stage of history. After Vietnam the antiwar movement struck me as not just the only rational alternative to political apathy, but the psychological alternative to madness.

A structural shift gradually occurs in the manuscript's second half as I, the memoirist, relinquish my centrality in the ongoing first person narrative in favor of a more distanced micro-historical study — buttressed amply by citations — of the New Left's political culture as practiced by a small band of radicals calling itself the Citizens' Commission of Inquiry on U.S. War Crimes in Vietnam (CCI), eager to organize antiwar veterans around the issue of American atrocities in Vietnam.

❖   ❖   ❖

The war and antiwar stories in this book are substantially about the abuse of Vietnamese civilians and about torture — torture being employed as SOP, standard operating procedure, in interrogations throughout Vietnam, a practice which many Vietnam veterans would confirm in public testimony under CCI's auspices. As this book goes to press the topic of the American military's use of torture in Iraq and Afghanistan, in Guantanamo, and in the secret prisons of the CIA sequestered at unknown locations around the world, is once again a question of grave concern to anyone who values the conventions of war and the sanctity of human rights. What CCI defined in the early 1970s as a *de facto* policy of torture, the United States government would now establish as policy *de jure*, sanctioned by Congress as the law of the land.

But the focus of this memoir goes beyond the political undertakings of the CCI principals and their veteran collaborators, and attempts to portray as well a certain time and place and way of being. Despite its origins in the culture of the Old Left of the pre–Vietnam era, CCI was categorically a creature of the New Left and the alternative culture of the sixties and early seventies. When New Leftists claimed that the "personal is political," it was not just an empty slogan we spouted to distance the politics of our generation from that of Leftists who came before.

For almost two years at CCI, or the Citizens' Commission, as we often referred to ourselves, I worked under the tutelage of, then alongside, Tod Ensign and Jeremy Rifkin. We comprehended politics as the achievable approximation of our distant dreams, as greater than our organized opposition within the pre-existing channels of power. In varying degrees we attempted to live our politics. Politics was not just an avocation, but a *lifestyle,* that word itself a by-product of the times when masses of young people strove not just to think, but to inhabit, the utopia we preached across the entire range of prevailing social and economic relations.

To honor these earnest, if utopian, aspirations, I have given some space to recording throughout the narrative how we interacted, behaved and even felt in the course of carrying out our contribution to ending the Vietnam War, which was our movement's greatest achievement. We did not make the revolution that many of us desired or imagined by mounting a serious challenge to an economic system we believed to be based inherently on exploitation. But our movement's collective experiments with alternative institutions and relationships and with cultural informality in many forms did empower a generational shift that gave rise to the existing landscape of identity politics with its not inconsiderable legacy of immediate benefits primarily to women and minorities.

Method and Sources

While the first section of this work, designated Book One, belongs exclusively to the genre of the memoir, the accounts therein do not depend entirely on the vagaries of memory. At my disposal while I wrote were various kinds of records, scrapbooks, yearbooks, photo albums, and, for the chapters on my army training and service and on the war itself, a full set of military orders, several notebooks, my war diary, and my own side of the correspondence I conducted with my parents from Vietnam. These materials proved invaluable in confirming, or in some cases correcting, recollections of events that had grown hazy over time.

Throughout the text I try to maintain some connection in voice and consciousness to the person I was when the events being described took place. At the same time, I can't pretend that these accounts are not in often imperceptible ways influenced, shaped and guided by the person I had become by the time of the writing. This murky ambiguity between past and present is, it strikes me, at the heart of every memoir.

The names of most acquaintances or comrades who appear in my narrative have been fictionalized, or identified by first name only, to protect the innocent ... and the guilty, except in the cases of those, who, like me, chose to make their experiences public or who were high ranking officers and officials, and therefore public figures with no claim to anonymity.

As a political memoir Book Two is written in the tradition of an eyewitness history. The text is heavily documented by accounts of CCI's political work which appeared in scores of newspaper articles, both here and abroad. As a formal entity with an office and staff CCI generated its own records, policy papers, incoming and outgoing correspondence, press releases, funding appeals, and the like. These records are housed in the Division of Rare and Manuscript Collections of the Cornell University Library, where I spent several days consulting them for this account.

The bibliography appearing at the end of this work is somewhat misleading, and pertains more to the general research and course work I performed in my doctoral studies than to the work at hand. At the same time the readings and study that informed me also inform the text in many places appropriate to the topics under discussion.

BOOK ONE

I

Days of Slumber

The suburbs exist without a rational past and without the
"big events" of history.
— *Robert Smithson*

The class of '61 began its final year at Babylon High in the late summer
of 1960. Two months later, by a slim majority, the nation elected John F.
Kennedy its first Roman Catholic president. Our own straw poll among the
seniors favored Richard Nixon two to one. Though very much a faithful
Catholic at the time, in this poll I too had cast my vote for the Republican.

In those days Babylon was small town–Republican in spades like most
townships on the once rural eastern half of Long Island. The GOP exercised
control over local patronage. I got my job at the town pool one summer
because I could say "Republican" when some local hack asked how my parents
were registered to vote. My being for Nixon in the high school mock
election was no expression of genuine political preference, just a kind of
socially conditioned reflex.

As for curiosity about the actual workings of the government day to day?
Zilch. Fortunately, a history teacher at Babylon High named Clyde (we all
knew he was *queer*) did provoke in me a tiny ripple of enthusiasm for events
in the larger world. Clyde's class was a time for debating international affairs:
Should Red China be admitted into the United Nations? Should Charles de
Gaulle get a swift kick in the rear as payback for his arrogant, relentless
anti–Americanism? After all we'd done for *him*!

Some taint of the isolationist stigma that runs so deeply in our culture
already had its stamp on my consciousness. I had based my choice of Spanish over French to fulfill a one-year modern language requirement exclusively
on the bitter revulsion I felt for de Gaulle and his alleged treachery. This was
the moral equivalent of a political act, and of the worst kind. Unlike my vote

Parading with my Cub Scout pack, Lindenhurst, New York, early 1950s. I am in the middle ground at right center, bisected by the staff of the guidon.

for Nixon, to whom I was totally indifferent, this twisted ambivalence toward the French involved emotions I neither controlled nor understood.

Such prejudices were easily inflamed by the indoctrination around patriotic sentiments that most everyone in mainstream America had been steeped in then from childhood through the ubiquity of our national rituals: we rose on little legs each school day to pledge allegiance to the flag, then sang "My Country 'Tis of Thee" (because even opera stars can't seem to bridge the octave range of our national anthem); we grew up little Pilgrims acting out the national myths, digesting the most rosy vision of our country's past and its exalted placement among the world's other inhabitants; and boys marched, marched, marched as scouts or Little Leaguers in militarily accented parades each Armistice Day and on the Fourth of July. We were in the army already, and didn't even know it.

By senior year in '61 I readily accepted the realities and limits of the American political system. By inclination as well as social reflex I had come to view active participation in the body politic as both unattainable and undesirable, a form of specialization reserved for those whose talent for power and craving for personal attention made them ideal candidates for public office. I was not to govern but to be governed, consigned, when I reached my majority, to the passive role of casting a ballot, ill-informed or otherwise, in the annual electoral

lottery which remains the philo-
sophical bedrock of what we call
democracy. This was not cynicism,
but realpolitik American-style.
And, frankly, it was okay with me.

It would have been the very
exceptional student at Babylon High
in 1960/61 who could have foreseen
the circumstances in which direct
confrontation with authority to
achieve some principled group or
individual objective might become,
not simply necessary, but unavoidable. And while I myself was still
a decade from being able to distinguish a principle from an opinion,
I could not deny having witnessed
throughout the previous year the
bold deeds of those determined
young Negroes we'd all seen on the
TV news sitting-in at Woolworth's
lunch counters throughout the seg-
regated South, demanding to be
served.

With my mother Margaret circa 1944 or 45.

But on what basis — even when one's mind rebelled at the very idea of
injustice, as mine often did — could we, the privileged children of comfortable white suburbanites, construct a parallel reality between the world of those
black youngsters and our own? We lived outside of history, or thought we
did, which amounted to the same thing.

The vanguard of what would become an alternative youth culture in the
final years of the decade was already taking tender steps toward Babylon by
1961. And not just with rock and roll (each generation seems entitled to its
own brand of musical madness, a kind of safety valve to channel or vent the
anarchic energies of its young). The still partially jammed messages of a deeper
alienation, which attacked the ethos of suburban conformism at its base,
emanated from the fringes of the beat and jazz scenes holed up within the
New York urban core some forty miles to our west; its signals floated toward
us on the winds of popular culture to find a fertile reception among those
already shadowed by instincts of rebellion.

I had just turned sixteen, a necking party in a girlfriend's finished basement, her older brother intoning by candlelight the title poem from Lawrence

Ferlinghetti's *A Coney Island of the Mind*, as we snapped our fingers the way we pictured hip patrons doing at some coffee house in Greenwich Village. These images came to us typically in ersatz documentary form through photo essays in magazines like *Life* and *Look*, or heavily parodied in pioneering comedies on early television. In such signs we might, when looking back, read forecasts of the culture-storms already in formation that would sweep away the suffocating Zeitgeist of the fifties.

Those barbs of dissension which made their way to early television were gentle enough; but their impact should not be undervalued. Among some baby boomers they pointed to the insurgent possibilities of merely raising questions. Take, for instance, the absolute alchemy in the zany antics of comic Ernie Kovacs in whose clutch the leaden alphabet of goofball slapstick was transformed into a genre of black humor oddly palatable to the very audiences whose straight-laced conventions it so tirelessly mocked.

Kovacs was an American Beckett, a master of the absurd morality skit. Witness his bizarre, hilarious Nairobi Trio (teaming Ernie with wife Edie Adams and, sometimes, a then virtually unknown Jack Lemmon). As the scene opens a combo of musicians, suspiciously simian, is seen seated at their instruments. One of them chomping a trademark cigar is obviously Kovacs. As the group's leader it is his duty to enforce the assembly-line-like tempo of the trio's single composition, played over and over with a rigidity that evokes the image of automatons responding to the hidden levers of a barrel organ.[1]

It is the tyranny of the metronome constantly subverted, however, by Kovacs's two recalcitrant sidemen, whose little riffs of improvisation win them withering double takes, if not a rap on their derby-domed heads with a baton. There can be no dissonance, Kovacs seemed to be suggesting, in the chain of command, no crack in the consensus of what amounted to an almost paranoid state of self-satisfaction which the fruits of power and prosperity had instilled in the American mind during the decade that followed the end of World War II.

In its infancy television was more chaotic, more spontaneous than today. After all, much of it was live. And the very culture of conformity, so stifling to genuine political discourse, gave rise to an explosion of satire, mostly in written form to be sure,[2] with a smaller infusion finding its way to the variety shows of fifties television. The Brechtian edge to this humor was as sobering as it was hilarious.

The short-lived, almost obscenely talented, team of Mike Nichols and Elaine May, whose act — invariably urban in setting and circumstance — possessed a fierce, in-the-know realism and knock-you-down intelligence, exposed middlebrow pretense to have no more substance than the crepe bunting we wound around our small town viewing stands for patriotic celebrations. Nichols's persona, for me, communicated the startling revelation that it was — or could be — cool for boys to be both smart ass and smart.

Then, of course, there was the peerless Lenny Bruce. But Lenny was seldom seen on television, and then only in some alloyed form which muted his highly charged and libertarian social commentary. Lenny was the true opposition, the *discouraging word* personified, and, therefore, suppressed, confined to the live, but small, audiences of the urban club scene. Before I had listened to his recordings, I knew of Lenny more as *cause célèbre* from highly publicized arrests for using dirty language in his monologues than from any firsthand exposure to his provocative and mordant wit.

I did gain one existential take on Bohemia during the first trip I'd ever taken into Manhattan without the confining presence of my parents and siblings. Just before summer break and eighth grade graduation in 1957, a buddy and I rode the train and made our way to Chinatown to buy Fourth of July fireworks for our classmates and ourselves.

This accomplished, following the usual make-believe cloak and dagger intrigues that neophytes and young boys thrive on, we wandered to the Village. And there we saw strange sights in the vicinity of Bleecker and Mac-Dougal. A hirsute heap of a man with long, full beard and dressed in coveralls straddled a folding chair on the sidewalk outside his bric-a-brac and old book shop; his *old lady*, done up like a tintype Frau from frontier times, but with thick wool socks and sandals, was handing him a cup of *tea*. We knew what that meant.

Direct brushes with big city life were rare, exotic exceptions to our normal social round, which, in those final high school years, remained decidedly, voluntarily, non-urban.[3] Even after we were old enough to drive, the idea that there was somewhere better to go or to be beyond the village and its surrounding watering holes remained a subject unexplored. Everything we needed was close to home; we wallowed in that insular atmosphere of provincial bliss.

If we chose to travel anywhere as far as forty miles it was always east to the beaches of Westhampton, where the club scene was as hot as a Brooklyn night in August. The beaches loomed large in our lives, especially in summer, but even in the depths of winter groups of us would sometimes cross the bridge and drive to Jones Beach to brave the icy winds blowing off the inhospitable ocean, while we walked the empty boardwalks under steel gray skies.

Mostly, though, we drove to local bars, like one favorite just across the bay from Babylon. The Oak Beach Inn was a rustic clubhouse set in the lee of the dunes. New York's legal drinking age was then eighteen, and the OBI catered mostly to a set of young people in their late teens and early twenties. But I was just sixteen, though barely, when I first went there, showing a friend's older brother's driver's license when we were carded at the door.

Our favorite watering hole, the Oak Beach Inn.

It was a moment of high drama in my young life. I was tall but baby faced; if I failed to pass I'd have to tuck my tail and ask my friend Billy, who, approaching seventeen, was already an OBI regular, to drive us back to the mainland where we faced the prospect of a boring evening beside the record player listen to the Kingston Trio sing "scotch & soda, mud in your eye," instead of quaffing highballs at the OBI. I had memorized the vital data and Billy quizzed me as we neared the dimly lit doorway of the bar's front entrance. But the bouncer, looking only for plausibility, eyed the box marked "date of birth," then waved me in without a word.

This subterfuge was not about drinking; our local culture did not prohibit young people from experimenting, more or less openly, with alcoholic beverages. With a wink and a nod we were schooled to hold our liquor. Being inside the OBI had more immediate social ramifications: it signaled that I could now mingle officially with the college crowd in a pseudo-adult world controlled, paradoxically, on behalf of the young by grownups who showed little inclination to function *in loco parentis*.

Since I would not turn eighteen until well into the second semester of my freshman year in college, and I began to frequent bars more or less regularly several months before my sixteenth birthday, I had come to rely for proof of age primarily on a false ID which Billy taught me how to manufacture. Babylon had a branch of the Motor Vehicles Bureau, and the blank forms for driver's licenses were readily available to anyone who walked into the office. What these forms lacked to make them official was the state stamp, a facsimile of which could be traced onto a blank license using a piece of carbon paper. It was hardly a perfect forgery, but I don't recall that anyone ever challenged my ID's authenticity on that or any other grounds.

This high school social whirl, organized around dances, bar hopping, private parties, or seasonal events like sail boat regattas, sustained the largest, most cohesive community in which I have ever functioned. No little measure of this cohesion was derived from a concrete accident of circumstance, privileged youth with its abundance of leisure; but geography was also a factor. From the intersection of the two main streets in *downtown* Babylon you could reach a village boundary by walking a mile or so in any direction. Half the members of this teen community lived within easy walking or biking distance of each other's houses.

On the set of *Ten Little Indians* at Babylon High School, 1960.

This circle of youths whose total numbered, perhaps, seventy-five to a hundred, and included underclassmen as well as seniors, was by no means open to all. Mere residence within the village, while important, did not convey automatic inclusion; nor did nonresidence necessarily mean exclusion. (A few of the kids, Italian for the most part, were from a nearby village and had been sharing our high school for several years while their own was being built.) You had to have the right stuff. Those from Babylon's old families were charter members; they formed the group's inner clique. But good looks, personality, athletic prowess, wit, and school spirit were attributes that might gain admittance for a given individual. Beyond the unspoken status conferred on those of the old guard, other restrictions of social or ethnic caste were somewhat vague, but most of the insiders tended to be college bound, on the school's academic rather than its commercial track.

It's not that I was so popular in school; more important, I was not unpopular. My position, while never tenuous, was somewhere on the mid-to-outer

With my sister Barbara Anne and father Wilbur on Fire Island, New York, August 1947.

rings, a source of insecurity or disappointment only on those few occasions when, having received mixed signals to move closer to the center, I found the air of friendship and compatibility too thin. But if acceptance by the innermost elites often eluded me, I was never one to push or curry favor. It already suited me to be an outsider on the inside. I had an easy way about me then and moved between the factions for the most part without provoking animosities. This endowment of my personality was recognized by one perceptive wag among my classmates who chose the legend for my senior photo in the yearbook: "Nice 'n easy does it." Only years later did I realize that this was not entirely a compliment.

This observation was confirmed, to my satisfaction at least, at my 40th high school reunion in August 2001. As I worked the banquet hall at one point greeting folks who, for the most part, I had never known and did not recognize, one gent commented, "I see that you still have that same agreeable personality." Though I correctly read his edge I wasn't the least bit offended, but rather, ironically amused. In fact, my war-trimmed "personality" has, for many decades now, been perceived minimally, by most I believe, as standoffish. If there had been old business to transact at that reunion I completely blew any opportunity of doing that. And that is the essence of my tale since Vietnam.

The Same Past in Wide-Angled View

Beneath that supposedly nice 'n easy exterior lurked nothing if not insecurity. A transition my own family had undergone in moving between what were two very different types of communities in 1955 had confronted me abruptly with the dilemma of class identity. In the village of Lindenhurst, only a few miles from Babylon, where I spent my first eleven years, our neighborhood had been essentially blue collar. Next door on one side was the family of a house painter, and on the other, an electrician who worked at Republic Aviation, a so-called defense plant, as did my father. My best friend's father was with the local highway department, and my sister Barbara's best friend's father delivered mail. There were some shopkeepers; a Jewish neighbor owned a small dry cleaner, and another man, a local garage and gas station.

Like my parents, many of our neighbors had occupied these new homes just as they were beginning family life. And some of the men, including my father, faced unparalleled opportunities in their careers, because war prosperity and victory had ushered in an era of upward mobility within the

Babylon High School senior yearbook photograph taken in fall 1960; I was sixteen years old.

United States the likes of which no nation on earth has ever experienced. Earlier opportunities for mobility — especially in the form of college credentials — had been shattered for many in my parents' generation by the Great Depression; now, an expanding economy would favor, first, the ambitious and the competent and help to compensate for those disappointments in the thirties. Income would become a mark of success and convey, at least within the confines of the new middle class, a status every bit as socially negotiable as a college diploma.

By the time I was ten or eleven this postwar sociology was just beginning to change the face of what I remember, perhaps with exaggerated fondness, as our distinctly non-status-conscious neighborhood. On our block my own family seemed to pace the new order; we were the first household within our circle to possess two late model cars. But the tallying of one's possessions to measure status had not yet risen much above a whisper among my playmates. That insidious notion that the social worth of one's family could be equated to the portfolio of its consumer goods was only beginning to undermine the unspoken, egalitarian solidarity which, in my imagination at least, characterizes all essentially working class neighborhoods.

But because of our two cars and certain other signs — the sweet smell of success had already altered slightly the manner in which my parents talked and carried themselves — I was vaguely aware that our family had begun its climb to another plateau. This sense of an impending change did not prevent me from being completely blindsided by the announcement toward the end of my sixth grade year that, in the summer to come, we would be moving.

This was not good news. No adolescent can be expected to view with equanimity the loss of a beloved childhood home — especially when it is the only world he or she has ever known. But in the adult mind, a voluntary uprooting such as this is small sacrifice for the excitement of exploring new horizons. Kids then didn't have rights, least of all the right to verbalize opinions and complaints; we had chores. So it was very much in tune with the logic of postwar mobility that, by 1955, when my father had moved securely into the ranks of middle management, we would decamp for a locale of more genteel surroundings: enter Babylon.

Babylon

One difference in the residential composition of the two communities was strikingly apparent, though, at first, it only vaguely registered in my own awareness. Where breadwinners among the old neighbors had been tradesmen, or occupied low level white collar positions, our new neighborhood was essentially professional. There were several lawyers, two school principals, an Episcopal priest, a bank vice president (when being a VP meant something), a department store buyer, two or three owners of successful businesses, a film company executive, a *Newsday* reporter, an optometrist, a justice of the peace, and a psychiatrist.

If Levittown, Long Island, had provided the residential model for mass suburbanization of an internal American migration after World War Two, our little enclave in Babylon — where each of the twenty original homes was an exact duplicate of its neighbor — was a prototype for the second phase of the same phenomenon. Here was a group that was making it with the means to custom-build or to buy an existing older home in the same village if they had wanted too. But they elected instead to create an instant community in which each member would begin on an equal footing with every other as a newcomer.

In their unique contribution to the saga of the American melting pot, these neighbors were truly exceptional. They had, in more cases than not, broken with the prevailing counter-tendency within the world of their parents by marrying outside their faiths, their national groups, and in some instances, their class.

The jab-hook combination of the Depression and the War may have set back the time table of career ambitions for my parents' generation as a whole. But those monumental upheavals also lent some credence to the ideal of a single national American identity by helping to foment a new outbreak of assimilation, the results of which were readily apparent in my own family and in the households of my new neighbors. Not only did we have a near-even count of Catholics and Protestants — plus a significant number of Jews — in this new development, but they were mingled through marriage in virtually all the permutations, both ethnic and denominational, that the composition of metropolitan New York's population then made possible; there was even a token Hispanic, though a Negro, it need hardly be mentioned, would still have been excluded under any circumstances.

My own parents typified the group; they overlapped ethnically — my father being all German, my mother German-Irish — but her side was Catholic and his Lutheran. Of equal, if not greater, impact than this religious difference on my personal formation was the fact that my parents were also from slightly different class backgrounds.

My mother Margaret's German people were more established than Dad's. They'd settled in Brooklyn in the 1830s; my father's side did not arrive until the seventies and eighties. Mom's Irish father was a college trained engineer, albeit the product of a night school education, and their family had enjoyed something of a middle-class life until her father died young and left them penniless. My father Wilbur's father was a master electrician who also made a good living, but the family's American roots still lay in shallow soil; their ties to New York German immigrant culture, while somewhat thin by the time I came on the scene, were by no means completely shredded. On my mother's side, moreover, a few men of her parents' generation had, like her father, already climbed into the professions, most notably her mother's brother, a prominent attorney, and one-time president of the Brooklyn Bar Association.

My own awakening to the existence of classes, however, was triggered by an incident in St. Joseph's schoolyard among my eighth grade classmates a year or so after our move from Lindenhurst. A group of boys huddled in serious discussion considering the options for high school in the following year. Two or three, somewhat pretentiously, were musing about their chances of attending an elite college preparatory school like Andover or Choate.

The talk knocked me off my perch. Hadn't it been assumed that those of us with the grades and financial means would go to private Catholic schools in the city? All that year we'd been taking entrance exams toward that end to narrow down our choices. Then, out of nowhere, came this alien chitchat about prep schools. In a gust of insight I began to grasp what it was that distinguished members of my middle class from theirs: the existence within this old Yankee village of a culture of manners whose social frames of reference lay outside the scope of my own experience.

The Catholic Thing

The first two years of high school I commuted on the Long Island Railroad along with a half-dozen other local boys to Archbishop Molloy in New York City's borough of Queens. Run by the Marists, Molloy, formerly St. Ann's Academy in Manhattan, was increasingly oriented toward the Long Island suburbs, where many of the natural constituents of such schools had been resettling over the past decade.

The mission of the Catholic teaching orders was not, except in rare cases, to nurture open-ended learning, nor to encourage independence of mind and spirit — scholasticism sought to replace all doubts with certainty — but to toughen the laity to defend the interests of the Church and its faithful against the hegemonic presence of American Protestantism, and to breed conformity to the will and wishes of authority. In fulfillment of these goals some of the Marists indulged sadistic proclivities, like one Brother Ludwig, who dropped me in the hallway with a solid punch to the solar plexus for talking during an outdoor prayer session where the entire student body stood in formation reciting the rosary under the hot sun for what seemed like hours.

I can recall little that was positive about my time at Molloy; indeed, I can recall almost nothing. My most vivid memories are of riding the 7:33 express from Babylon to Jamaica every school day for two years posed as a miniature businessman in a suit and tie, reading the daily sports pages, playing cards and smoking Camels. But the school itself with its oppressive, institutional atmosphere has left a faint but foul taste. Which makes it all the more curious that, at the start of my junior year, I entered Marist Prep — a kind of seminary — having temporarily deluded myself about receiving a call from God — a vocation, in Catholic parlance — to join the very religious order I by now thoroughly despised.

My motives were inseparable from a secret ambition to attend "prep school" which first sprouted in that eighth grade school yard; and while Marist Prep was hardly what my classmates had been talking about, it was the only shot at boarding school I was ever likely to get. The power of this fantasy reveals how I chose to pattern my identity on the ideals of Babylon over those of Lindenhurst, and in this way, resolve whatever confusion or guilt I felt about

being caught between the classes. Later I would complete my external transformation by consciously adopting the Ivy League look: hair cut short, yet
parted; the uniform *de rigueur* of chinos, broadcloth shirts, and penny
loafers — having passed rather quickly around age fourteen through the alternative pompadour-coiffed, continental style of the rival, essentially working
class faction, the "hoods."

At fifteen I was chaffing at the bit of parental control; I dreaded returning to Molloy for another year. Since the option of transferring to Babylon
High was never raised, I conjured the smoke screen of a religious calling to
provide necessary cover for the radical change of scenery I seemed so intent
on bringing about. Still it would be inaccurate to imply that my vocation was
a conscious fabrication, or that I had in some way severed the umbilical that
linked me to my faith. I was, like many teens, a reluctant practitioner. But
Catholicism continued to feed my spiritual fires and to enrich my inner life
in immeasurable ways, providing a cultural framework that, even after decades
of separation from the Church, has never ceased to influence my thinking.

What I learned during those six months in the Marist juniorate at Esopus, New York — housed in the old Paine Whitney estate on the craggy wooded
palisades overlooking the Hudson River — was that communal life is anathema to someone with my peculiar brand of abashed individualism. From that
point onward I would grow increasingly aware of my need for anonymity of
a type that, paradoxically, submission of the self to a group does not permit.

Seminary provided the occasion for another important self-discovery; on
those Sundays once a month when families came to visit, my hormonal hack-
les would rise to fever pitch whenever I met this or that fetching sister of a
brother seminarian. And I knew then that I could never accept a vow of celibacy.

Finally one wintry Friday afternoon, having convinced myself that I
could no longer tolerate Esopus another day, I marched into the office of the
headmaster and announced I would be leaving on the morning train for home.
Within a week I asked — and received — my father's permission to smoke in
public, and by the week thereafter I was in the arms of a buxom sixteen year
old from a neighboring village, furiously petting every chance I could get. I
had transferred to Babylon's public high school, and for the next year and a
half, reveled in the high water of my teenage years.

1961–1968

Between that magic summer of 1961 and the hour I was called to war in
1968 lay the seven years of my life that I understand the least. Many important
memories populate that period, but, overall, it was a time of ill appropriated

opportunities which began not quite five months after my seventeenth birthday when I arrived in Olean, New York, to enter St. Bonaventure University as a freshman.

This choice of schools reflected an obvious continuity with the course my education had taken to date. Except for that brief interval at Babylon High I had always attended parochial schools. Quite logically the guidance counselor at Babylon had promoted this particular college for myself and five other graduating Catholic boys on the grounds that we could all get in, and none of us had strong opinions about going anywhere else.

Under the tutelage of Franciscan friars St. Bonaventure retained the air of a medieval monastery. Freshmen wore beanies and special neckties and underwent a month long hazing. Chapel on Sundays and Holy Days was compulsory, as was membership in ROTC for the first two years, a condition linked to Bonnies' status as a land grant institution. Each evening we were required to sit at our dorm room desks from seven to nine with doors wide open, while the resident monk patrolled the corridor reciting his beads or his breviary. Only on Saturday nights were freshmen allowed an escape from campus, and then only till midnight. I made the dean's list both semesters, and at the end of the year, transferred to Georgetown University.

I had mutinied against the confinement, the harsh winter of upstate New York's snow-bound southern tier, the rust-belt dreariness of the town's depressed economic life. But at St. Bonaventure I not only acquired the academic credentials to transfer to a better school, but the rationale for making the move appear a necessity.

Unlike many Americans who routinely founder in modern language studies, I had discovered late in high school a knack for Spanish. At Bonnies I was perhaps the top Spanish language student in the freshman class. We were allowed to leave our rooms during the nightly study period to consult a classmate on some homework-related question; people literally lined up outside my door to get help with their Spanish. But Georgetown, with its Institute (now Faculty) of Languages and Linguistics, was the place to specialize in modern languages, not St. Bonaventure. And Georgetown, whose prestige among Catholic families ranked it with the best colleges in the country, was located in the nation's capital, that sprawling black ghetto with the small white city at its core ... but a city nonetheless.

Georgetown

Within that core was the neighborhood of Georgetown, an urban village not radically different in size, but in its cultural amenities and social diversity, light-years from my hometown of Babylon. My rented room just south of Wisconsin Avenue, Georgetown's main thoroughfare, was an easy mile's walk to the university campus. For the only time, my parents installed me in my college digs, the private home of an aged and proper Southern lady who had let rooms to another Babylon boy, a high school acquaintance named Jay, on whose recommendation a remaining bedroom was made available to me.

My four-year-old sister, Maggi, the only of my three siblings to accompany us on this trip, expressed delight and confusion about the little girl with the "chocolate face," the daughter of the cleaning woman who had played with her on the stoop while I was being established within. This was clearly the first encounter with a person of color that Maggi registered consciously, an interesting social artifact and commentary on the *de facto* apartheid very much in force throughout Long Island in 1962.

At registration for classes I decided to not rejoin ROTC; that brief exposure to enforced military service at St. Bonaventure had evoked the same responses of ennui and powerlessness I had once felt in an even briefer stint with the Boy Scouts. The draft was not a serious problem then. Practically anyone from the middle class could avoid service (though many chose not to) without drawing on the prerogatives or evasions that would become commonplace within three short years with the rapid escalation of the war in Vietnam.

To say that Vietnam was invisible to me in 1962 would be an understatement. Laos, okay. "Lay-os," Kennedy pronounced it. I'd heard about that conflict on the nightly news, which, if I watched at all, was probably only for the chance of seeing and listening to some clip featuring our charismatic president. Not what he said, but the way he said it. I am convinced that, for many young folk coming of age in the early sixties, the content of Kennedy's speeches was of no more significance than the name of the tune played by the Pied Piper. Kennedy fascinated me for the same reasons I enjoyed any movie starring, say, Jimmy Stewart or Cary Grant. Kennedy projected the élan and vitality of a marquee idol.

My gut orientation in politics had by now shifted toward middle of the road liberalism, the influence of a very bright classmate at St. Bonaventure. We were both disk jockeys on the college radio station. I loved rock, and devoted my entire program to playing it with only a brief note to introduce each tune. But where I gyrated voicelessly behind my mike to the Isley Brothers, Kevin talked. He subscribed to *Commonweal*, and he spun brilliant monologues on the air lampooning the extreme right, especially Robert Welch, the candy industrialist and founder of the John Birch Society. What had first impressed me about Kevin was, like Kennedy, not so much what he said, but the aura of self-confidence surrounding his outspokenness.

A realization that I too had a deep desire to express myself was gradually stirring, causing me to engage the world more closely and to sharpen my opinions. Even so I was to remain more audience than participant for some time. Only in tavern bull sessions or at supper table debates with roommates would I really vent my views, which already placed me on the bleeding heart fringe in the company of conservatives. These boys were smart enough but thoroughly conventional, bound for careers in banking, big corporations, and the law. Yet — with the exception of a few chums from the Language Institute, all very apolitical — this was my primary circle of friends.

One business student, a very active Young Republican who had also transferred from St. Bonaventure, where I knew him only slightly as a fellow-booster of the young heavyweight Cassius Clay, would soon become my closest companion. John was a plain looking Irish-American with a winning personality and deeply conservative political convictions from one of New Jersey's affluent northern suburbs. The well of distance between his political instincts and mine was bottomless, but no hint of acrimony ever entered our disagreements or spoiled our friendship.

For years I tagged along with John to dozens of college Young Republican functions, looking to meet girls and sponging off the party's well-stocked hospitality suites — their confabs typically hosted in one of Washington's better hotels. But nothing ever clicked for me at these events. I never actually met anyone — girl or guy — that I felt drawn to.

John was with the party's majority center-right wing, the Nixon people, who even then struck me as slimy beyond belief. But John was different. He had a gentlemanly quality, almost courtly, which allowed him to accommodate through many cordial rounds of horse trading certain sensibilities of the party's smaller moderate factions. When it came to the larger and more vocal right flank occupied by the Young Americans for Freedom, John was uncompromising. He and his cronies waged endless parliamentary warfare with the YAFers, the Buckleyites, whom they seemed to view, not just as competitors for control of the college party, but as extremists, and therefore somewhat dangerous. This amused me no end, since John himself was an avid Irish nationalist, and many a night, after closing a local bar, we'd cruise homeward in his black MG cursing the British and bellowing choruses from "The Rising of the Moon."

In the Language Institute my friends were of a totally different tint. One distinguishing feature was that performance for a language student is measured in the most concrete way: fluency and literacy in a foreign tongue. One could not easily fudge one's proficiency; you either made palpable progress in acquiring the language in question or you didn't. So Institute students — at least mechanistically — tended to be more studious than those in the university's other colleges. In fact, the operative code among my business student friends was that any grade higher than a "hook," a "gentleman C," reflected badly on your character. Honors, if achieving them meant being a grind or sacrificing social time, were viewed with much greater contempt than failure. Failure, at least, was funny, and one was never more of a good fellow in this company than when cast as the object of good natured derision for having tanked some course that everyone else managed to pass without raising a bead of sweat. There's solidarity, Virginia, in the class chosen to govern.

The three lads I had most contact with in the Institute were from backgrounds that placed them outside the ranks of Georgetown's socially ambitious elites and achievers. One of them, George — whom we sometimes called "Fingers" — was a musical prodigy who had mastered both flamenco guitar and five-string banjo. In appearance George was striking, with thick jet black hair and skin white as porcelain, vaguely Hispanic, though with a German surname. With our buddy Mike, a lanky, sweet natured Virginia boy from nearby suburbia, the three of us formed a study circle to tackle the impossibly difficult examinations in first year linguistics. That subject was more foreign to me than any language, inaccessible the way math had always been. I flunked it first semester, the only course I would ever fail in college, and in the field that would eventually became my major.

Whenever we studied at his parent's home, Fingers — bowing modestly to our relentless but sincere entreaties — would play for us, first flamenco, then bluegrass banjo. The musical cultures of Manitas de Plata and Earl Scruggs are leagues apart, yet, already at eighteen, George possessed both the technical skills and the sensitivity to bridge them seamlessly.[4]

During those first years at Georgetown I specialized in intensive language study, Spanish and later Portuguese, which I'd come to under peculiar circumstances. The corridors of the Language Institute were a modern Babel; at a given moment most of the world's major tongues could be heard, and were soon easily recognizable to me. Until one morning during my third semester, I was passing between classes and heard a group of students speaking with a very Latin-looking woman in a language — with what, Slavic overtones? — that I couldn't peg. Rumanian? I muttered. No, a classmate named Joseph answered; Brazilian Portuguese. The language had developed a small following that year, and was one that he himself had begun to study. I needed a minor, Joseph went on, and really it was much closer to Spanish than it sounded. Why not sign up for Portuguese in the coming term? It was a fateful moment.

Accepting this advice led to my first close association with an African-American and a homosexual, both of whom were Joseph. In those years, Joseph seems to have shared his minority status in the overwhelmingly white student body with only two or three other American blacks; there were also a number of visiting students from black Africa.[5]

In his public mask Joseph reminded me of a minstrel, a somewhat fractured version of the caricatures in blackface created by the likes of Al Jolson and Eddie Cantor in those musical talkies of the early thirties. Joseph, always "on," always performing, seemed to have patterned his social persona on precisely such archetypes, perhaps because they were already familiar and acceptable within the virtually all-white milieu where he had chosen to pursue his undergraduate studies.

His Puck-like antics were patronized, and made Joseph appear more popular than he really was; the actual respect he merited and gained went much deeper than his apparent popularity. Joseph was among the most gifted polyglots in the entire institute. His mind was first rate, and his ear and eye for the nuances of sound and behavior across cultures had armed him with rare talents for navigating the international waters of academia, business or diplomacy. It was, I imagine, Joseph's gayness (in both dimensions) that prevented us from developing a closer friendship, even after we were thrown into each other's company during 1964 when we both spent the year in Rio de Janeiro.

My involvement with things Brazilian evolved rapidly. By the middle of junior year in the fall of 1963, after I had been studying basic Portuguese for a single term, a groundswell of enthusiasm swept through the Portuguese department which numbered — at most — a dozen students, carrying more than half of them off to São Paulo in the new year courtesy of scholarships provided by New York University. Again it was Joseph who directed my fate. Sao Paulo is boring; there's no beach. Let's go to Rio, he said.

I didn't even know I was going. I'd missed the application deadline for the scholarship. My Portuguese was progressing well, but — unlike Joseph — I did not yet speak nor understand the language. I had no money. No arrangements had been made with the school administration, nor with any corresponding university in Rio. Yet, I was truly envious of my fellow students who were shipping out to São Paulo, all expenses paid. The same impulse to spend the next year abroad had been implanted in me just as intensely as in them by all that wild enthusiasm, that frenzy to be off.

For the moment I had no ties, or at least it felt that way. I'd fought terribly with my parents, the culmination of many childhood tensions, and had not spoken with them since Thanksgiving. At nineteen, I was an emancipated man, paying my own way, including for the first time my tuition. That first year-and-a-half at Georgetown had seen me try my hardest to adapt to the rhythms of campus life, despite a feeling of being tugged between the opposing poles of two sets of values, two sets of friends. I would break with neither, but from here on I began to cut my own path through the world.

Work now occupied most of every waking hour as I balanced a full academic schedule with shifts waiting tables in the Tombs, the basement pub of the 1789, a restaurant just across from the quad of buildings where language, business, and foreign service students attended classes. The East Campus, as this complex was called, was a self-contained world, and the clubby vapors emanating from its wings, intoxicating. In the daytime students shuttled between their classes and the '89 or Clyde's, another popular ginmill down the hill on M Street; whether patron or employee, you were never out of the loop.

In-between times the city — with its cultural emporia and off-campus dating circuit — was our oyster, our movable feast. I frequented the National Gallery, often for the art, but mostly on Sundays for the chamber music, to test by daylight the depth of some infatuation formed the night before at a private party or a mixer at one of Washington's seemingly infinite number of private girls' colleges and finishing schools. I played lacrosse that first year, very badly, enduring frosty workouts at dawn each morning until I broke my arm in a scrimmage.

The school calendar offered its own flow of attractions, conventional college fare like sporting events where the student body assembled *en masse* to cheer the home team — years before Georgetown became a national basketball power — or themed weekends with name entertainment: Count Basie over cocktails, a hootenanny featuring the Kingston Trio, poolside with the Young Rascals. Prominent figures from the world stage of political and intellectual life materialized regularly to address convocations. The range was dizzying and provocative, blending the voices and ideas of such impossible opposites as Haile Selassie, Madame Nhu and Dwight Macdonald. There was even once a despotic message beamed directly to the university via closed-circuit television from Pope Paul VI, whose dark persona echoed, for me, a strange association to the Flash Gordon nemesis, Ming the Merciless.

So remote was the Jesuitical presence at Georgetown that the student pols seemed to govern everything, particularly on this satellite campus — a block from the main gate — where by 1964 a young Bill Clinton, class of '68, was already helping to steer student events as president of his freshman class. My old roommate Jay once reminded me that Clinton arrived at Georgetown bearing ballpoint pens with his name on them.

The contrast between threadbare, cloistered Bonaventure and glamorous, worldly Georgetown couldn't have been more dramatic. The one reeked of piety, the other of power. There was money at Georgetown, a hint of the top drawer. Scions of the nation's Catholic aristocracy; the offspring of Washington's embassy row. Toffs might surface at school polo matches, held in nearby horsey Potomac, Maryland, in tieless tuxedos rumpled like pajamas and sock-

less tasseled loafers swilling Moet from jeroboams while perched on the rumps
of sporty cars pawing their breathless world class beauties.

This was the world, a small fraction of the Georgetown student body's
social make-up to be sure, that my eighth grade classmates had tried to conjure with their talk of "going to Andover or Choate"— the world Calvin Klein,
Ralph Lauren and their ad-men once sought to impersonate in the Sunday
New York Times Magazine with story-board photo spreads of the tweedy rich
and idle, projecting the bloodless narcissism of professional models where the
lusty *je ne sais quois* that comes so naturally to the ruling gentry ought to be.

Despite the oft heard disclaimer that sustains our national mythology
that we live in a classless society — "I'm (you're, we're) just as good as so and
so"— every American is well aware of his or her class position in relation to
everyone else. But it has never been popular in the United States, except during rare periods of labor militancy, to nurture the consciousness underlying
this reality. To most Americans, not *class*, but the *climb* is everything; as a body
in motion owing to the marvel of postwar mobility I myself was able to quickly
gauge at Georgetown how far I'd come, and how far I still had to go.

But an appetite for position is not equivalent to the ambition for its
attainment. What began as mixed feelings, fascination laced with resentment,
toward the monied elites in whose company I was suddenly thrust, gradually
evolved into an immobilizing state of alienation which seemed to freeze my
psyche in its tracks for years to come, opposing my lust for the accouterments
of power and affluence with my disgust toward those who sought such blan-
dishments by turning a blind eye to the inequities of life that my own conscience was by now increasingly attuned to.

From an early age the inconsistencies in a whole range of society's per-
formances have impressed me deeply. The first source of youthful disillusionment, of course, is always the family — mine had its share of garden variety
dysfunctions that typified the times — the second, the Church. I for one was
naively oversensitive to what I perceived as hypocrisies in the practice of
Catholicism; how little the beauty of the Word seemed to penetrate the hearts
of the faithful.

When I think of the inordinate number of my own Catholic men friends
from high school and college who became lawyers, bankers, stock brokers,
corporate executives and the like, this lack of piety is hardly revealing. What
has always irked me, however, is how indifferently these honorable folk worship on, emotionally, intellectually, spiritually blind to the chasm separating
their actions from the ideals of their faith. We who are lapsed Catholics, on
the other hand, often behave like former drunks, making a religion of our
recovery, searching endlessly for an aesthetic that can rival for uplift or beauty
the old Latin mass and the mysteries of its priestcraft.

Not surprisingly, it was in this realm of aesthetics (not politics *per se*, but politics as *culture*) where I made all my initial breaks from the mainstream in those early years at Georgetown. Every space I occupied, mentally or physically, was gradually being transformed into some plot of alien ground, leading to a second major episode in my life — this time a foreign adventure — where I sought temporary refuge from my now chronic aimlessness.

Brazil

When I boarded that Pan Am 707 in New York a few weeks after New Year's in 1964 with about three hundred dollars in my pocket and a one-way ticket to Rio de Janeiro, I was nineteen years old. A brief and tearful reconciliation with my family did not alleviate my melancholy state. Or was it all a pose? My list of standard disappointments magnified through a lens of adolescent self-preoccupation?

And yet my crisis was not entirely individual or subjective. These were sad and heady times for the young of my generation. The shock of the Kennedy assassination can not be underestimated; it left many youths in a wake of hopelessness, however irrational that may sound even in my own ears given the less-than-glowing opinions I hold today toward JFK and the politics of his administration. Yet it is true. That same November afternoon after the news arrived from Dallas I knelt in the Georgetown church where Jack and Jackie had once been parishioners, and wept. For what or whom I cannot say.

Two earlier incidents involving the U.S. and Cuba also had a sobering impact on how many young Americans now viewed our nation's position in the world. With the Bay of Pigs fiasco, children of the postwar period got their first real sign that American power had its limits. Many of us — even when largely apolitical — did not see our own reflections in the pervasive ideology of anti-communism; if we thought of such matters at all, it was as old fogy stuff. We saw promise in Fidel, while Batista stood so transparently for corruption and dictatorship in the tradition of the old banana republics.

The Cuban missile crisis too had caused considerable trauma, in contrast to the mock-terror of the atomic political theater of the fifties. Civil defense exercises had actually been welcome breaks from the tedium of grammar school routines, and fallout shelters the envy of any child who spent his playtime building forts from packing crates that once housed home appliances. There were somber moments when it began to dawn on those within my ring of acquaintances that this U.S.-Soviet confrontation over ICBMs in Cuba might be the live atomic exercise that all the prior hoopla surrounding the race toward nuclear Armageddon only masqueraded as.

The civil rights movement spoke of pending crises of homegrown origin. By the early sixties it was becoming clear that Jim Crow (and the legacy of slavery on which it was built) was a time bomb whose inevitable detonation had institutionalized racial conflict as the defining characteristic of American life during the final quarter of the twentieth century, and is by no means resolved as we go forward in the new millennium.

My own experience can be cited to illustrate why racial bias has remained so intractable. I can actually trace a measurable rise in my personal fear of blacks as the irreconcilable *other* from the very event that marked a seminal advance for African-Americans themselves in their struggle for civic equality. I am referring to the 1963 March on Washington when Dr. Martin Luther King, Jr., delivered his now legendary "I have a dream" speech.

Like many northerners of liberal persuasion I was passively sympathetic to the goals of integration. Yet I am equally certain that I viewed the "Negro problem" as essentially a symptom of Southern racism. When the moment came that tens of thousands of black folk swelled the boulevards of Washington, I spent the day in bed, having stayed awake through the previous night reading, of all things, *Advise and Consent*. And I knew very well, even then, that my motivation for this totally uncharacteristic behavior — pulling all-nighters has always been an almost metabolic impossibility for me — had something to do with avoiding contact with the marchers. Apparently, not only the presence of so many blacks, but the very fact of their mass politics, threw me into a kind of quiet consternation and drove me into hiding.

Today I think of myself as a recovering racist (much in the way I consider myself a recovering Catholic). And, looking back, I now understand that my relationship with Joseph, the black classmate in whose company I was now going to Brazil, was doomed as much by unexamined racism on my part as by whatever discomfort I felt about his exaggerated personality and his sexual orientation.

And, undoubtedly, Joseph sensed our incompatibility even more poignantly than did I. Because on our second day in Brazil, as I stood very tentatively scanning Copacabana beach from a top floor window in the apartment belonging to the family of another Georgetown classmate whose father was the number three man in the U.S. embassy — probably the CIA station chief, I have since concluded — Joseph suddenly appeared at my side, yelling "come down to the beach. There's an American guy down there you'll really like."

Thus I met Chris and formed one of those sidekick romances common among straight men that feminists today, half in jest, half in despair, disparage as male bonding. Chris (whose uncle was the number two man in the U.S. embassy, and his cousin, one of Georgetown's São Paulo contingent) had just blown in from Switzerland where he'd been living as a ski bum. We hit it off instantly. He was a red haired Yankee version of Jean Paul Belmondo who quickly informed us that he'd picked up an Argentine beauty that morning and promised her a ride on the cable car to the top of *Pão de Açucar.*[6] We exchanged addresses and agreed to meet at his place the following day.

Chris had been hassled by two plainclothes cops his first night in Rio at some strip dive where he'd had a few too many. But he so charmed the cops that they'd invited the all-but-indigent gringo to share their flat, where I found him late the next morning and was promptly introduced to detectives Mario and Fontinelli, the former a tall, ruggedly handsome man with the manner of a gangster, the latter wiry, alert, and good natured. The place was a warren of rooms with sliding French doors out of which paraded an endless stream of girls in various stages of undress, whom the two cops shooed away after bussing their cheeks and wishing them *bom dia.*

All told those first few months in Rio were an idyll. The fortuitous arrival of our other classmate had allowed Joseph and me to camp out in style at her parents' digs in the *Edifício Chopin,* a luxury building where Brazil's president João (Jango) Goulart was also residing at the time, right next to the elegant Copacabana Palace Hotel. We commuted to classes by *lotação,* a squat little jitney that never came to a full stop while adding or discarding passengers before the conductor pulled the signal cord and cried out to the driver, *"vai embora*— get a move on." And we both matriculated in *cadeiras isoladas,* a smorgasbord of electives offered at the *Faculdade de Filosofia,* the Catholic University's liberal arts college. Other than the fact that the lectures were initially incomprehensible to me, my only strong recollection of those early days at the university is of attending a polemic delivered by a sister of Fidel Castro who had turned against the Cuban Revolution and was touring South America to bad-mouth her brother.

I spent most evenings with Chris those first two months in an oceanfront café at the Leme end of Copacabana Beach drinking *batidas,* chilled cachaca — a kind of native white lightning — cut with sweetened lime juice, and beer from tall, green-tinted bottles of *Chopp da Brama,* Brazil's most popular brew, for chasers. One night I got so smashed I took off my clothes and ran naked along the water's edge to the howling delight of several companions.

By the end of March all of Brazil was in turmoil; a military coup had overturned the left-leaning Jango's democratically elected government. On April 1st I awoke to the sound of tanks rolling up the avenues, and saw soldiers armed with burp guns posted at every corner. Rumors were rampant. Resistance was said to be forming in the country's south led by Jango's brother-in-law, Leonel Brizola. The universities would be shut down, mass arrests would follow. But nothing came of all this yet, and in a week or two, life was back to normal so far as these events affected the lives of a few visiting American students. The hard core repression which would become the trademark of the generals' long tenure in Brazil was still a year or two from being fully established. With the restoration of democracy in 1989 Brizola returned from exile, and remained a prominent politician in Brazil into the twenty-first century.[7] Indeed, the old lion contested the vice-presidential spot on the ticket of Luis Ignacio (Lula) da Silva of the *Partido dos Trabalhadores* (Worker's Party) in Brazil's 1998 national elections, one of three defeats by Lula before he finally achieved the presidential office.

The university campus had been in an uproar for several weeks prior to the coup. Everyone knew it was coming; the papers were full of warnings about the generals' threatening to "leave their barracks" to "restore order." Jango's crime, in part the association with his openly anti–American brother-in-law, was that he was indeed moving Brazil out of the American orbit toward a policy of non-alignment, and Rio's most militant students were agitating tirelessly to defend him. I remember clearly a discussion with an engineering student who was trying to convince me that the U.S. was active behind the scenes in support of the military overthrow, and how he'd used the word *imperialismo*, the first time I'd ever heard the term. As any student of Latin American history may easily verify today, he was right.

In the middle of April I turned twenty, and the morning of my birthday Chris insisted I come over to his place, that Mario and Fontinelli had a "surprise" for me. No sooner had I arrived than the two Brazilians cops, grinning ridiculously, ushered me into a bedroom alcove and closed the door. A minute later a girl appeared dressed in bra and panties. It seems *meu amigo* Chris, in whom I had confided the most intimate details of my past, felt strongly that a man should not pass his twentieth birthday and remain a virgin. The deed done — for truly it was a perfunctory act — I was backslapped by the boys, feted with champagne and dragged about the local cafes for a round of daylight merrymaking that is Rio's special province — the girl, a mere bit player in this mini-debauch, soon forgotten.

If I had been a virgin, it was only in the most technical interpretation of that state. I had been seeing the same person for over three years, Katie, literally "the girl next door" in Babylon. Katie and I were friends, companions and playmates, and had been discovering the pleasures of teenage sexuality in each other's company for some time at a pace we both found satisfactory. As Catholics we voluntarily abstained from actual intercourse. Beyond that...

Shortly after my birthday Chris ran out of cash but managed to find a job up the coast as a diver, scraping the bottoms of oceangoing vessels as they moored in the waters off Vitoria, waiting for their loads of iron ore. His departure was a blow, but it forced me to immerse myself in the Brazilian reality, after which my Portuguese improved rapidly.

Carnaval had come and gone. Typical of the differences between us, Joseph celebrated on the streets, while I joined my own circle of Brazilian friends at lavish dances in the private clubs of a neighborhood called Lagoa. We soon moved again to separate locations and began to see each other less and less frequently.

By July I was really on my own for the first time, living in a simple *pensão* at the foot of a Copacabana hillside on the opposite slope of which the shanties of a small *favela* were scattered in dense profusion. Slum clearance in this swank neighborhood, heavily contested before the coup, was soon thereafter pushed through to its grim completion.

On horseback in Brazil, 1964.

A sprawling cement apron had been poured in the vicinity of my boarding house, and every Thursday evening the *favelados* assembled there to rehearse the samba routines they would parade during the next year's *Carnaval*. The percussion band provided a stabilizing activity for *favela* youths much the way a drum and bugle corps might perform a similar function in a neighborhood of poor American blacks, but the rhythms of Brazil, the *batucada,* were preserved from the culture of the slave, not the master, ancient Africa's gift of sheer transcendental joy to any human spirit that has ever had the good fortune to fall under their spell.

It was now the depth of winter and classes had recessed until the beginning of August. Rio's weather, in turn sunny or overcast, determined whether or not my two fellow boarders and I would trudge off to the beach first thing each morning and dive into the ocean for a wake-up plunge. The owlish Rodrigo came from a town in Minas Gerais where his father was president of the local *Banco do Brasil*. And Antonio Geraldo, a tall and kindhearted country boy built like a cornerback, was the son of a coffee planter from the interior of São Paulo state. Both lads, recalcitrant scholars, were in Rio to finish high school, though Rodrigo was near my age and Antonio Geraldo, a year older — the sons of Brazilian gentry were permitted, if not always encouraged, to sow their wild oats well into their thirties.

Rodrigo's parents summoned him home for a week and he took me with him. The town was surrounded by enormous cattle spreads, one of which belonged to Rodrigo's girlfriend's father, where we spent our first day riding horseback over rolling, fenceless pastures. That night I ate dinner from the mantle because the welts on my thighs and buttocks were too raw to allow for any other posture. My hosts were as sympathetic as they were amused, for they seemed to find my excessive spontaneity refreshing and happily at odds with their idea of the typical *Americano* as a red faced, overbearing loud-mouth. I had, moreover, achieved a certain command of Portuguese, and this pleased Brazilians a great deal, as they had become accustomed to hearing their language butchered by foreigners, and found the labored American accent particularly offensive.

Before the week was up we attended a *churrasco*, a barbecue where a huge bull was roasted over an open pit to celebrate first communion at a local fazenda for the children of the land owners and the field hands alike. I was the only adult male to receive the sacrament that day, and after mass the other men crowded me and pumped my hand as if I'd just committed some rare act of courage or devotion, I could never determine which. But it made me feel like a horse's ass, and I blushed to the point of giving credence to at least that single element of their gringo stereotype.

Chris suddenly reappeared in a panic. His draft notice had come; to honor it meant an immediate return stateside for an induction physical and the end to his wanderlust. In the cafes of Leme we hatched a scheme to make for the Amazon and fade from sight. I would chuck my classes and play Sancho Panza to my friend's Quixote; in truth my own inner restlessness required no more justification for an escapade than whatever the occasion at hand. I also sympathized with Chris's dilemma. Didn't I also intend to avoid the service if possible? The sweeping mobilization of forces for Vietnam that would challenge that vague inclination was still a year in the making. Political news continued to pass through me like x-rays through a wooden door. As Chris and I plotted his escape, the Tonkin Gulf charade would have been much in the news, but it failed to leave even the most shallow indentation on my memory.

We headed north by rickety bus, much of the coastal road still unpaved, twelve long, rainy hours to Vitoria. Resting a few days we then set out for Minas, hitching, and our first ride, nested in the canvas top of a large truck, took us as far as Teofilo Otoni in the heart of Brazil's gemstone country. We had stayed with a U.S. government official in Vitoria whose work was linked to the Alliance for Progress; in his case that meant organizing agricultural co-ops to rival those dominated by the *partidão*— the "big party" — as the pro–Moscow Communists were called to distinguish them from the smaller Peking-oriented faction. And in Minas an American engineer, who'd helped lay out the rail line that carried ore down the mountain to the sea, put us up in a chalet guesthouse reserved by the railroad for visiting VIPs; the engineer had gone native like a man shipwrecked on a South Sea island, and had fathered many children by his Brazilian spouse, a simple country girl.

The bus next carried us to Feira de Santana, a dusty market town in the Bahia outback, then on to the coast, to Salvador, which unexpectedly turned out to be our final stop. After a few glorious days in this exotic African-scented city soaking up the *macumba* culture and combing the beaches, living on grilled shrimp, fresh fruit and *caipirinhas*— the local concoction of lime juice and fire water — Chris announced, out of nowhere, that he could not go on. I felt betrayed. I had hitched a ride on Chris's fantasy, and suddenly he just caved in to the specter of Uncle Sam that we had been boasting so glibly of defying. But I couldn't protest, knowing full well that it was my free spirited friend, not I, who was facing Uncle's wrath.

Chris's real uncle, the diplomat, arranged for us to fly back to Rio a day later on one of the daily runs the Brazilian Air Force made in their vintage DC-3s. Salvador's airport made such a strong visual impression on me that the image remains indelibly vivid in my mind: a Hollywood version of what a sleepy South American airfield was supposed to look like. I now realize that in 1964, the whole world still looked the way it had before the Second World War. Only the United States was modern in ways that must have struck the rest of the planet's inhabitants as fantastic.

We'd been on the road for perhaps three weeks. After taking leave of Chris my Brazilian adventure began to lose momentum. I felt homesick and alone. I returned to my boarding house and took up classes again at the university. Rio retained its magic to pleasure and distract, but the next few months dragged on listlessly and remain something of a blur in memory. By mid–December I decided to go home, having secured free passage on a merchant ship thanks to a program the U.S. State Department created to transport youthful Brazilian leaders it was courting to Washington.

Once again I made my way to Vitoria, my spirits about as low as they had been eleven months before on leaving the U.S. The Brazilians call this mood *saudades*, bittersweet nostalgia spiked with melancholy, a sentiment not inappropriate to moments of separation such as this. But for me it was the old feeling of being adrift again, a pilgrim without a destination. A few days before sailing I boarded my ship, then went ashore to spend Christmas at a whorehouse. By the New Year we were somewhere off the coast of Trinidad toasting 1965 at the captain's table with rounds of akvavit. The ship, a Japanese-built behemoth of an ore-boat with a Norwegian crew, took nineteen days to reach Baltimore, much of which I spent feeling seasick in my cabin, or engrossed in *Lady Chatterley's Lover*. The very instant I touched American soil the culture shock all but overwhelmed me. Fire belching smoke stacks from steel furnaces on the nearby wintry horizon and the chainlink fence around the wharf made everything seem bleak.

Clouds of War

The visual landscape mirrored my immediate prospects, which were not promising. I'd failed to bring any paperwork from Brazil to certify my time at the university, and Georgetown awarded me just six credits for the entire year. This meant staying in school until June of 1966 to fulfill the requirements for a bachelor's. I'd managed to thrive in Brazil for almost twelve months on just seven or eight hundred dollars; now I had to scramble for a lot more cash than that to support myself, while another installment of defense loans would pay the college bills for the year to come.

All that semester I skulked around campus in a faded suede blazer, thin and dissolute, like an out-of-work tragedian. There was much talk about the draft, but precious little on the troop build-up *per se*. One couple I knew did rush their wedding plans by a year or so to June of '65, since only single men were vulnerable to the call until they reached the age of 26. Many others wavered on this path as well, or looked for outs in other quarters. Everyone wanted to avoid the draft, not the war, which was still a remote threat in a far off land.

The Marines had landed on China Beach in March to much fanfare and publicity. But the television footage, far from communicating a sense of urgency, conveyed the dated look of an upbeat newsreel from the forties, a la MacArthur's return to the Philippines, while the lighthearted mood captured on the faces of the American troops suggested Vietnam would be a cakewalk. A demonstration in Washington that April marked the equally historic inauguration of mass protest against the war. But I was totally oblivious to this organized antiwar presence only a dozen blocks away, so separate was the world of opposition from that of the vast majority whose conventional perception of events I continued to share, if only by default.

I got a break that summer when the United States Information Agency chose me as an intern. The program, which paid surprisingly well, began with a whirlwind orientation lasting a week. Not only were we presented with endless flowcharts describing the Information Agency's worldwide mission and organizational structure, but we also joined our intern counterparts from other agencies at what were essentially government propaganda rallies, where such luminaries as Vice President Hubert H. Humphrey and the junior senator from New York, Robert F. Kennedy, regaled us with their visions of civic virtue in the great reception hall at Foggy Bottom. Hubert was seen as a terrible stiff, but the pugnacious Bobby remained a crowd pleaser with the young.

If I can be said to have had any career ambition by this time, it was to join the Foreign Service, perhaps opting for the path of least resistance, the less prestigious Information Agency over the truly formidable challenge of the State Department. Brazil had fueled my taste for a life of genteel transcultural commuting. I dreamily imagined myself shuttling between South America, the Iberian Peninsula, and agency headquarters on K Street, jabbering away in Portuguese and Spanish and contributing my share of data to flowcharts that subsequent waves of youngsters would stare at numbly in the years to come.

On the final afternoon of our initiation to government service, the interns gathered in the agency's auditorium for a film. I sat beside my new friend, Cia, who was giggling uncontrollably. Her father, William S. White, a nationally syndicated columnist, was a boon companion of the man whose basset hound features filled the screen before us. Cia settled down just in time for us to hear Lyndon Johnson pose, rhetorically, the question that the rest of the nation has been trying to answer ever since: Why Vietnam?

II

Days of Wakening

A question's not really a question, if you know the answer too.

— *John Prine*

"Why Vietnam?" Thus spoke LBJ, staring me straight in the eye like Big Brother from a recruiting poster. But the message of the war's immediacy, rendered even more remote by the president's sepulchral cold war tone, did not transcend the medium. After living in Brazil it was hard to swallow that the U.S. could be the victim of some undernourished peasant society. Beyond that I had no problem with the idea of war, which, in my mind, remained a tempting rite of passage. What I detested, even feared, was the prospect of submitting to the prison-like conformity of military life.

As we half-watched the government film Cia and I traded asides and chortled about the absurdity of it all; we were fast friends that summer, and, one night, Cia invited me home for dinner. Around the table Cia and her younger sister, Victoria, writhed in bemusement at every topic their poor parents tried to introduce to keep the conversation in motion. The girls' irreverence was infectious. Once, when Mr. White asked if I was kin to Alexander Uhl, our ambassador at Berlin before *the* war, I snorted, "Do you mean Alexander Graham Uhl?" It was a cruel, stupid trick which I regretted almost instantly; but the girls thought my wit ranked with Oscar Wilde and practically rolled off their chairs in stitches. The grownups took it in stride, every fiber in them straining to avoid a scene. But I felt ashamed for playing to the gallery when my natural inclination is to always empathize with underdogs. In this case, it was Cia's parents who, undeservedly, were getting the worst of it.

That fifth year as a Georgetown undergraduate began in September 1965 with a rude awakening. The draft board sent notice that my student deferment would expire on the first day of the coming year. For failing to complete my degree in the required four years' time, I was to be re-classified 1-A, draft bait, subject to military induction without further warning.

The crisis was palpable: I knew myself well enough to realize I could not make it as an enlisted man. My fears and premonitions were quite literally of being dragged off to the stockade, much the way I had been routinely dispatched to the principal's office at Babylon High for disrupting my favorite teacher Clyde's history lectures with some wisecrack. (Toward the end of senior year a recording of the school anthem was played over the public address; what did we think of it, Clyde asked? "I'll give it an 80; I like the music but it's hard to dance to." Laughter all. Exit Michael.)

My first impulse — again — was to flee from the Selective Service. I would go back to Brazil, find work, sit out the war. The idea of exile had romantic appeal. But at twenty-one I worried that the potential lifelong consequence of abandoning my homeland was to never be permitted to return, to wander the earth a man without a country. At that age one thinks in absolutes. The options seemed black and white; exile would become unbearable in the long run, so I ruled it out. Next, I applied to the Peace Corps. Despite my failure to meet the minimum qualifications — a college degree or a demonstrable trade — I was invited to join a group bound for Brazil on the strength of my fluency in Portuguese.

This plan foundered on another unacceptable consequence. My blue collar gut equated college credentials with a worker's union card. Two currents of folk pessimism, the potato famine and the Brüder Grimm, coursed the subtext of my upbringing, and no degree of affluence or security seemed to still their dire prophesies. Once again the wolf was at the door, the poorhouse gate in view. If I left school now I'd never go back; I'd be bagging groceries at the Big Ben for the rest of my life. A mind in conflict attracts the devil; he came as a classmate merely stating the facts: the ROTC program was now offering a "compressed course" for those, like me, who faced the threat of being drafted out of college. The next thing I knew I was having a friendly chat with the sergeant major.

The bargain sealed, I committed myself to remain at Georgetown for, not just one, but two more years, a virtual ROTC major over the final stretches. My coin of social anxieties had bought me a two year hitch as an "officer and gentleman." But when word came down that I'd been assigned to Army Intelligence this compromise began to strike me as a sound career move. Hadn't so many of the old hands at State served in the elite spook network OSS — the Office of Strategic Services — during the Second World War? This, I thought, will look good on my record.

❖   ❖   ❖

Had I graduated in 1965 it seems almost certain that my life must have followed a different trajectory from that which guides these reflections. Those additional two years at Georgetown wedded me more deeply to the central dramas facing the Vietnam generation than most of my contemporaries who had managed to slip the net just as the war's escalation was being planned and put into play. My own choices meant that I would get to Vietnam as the war was peaking in late 1968, a twenty-four year old lieutenant in a war where the average age of the fighting man was nineteen years, ten months.

The other profoundly important aspect to my being sidetracked on campus from 1965 to 1967 was that these were the years when the ideas and values of what we call "the sixties" began to spread from their hothouse origins among a tiny bohemian or radical vanguard to wider and wider cohort of students and youths. The collective alienation long in ferment among those growing up in the fifties was now steaming toward a critical boundary, its dominant substance first and foremost cultural, not political. A transformation from cultural alienation to oppositional politics followed a considerable period of incubation, and then embraced only a small minority among the vast numbers caught up in the overall generational upheaval.

Only after late 1969, and until roughly the end of 1972, spurred by a generalized war weariness and by popular disgust toward such horrors as the revelation of the My Lai massacre, the invasion of Cambodia and the killings of students at Kent State and Jackson State, the terror bombings of Laos and of Hanoi and Haiphong — and because the antiwar stance had by then become something of a fad — did radical politics and the counterculture merge briefly into a single expression of disaffection among vast numbers of youths of virtually every social and economic background.

I believe my own evolution in this regard was entirely typical. Well, up to a point. A predisposition to not take the world at face value did seem to have me earmarked for social experimentation somewhere down the line, but always within those restraints of background and personality I have already sketched above. If one can be a late bloomer by constitution, that's what I was, hovering, watching on some periphery until pure impulse propelled me headlong toward the unknown. Marijuana is a case in point.

By 1966 pot was beginning to circulate on the fringes of college life; Georgetown, worldly but conservative, was probably somewhat behind the curve of the national turn to recreational drugs. For me *pot* was just a word, a taboo, something artists and musicians did ... maybe. That's how I came to it anyway. My classmate Fingers was now part of a folk group, its lead guitar. The band played weekends at a rathskeller near Dupont Circle, warming up audiences for touring headliners. One night in particular comes to mind because the great three-finger blues picker Mississippi John Hurt was featured. Somehow during the break the conversation led to drugs, about how the sidemen were all out back getting high.

How exactly this led to an apartment across the Potomac in Falls Church, Virginia, on a completely different occasion, I can't quite piece together any longer. A fragment of memory insists on the connection, but I can't even recall who was on hand. We were a group of three or four who had gone there to smoke reefer, me for the first time. The moment is remarkable for the ritual we followed before lighting up; all the doors and windows in the room were masked with tape to keep the pungent telltale fumes of the burning hemp within the room. This was a common precaution in those days, or so I was told. The clandestine atmosphere made everyone uncomfortable; no one spoke, eyes were shrouded giving the appearance of faces in pain, and fleeting glances darted from door to window and back again. I distinctly remember not getting high.

A few months later I boarded a jet at Dulles Airport, dressed in an ROTC uniform, ill-fitting and unpressed, and flew to San Francisco to visit my friend Cia who was now at Stanford. The humiliation of traveling in uniform was only partially salved by the half-price ticket the charade afforded me. I bounded through the gate on arrival, and rushed past my friend to the men's room to shed the despised costume, feeling like a total square. We then drove south to the campus in Palo Alto, and Cia pointed out the little multi-colored houses in Daly City "made of ticky-tacky" that inspired a Malvina Reynolds folk tune Pete Seeger had somehow managed to spin into a top-fortics hit a year or two before.

The week I spent with Cia was a crash course in deciphering the symbols and manners of the emerging "freak" culture. In her cheery way Cia gave me the Cooke's tour, the Haight, a concert and light show at the Fillmore, a long, romantic drive to Big Sur that made me wish I was her boyfriend instead of that creep who kept trying to get her to flee to the desert all week because he was convinced an earthquake was coming. Back on campus at a pacifist teach-in we listened to Joan Baez, demur in blue serge and a study for Major Barbara in her righteousness, as she preached a militant antiwar sermon bordering, in my sheltered imagination, the limits of free expression. It was around this same time that Baez's intended, the draft resister David Harris — then a highly visible student pol — had his long hair shaved to the scalp by a mob of Neanderthals from a Stanford jock fraternity.

Cia hadn't really changed, but her crowd, especially the men, were very hip, one guy dressed in suede and buckskin with a stash swinging ostentatiously from his belt in a little pouch. I didn't take the joint when it came my way, and wouldn't smoke reefer again till I was out of the service. I think I believed, based on that single uptight hit, that being high was an act people put on to appear cool. Cia and I had little contact after this. I was glad to leave for home. The whole scene around Stanford made me nervous; Cia and her friends kept time to the Stones and Dylan, and I was still partial to the Beatles.

By 1967 Vietnam had settled into its slot as lead story on the nightly news. But in my world, one's position on the war was still argued within the bounds of the mainstream debate between hawks versus doves. No one I knew questioned the assumptions surrounding U.S. involvement; and certainly no one grasped the nature of, much less championed, the Vietnamese struggle for self-determination. My own views were vaguely pacifist, theological more than political. In a class on military history I would repeatedly condemn war as intrinsically immoral, rooting my argument in the realm of a pure and lofty rationalism. And I made it clear that I myself could never fire a weapon at another human being.

The course was memorable and the teacher, a major of infantry, one of the best I would encounter in all my college days. He had an amateur's passion for history which was contagious, and he tolerated, even encouraged, viewpoints like mine that were antithetical to the narrow traditions of military orthodoxy. And yet, my distaste for regimentation notwithstanding, I never claimed my moral scruples would prevent me from serving, or even going to war. Quite the opposite. I looked on war as a generational given; and I always imagined that my generation, like my father's and his father's before him (though neither had actually served), would have a war of its own, and that, in some fashion, I would be a participant. The major was not put off by these contradictions; he seemed to embrace them.

Antiwar opposition at Georgetown was marginal. There were no teach-ins on the campus during those years. Or if anything even remotely comparable to such a forum did occur, it was so insignificant as to have been virtually invisible. Every Saturday in the spring of '67, when army ROTC performed its insufferable but mandatory parade on the university athletic field, we were picketed by a small contingent whose placards identified them as the Georgetown chapter of the SDS. But in the atmosphere of total acquiescence to the war which pervaded campus and off-campus life at Georgetown, they seemed as out of place as a band of millenarians in sack cloth predicting the impending End of Days.

On June 5, 1967, I finally graduated from college. The commencement speaker that year, Undersecretary of State Nicholas de B. Katzenbach, reflected Georgetown's essentially pro-administration stance on the war; his presence was greeted without a murmur of protest. Katzenbach, a domestic liberal, was very much a hawk on Vietnam; as acting attorney general under Johnson in 1964 he had argued forcefully for the president's right to conduct hostilities abroad without the consent of Congress. Katzenbach would later refer to the Tonkin Gulf Resolution as the "functional equivalent" of a declaration of war, acknowledging that Lyndon Johnson and his cabinet exploited the dubious Tonkin Gulf incident to gain *de facto* approval from a by-no-means reluctant Congress for the Administration's war policies without having to subject them to public scrutiny or open debate.

❖ ❖ ❖

Twelve days after graduation I reported to the Indiantown Gap Military Reservation near Hersey, Pennsylvania, for six weeks of ROTC boot camp. The gung-ho troopers, the superannuated boy scouts who loved to play soldier with real war toys and uniforms, thrived in this setting. For them it was fun; for me it was a matter of going through the paces, counting my blessings, which under the circumstances were many. I was not, for example, an enlisted man, subject to round-the-clock harassment by a team of sadistic drill instructors. Our company sergeant was a human being who lacked the dark psychological agenda that characterizes so many of his species.

By day he worked us hard, the physical conditioning relentless but not intimidating unless you were overweight or without any athletic aptitude whatsoever. Most evenings, barring scheduled events, the company engaged in petty drudgery, preparing for those mickey-mouse inspections that the army hierarchy believes will encourage bonding among its underlings, a medium for channeling into group loyalty the anti-authority feelings a given individual might otherwise direct against the institution. To my surprise and relief I was exempt from much of this extracurricular busy work thanks to the military principle known as RHIP — "rank has its privilege."

As a graduate I would be commissioned at the end of camp; whereas the rest of the company, except for one other guy, still had a year of college remaining. Our seniority permitted us to frequent the officer's club after normal duty hours. By five most evenings I would be standing outside the barracks in my Madras sport coat waiting for Duke to pick me up in his white convertible.

Duke, so named for his uncanny ability to mimic John Wayne, was an old chum from the Georgetown Business School, class of '65. With only a few months left in the service, now a first lieutenant, he had been assigned to headquarters at Indiantown Gap. Maybe because Duke was far from being a hard ass and didn't pull rank on any of the cadets I introduced him to, no one in my unit ever expressed resentment about my country-club indifference toward the military; the other graduating lieutenant was not so lucky.

When we returned one night just before lights-out, well into our cups, he stumbled toward his bunk and found it missing. It had been dismantled and re-assembled on the landing of the second story fire escape.

I distinguished myself in one other small way over the course of training as the only one in my company who "bolo'd," failed to qualify on the rifle range. Try as I might I just couldn't shoot straight, except once behind a humongous fifty-caliber machine gun aimed at some huge rusted hulks of armored vehicles aligned on a distant ridge line. You were a sitting duck on either end of that equation, I suppose.

In all it was a painless, monotonous six weeks, punctuated by a single, if bizarre, cultural highpoint. One afternoon, probably a Sunday, the entire corps was herded into a field to attend a USO show. Featured was a singing group called the Inkspots — a relic from the big band era — three or four older black guys set up on the flat bed of an army truck, one of whom kept time with a pair of brushes on a single snare. With this gig those poor souls had really hit the bottom of the barrel.

Active Duty

Toward the end of October a letter arrived from the Department of the Army ordering me to report to Infantry Officers School at Ft. Benning, Georgia, on the 27th of November. Though ultimately slated for counterintelligence, I would have to qualify first as an infantry platoon leader. This was in the tradition of the old combat spooks who went behind the lines to rally partisans, blow up trains, or spy on the enemy. My girlfriend, Katie, had agreed to accompany me as far as Atlanta.

Katie and I had been going together for over six years, with a few short-lived breakups in between. We had stayed close until a year or so after my return from Brazil. Now we were drifting apart, something I felt and resisted but couldn't really bring myself to acknowledge. For reasons I never entirely understood, she had always been adamant about my not going into the service. This was odd since her views were neither anti-military nor anti-establishment; in fact, her father was a bird colonel in the Air Force Reserves, and the two of them were very close. It is belatedly obvious that Katie was more invested in our relationship than I realized; by the fall of 1967 she no longer felt that way, and she was finding it difficult to break the news.

In photos of that period the tension in her face tells the story that Katie could not fashion into words until almost a year later. The whole trip south our contact was strained, and then we made a bad parting; in a little volume of verse Katie gave me, *The Rubaiyat of Omar Khayyam,* and asked me not to open until after she'd gone, was a note saying that no matter what she said or did, she would always love me. Even by then I was too dense to get it, because I was so desperate to put the best spin on her cryptic message.

The next morning my lumpy old Saab — one of those three-cylinder affairs with the two-stroke engine — limped into Ft. Benning. Young lieutenants were gathering from all over the country, finding their units and billeting assignments, chang-

With my mom, sisters Barbara and Maggi and brother Tom in 1967, just before entering the army.

ing into fatigues for the first school-wide formation. My company stood before its commanding captain, a vicious little twerp who'd gone to Officer Candidate School. He was a ninety-day wonder, not a college trained product of ROTC, a source of deep-seated bitterness he made no effort to conceal.

As he moved through our ranks all ruffled with his resentments, he abruptly paused before me, ordering me to step out and remove my "cover," military for hat. Was Lieutenant Uhl (or however he butchered my name) here to audition for a rock & roll band? he screamed in my face. I'd been sporting fashionably longish hair and a mustache since the end of basic, but the night before in Atlanta I'd had my head closely cropped and my whiskers shaved off; it had been a decade or more since I'd worn my hair this short. A classic crew cut with nothing left to part. But not close enough for young Captain Queeg. I quickly resigned myself to a long nine weeks ahead.

Slightly more than half our company was in the infantry, bound for advanced combat training after finishing this course in small unit fundamentals, or, in some cases, right to line units in Vietnam if they drew short straws. The rest of us were headed for Army Intelligence School at Ft. Holabird in Baltimore to acquire the elemental tools of spookcraft. An idiot could distinguish those of one branch from the other. The infantry officers wore starched, custom-tailored fatigues; the intelligence officers looked like they'd dressed to wash their cars. Appearances, however, were superficial; one naturally assumed the style of one's caste. Our diminutive commanding tyrant made many futile attempts to widen this divide, but the camaraderie throughout our company tended to cut across these irrelevant differences; for each of us was expected to play out the school's demanding script, regardless of the insignia he wore on his lapels.

One aim common for both groups involved "getting into shape." Each dawn I joined my infantry roommate, Peter — a very polished fellow of White Russian stock — for a five-mile run before mess call. We all knew that a certain amount of stamina would help get us through the many sleep-shortened nights. Gradually, even the most baggy-pants professor-types began to sharpen their line; it was always a hassle in the army to stand out, as I'd learned that first day. So I too discarded the clunky "McNamara boots" that were standard issue, and replaced them with a sleek pair of Corcorans like the paratroopers wore. Each night, Peter and I placed our mud-caked footwear outside the door of our two-man room as if we were at the Waldorf. For a small fee, a man known as the Black Ranger returned them by morning all spic and span and spit-shined.

Training at the infantry school was split between classroom and field work. Since army pedagogy is rote-oriented, the content of a given block of instruction tended toward the banal. They'd sometimes get your attention, but seldom in the manner intended — like the badly acted, worse written, psyops films we were shown on one of the more entertaining afternoons, especially the film which was meant to portray an American community being pacified by "aggressors" after some hallucinogenic drug had been dumped into its water supply. It's not as if the military institution lacked the budget to produce a more subtle piece of propaganda, but that the army's take on the world-at-large instantly struck this skeptic as ludicrous, a study in self-caricature. These Defense Department films embodied the provincial superstitions of the classic one reeler *Reefer Madness*; it was a state of mind in the army, not just a genre preference.

When it came to production values, Ft. Benning wasn't even as close to reality as the dismal standards set by Hollywood. Nothing of the true feeling of Vietnam and its war was communicated in their little mock-up Asian villages, as I was soon to discover. Only once did I see an exhibition at Benning that squared with what would be my own wartime experience. A very fit young sergeant, short and wiry, had been a tunnel rat in Vietnam, and he was being showcased as much for having won a silver star through some act of personal bravery as for his ability to demonstrate a special talent. We were told to imagine that the enemy was concealed in the tunnel before us, and that our man was going to show us various contingencies for dealing with the situation. He approached the entrance on his belly probing its lid with a long stick, popped it open and spoke incantations in pidgin Vietnamese to lure the enemy into surrender. When no foe appeared, he slithered into the hole head first with a flashlight in one hand and a forty-five in the other, and disappeared — emerging seconds later to hardy applause for his spirited and virtuoso performance.

In the field, our two crescendo events were to be the live ammo drill — a tactical advance of a line company actually firing its weapons — and an overnight romp in the bayou called Escape and Evasion, during which we would be "hunted" by aggressors. Supervision during the former, what with all that lead flying about, was never tighter during those nine weeks. The rest of the time only the trainees ran the risk of being hurt; during this tightly orchestrated shoot-out, an instructor too could suddenly find himself in the line of fire.

Escape and Evasion was the highpoint of excitement for the outdoor types, mostly country boys on the infantry side who'd been carrying guns into the woods since childhood. To me, the confines of the Okefenokee swamp were not inviting; despite hours of training in the use of compass and topographical maps, all the trees and the terrain still looked the same to me. We were to use these newly learned skills to find our way to "friendly" territory after being plunked down in the middle of nowhere. At all costs we were to avoid the roads, as they would be heavily patrolled by the aggressor; and God help us if we fell into *his* hands, especially if we were discovered bending the rules. Horror stories abounded of being confined to foot lockers and peed on by all and sundry. My solution was to follow the road from just inside the wood line straight to the finish, ducking from view when the sound of motor vehicles approached. Any other way, I'd still be out there.

Infantry school was not all work and no play; unlike our counterparts in the enlisted ranks, we actually had free time, occasionally evenings and weekends. Columbus, Georgia, like most military towns, was a pit. But the outskirts offered some interesting Southern institutions, mostly having to do with food. We found one place where a black woman, a housewife, served great barbecue from the back steps of her kitchen. But the favorite for our over-stimulated appetites were those all-you-can-eat chicken and catfish joints.

My only really bad experience was being pulled over by a gang of Bull Connor clones in police uniforms who extorted a cash "fine" on the spot for some trumped up speeding charge (in that Saab?) as I was driving north through Georgia on my way home. Okay, I thought, I have New York plates, fair game for these crackers. But I'm also an active duty officer in the United States Army — not the Union Army; doesn't that cut some slack? Not with those boys.

❖ ❖ ❖

Ft. Holabird was light and pleasant duty. Half the time, you could almost pretend you weren't in the army. Except for a handful of lifers making career changes, most of my classmates were recent college grads in for their two year hitches. It was a crowd bound for the professions, law, the academy, maybe government service. Most of us lived off-post in a high rise complex near Charles Street surrounded by Baltimore's most charming residential townhouses.

The curriculum at the counterintelligence school was a nuts and bolts affair, with a few accessories to suggest the more exotic elements of spookcraft that most of us would never practice. Every morning, six days a week, we spent two hours behind our manual Underwoods, as a doughty old matron cruised the aisles with her pointer reminding us that lowly lieutenants — which most of us were — didn't "have clerks in this man's army to type up their Agent Reports." God bless her and Uncle Sam for teaching this poor dyslexic how to use a typewriter; a crippled penmanship, compounded by lousy spelling despite my love of reading, made me dread composing anything in longhand.

The second most concentrated block of instruction at Ft. Holabird involved hours of role playing as we learned to conduct background investigations for security clearances, the drone side to the counterintelligence mystique. And since this mission absorbed much of our branch's manpower, I gathered that most of us would be assigned to the boring, but far from hazardous, domestic chore of canvassing the hometown neighbors of those now "being considered for a position of trust and responsibility in the United States Army," seeking to determine, among other things, if so-and-so "had ever been known to engage in acts of moral turpitude." Thus, a former rowdy teen who'd once punched a hardball through Mr. Grump's beloved sun porch window might now be denied his top secret clearance on the basis of some longstanding small town grudge. The modus operandi of intelligence gathering, I was beginning to understand, was rooted in gossip.

In "flaps and seals" we were shown how to whittle Popsicle sticks for opening mail, lifting away the glue from the rear flap of the envelope without tearing the paper fibers and leaving evidence of tampering that could be detected under ultraviolet light.

DAME, "defense against mechanical entry," was pure performance art. Rumored to be the most "outstanding" class on the counterintelligence agenda, DAME lived up to its billing. Facing us as we filed into the classroom was a Plexiglas door set in a stand-alone frame, armed from top to bottom with locks and fasteners of every variety. As soon as his student audience settled down, the instructor sprang into furious action from behind this transparent display, and, within thirty seconds, had succeeded picking each of the locks in turn. The latch clicked and he opened the door with a flourish, only to have it stopped short from the inside by a security chain. What to do now his perplexed expression seemed to ask? Cutting the chain was not an option; this was to be a covert entry, he cautioned. No tracks.

That said, the instructor produced three small items, a heavy rubber band, a large paper clip, and a strip of duct tape about six inches long. These he fashioned into a kind of necklace, joining the paper clip to one end of the rubber band and duct tape to the other. With this odd assemblage in hand he reached through the opening and hooked the paper clip to the knobbed end of the security chain. Then by nesting his shoulder into the space between the door and the jamb, he inserted his arm and stretched the rubber band — still hooked to the chain — toward the center of the door where he taped it fast. As the door snapped shut, the chain miraculously popped from its containment, and the instructor glided though the threshold to the approbation and delight of all.

Against such rare moments of initiation into the secret rites of the spy trade the dull pace of classroom instruction lumbered on while, outside, spring gradually unfolded, dissolving one mild day into the next. And spring fever was never more keenly felt for most of us than during a day-long lecture on constitutional law, a tortured effort to layer some pretense of legality over the dubious practices of agencies such as ours. With unintended irony, the command had chosen as teacher for this instruction an Eastern European refugee, whose thickly accented English and bitter anti-communist invective made him appear far more sinister and alien in my eyes than the red menace he could only invoke through abstraction.

It was always a great relief to escape the dingy classrooms, even — perhaps especially — when the unreality of the curriculum plummeted from the merely preposterous to the patently absurd. Such was the case when we moved to the streets and sidewalks of downtown Baltimore to apply the methods of surveillance we'd been drilled in — quite superficially — back at the post. The car chase was a complete fiasco. None of the radios seemed capable of communicating more than incomprehensible squawks among the three identical Plymouths from the government motor pool that our team occupied during the pursuit, and we quickly lost our subject in a tangle of under paths and ramps leading to an expressway.

For the street exercise our mark, or *rabbit*, was a career noncom in civvies wearing shiny military dress shoes and white socks, who, we joshed among ourselves, stood out like a beacon in a shroud of fog. But when he ducked into a large department store and hopped an escalator, he too soon eluded us among the throngs of lunchtime shoppers. Still we soldiered on in a vain quest to find our man, adapting the prospects of certain failure into a ploy for extending this open air excursion well into the afternoon.

As for news from the front, barely a whisper reached us within the confines of this secluded hothouse. Only on a morning devoted to the fine art of prisoner interrogation did the old warhorses gather us around them during breaks and spin their tales of Vietnam horrors, about "gooks" being flung from choppers at 5,000 feet, and of the other forms of mayhem and malpractice inflicted on "those slant-eyed bastards" to make them talk. While inside the classroom, the conventions of war and rules of engagement meant to regulate the humane treatment of friend and foe alike were taught with all the earnest piety humans can muster when they wish to disguise what they preach from what they practice.

It must have been a Saturday, two days after Martin Luther King's assassination on the 4th of April 1968, when I took my overnight pass and boarded a train bound for New York City. At Penn Station I flagged a cab and raced down to the Village, where my friend Katie had made reservations for dinner in what she called "the oldest restaurant in the city." Still in uniform, I imagined myself the object of many hostile stares as we waited for our table, and I thought, how different it must have been during World War Two to appear in public wearing the uniform of one's country, a time when a young man *not* in uniform might have drawn the glaring disapproval of the populace.

My only other memory of that abbreviated weekend was going after dinner to the White Horse Tavern, down the block from the flat Katie now rented since moving into the city and taking a job as a social worker. This bar was an institution in the Village, a literary haunt where, during the early fifties, Dylan Thomas once held forth in bouts of sodden eloquence. A year and a half later as an NYU grad student I would return frequently to the White Horse. But by then, almost everything about my prior life, including my former girlfriend, had become history.

I was feeling down when I left New York the next evening, the strain, I suppose, of trying to sustain an emotional connection that had run its course. Rain was falling lightly by the time the train reached Baltimore, where, to my astonishment, the station was encircled by a unit of the Maryland National Guard. The repressed fury of the black community had been uncorked nationwide in reaction to the murder of Reverend King, and the convulsions of violence in Baltimore had caused then-governor Spiro T. Agnew (later vice president under Nixon and forced to resign in disgrace for taking bribes) to declare a state of emergency.

A nighttime curfew was already in effect, and the weekend warriors were ordering passengers to get off the street as quickly as possible. Again my uniform was a distinguishing mark. Spotting me in the crowd, a soldier approached and saluted. When I told him I lived nearby, and would prefer to walk home rather than being obliged to join the line of civilians waiting for a taxi, he promptly escorted me through the barriers. In my dejected state, walking slowly through those dark, empty streets, I felt weighed down by an enormous sadness, not just for myself, but for my country.

Images from a Czech art film, *Closely Watched Trains*, that my army friends and I had seen a few weeks earlier began to filter through my mind. It was the story of a lone saboteur's private war against the Nazis, and certain dark emotions from that film resonated with the moment I myself was living. Pulling the lapels of my trench coat tighter to ward off the damp night air, I entered the spirit of that film and followed a trail of wet reflections from the street lights that led to the door of my building. A few days later orders were posted at Ft. Holabird assigning what for most of us would be our first real duty stations. I drew an intelligence detachment at Ft. Hood, Texas, where I was ordered to report by the middle of May.

❖   ❖   ❖

Ft. Hood was the army writ large: a vast military reservation on a godforsaken patch of scrub-growth half the size of Delaware, smack dab in the middle of the Lone Star State; a domain unto itself, where that paradigm of army towns, Killeen, a municipality more military than civilian, stuck to one border of the base the way a bunion grips a big toe.

Till Texas my first six months in the service had been something of a lark. Ft. Benning was a nine-week Boy Scout Jamboree for post-adolescent males, and Ft. Holabird, a variant of academic life in khaki. As officer-in-charge of Ft. Hood's counterintelligence unit, I would now, presumably, begin to earn my keep. The army table of organization called for a second lieutenant to head this office, but I soon discovered that my status was purely titular. Real authority rested with two career special agents, who, when not in civilian clothes — the uniform *du jour* for our staff of seven — wore the insignia of chief warrant officers, a hybrid grade in the command chain between enlisted ranks and officer corps.

In practice, newly minted lieutenants who attempted to lead subordinates infinitely more seasoned in military matters than themselves quickly became objects of derision. Seldom, except perhaps by some recent inductee as raw as he, would you ever hear an army second lieutenant being addressed as "sir." If appropriately modest he was treated with indifference, and simply called "lieutenant." Should he make himself obnoxious the pronunciation of his title was squealed — "Loooo-tenant" — to hog call proportions to remind the bearer of this insignificant "butter bar" insignia of his true ranking in the barnyard of command.

Happily for me army intelligence tolerated relationships among the ranks

that were more collegial than military. Having quickly taken my measure as
a guy not bent on going by the book, my new coworkers welcomed me on
terms of forbearance akin to those extended to the wife's favorite brother. The
two chiefs installed me as their latest figurehead-in-residence, paying due
respect to form by giving me the unit's largest office. Then they went about
their business as if I wasn't there, friendly enough, but with little pretense of
involving me in the planning or decision-making of their operations. I was
presented with a set of "box tops"—badge and credentials number 2432—a
snub-nosed .38 revolver, and, to further enhance my cover, a green civilian
sticker for the small Honda motorcycle I purchased within days of my arrival.
With no real duties to speak of I assumed my pose as Special Agent Uhl, permitted, for the most part, to come and go as I pleased.

I was well aware from the beginning that the two chiefs in my office were
engaged in a witch hunt. They spent hours each day trying to identify disaffected GIs spreading antiwar sentiments among the troops, especially the
leaders, whom the army hoped to arrest and punish or, failing that, brand as
undesirables and discharge from the service.

My natural, if inactive, sympathies were with the disaffected; there were
generational vibes which eluded the old farts in and out of the military who
were still fighting World War Two. Where they sensed danger, I saw only the
mundane. But a deeper national feeling gripped me beneath the crude surface of that tired Cold War ideology, and I wasn't such a dilettante or, as yet,
so resolutely alienated from the army, that I didn't make some small effort at
first to swim with the prevailing current.

There were files on hand, mostly devoted to an antiwar coffee house
called the Oleo Strut, which had only recently opened on Killeen's main drag;
and dossiers recording the movements and actions of the civilian and GI
activists who worked there. And there were other files at G-2—general staff
for intelligence—providing background on the antiwar movement. I had better study these too, the colonel told me, since I would probably accompany
troops from Ft. Hood going to Chicago should opponents of the war carry
out their much publicized threat to disrupt the National Democratic Convention, set to open there in August 1968.

The quality of these G-2 files, a few articles seemingly clipped at random from *Time* and *Newsweek*, profiling antiwar personalities like Rennie
Davis and Abbie Hoffman, offended even my muted expectations of spycraft
professionalism. Added to a belief that opposition to the war, for soldiers as
well as civilians, constituted free expression, not subversion, was my genuine
shock that a major command like Ft. Hood relied on the popular media for
information about a set of adversaries its soldiers might be called on to con-
front as early as the coming summer.

I have focused on these two sets of files because they were the key external stimuli I can identify that caused a shift, however slight, in the ballast of my own political evolution. Thereafter I was able to psychologically distance myself from any obligation to carry out the mission of my office. And to this day I'm not at all certain whether it was my reluctance to play the bully in relation to a bunch of GIs whose antiwar attitudes had pissed off the almighty command, or my disdain for the intellectual shoddiness of my colleagues and superiors, that played the more decisive role in this spontaneous resolve. In the absence of any deeper convictions, however, I soon became all but overwhelmed by feelings of isolation. From that point on, the army would become an increasingly uncomfortable place for me.

My civilian cover mitigated some of this discomfort. Just being free of the uniform meant I could sidestep the more robotic military humiliations, all the bowing and scraping. Most people I encountered at Hood, including senior officers, assumed I *was* a civilian. Another advantage was being allowed to live off base, though here the tradeoff was questionable. Killeen, a visual and cultural wasteland, offered little more than a bit of geographical separation from the numbing homogeneity that characterizes life on most U.S. military bases, Ft. Hood being no exception.

Many years later I came across a copy of *Sing Out!* magazine in which blues singer Barbara Dane described perfectly how Killeen looked in those days "with its strings of greasy spoons, pawn shops, loan sharks, used car lots and motels, without even a decent movie or bookstore to offset the pin-ball palace and the pool room." Still I suspect it was mood as much as means which led me to that crummy one-room efficiency in a converted old motel.

I had no friends as yet, no instant pool of roommates, like at Holabird, to help defray expenses for better quarters. But the impulse to slum was an innate pull toward anonymity which my silent withdrawal from the machinations of army intelligence now gave me the freedom to indulge. Ironically this latent antisocial trait might have adapted me well for the role of ideal spy, if only I'd been armed with fewer scruples. As it was, circumstances did not permit me to completely skirt the intrigues developing around me.

Seen in one light, the role I would come to play at the Oleo Strut was, *de facto*, that of a double agent. But this is to suggest something reckless, even heroic, on my part, which was not the case. My own interests dictated that I avoid a clash with military authority. I was willing to court only minimal risk. If I made some meager contribution to the welfare of the antiestablishment coffee house and those who staffed it, this rested ultimately on my stance of strict neutrality.

There were heroes enough at the Oleo Strut, civilians and GIs alike, but I wasn't one of them. The mere presence of this evangelical outpost in a region dominated by patriotic orthodoxy and political reaction, where not just hostility, but sinister, even murderous, intentions dogged its organizers' every move, was — to me — an act of pure courage as awe inspiring as it was incomprehensible. A score of such projects would be established over the course of the war in towns abutting major training posts across the country, guided and supported by a coalition of radicals, including elements of Students for a Democratic Society, calling itself SOS — Summer of Support, and later the United States Servicemen's Fund (USSF).[1] But none of these centers of GI resistance proved a greater threat to the "good order and discipline" of the U.S. armed forces than the Oleo Strut.

I might not have started going there at all had the town offered any reasonable alternative. But after a few deadly evenings shooting pool, I cruised slowly past the Strut, and the scene there appeared leagues more inviting than anything Killeen's other leisure dives had to offer. The organizers had created an informal — but hip — café setting, where a spinning light on the ceiling strobed wall posters of rebel political icons, alongside a busty, but otherwise incongruous, Raquel Welch. Of the patrons, overwhelmingly off-duty GIs, a few had their noses buried in newspapers or magazines. The majority percolated around the small tables in animated conversation, while the activists who staffed the place, both male and female, circulated among them. Here was the antithesis of the nonverbal posturing and compulsive boozing that so typified the holding pens where most American servicemen spend their idle hours.

To cover my ass I decided to inform the boys back at CI that, from time to time, I was going to pop into the coffee house to see what I could see. The sudden appearance of an underground paper, *Fatigue Press*, had the command in a snit, but it gave me the rationale I needed. The CI section was urgently trying to discover, not only the names of its GI editors, but also confirmation of a pet theory that the paper was being laid out in the back room of the Strut, and then run off on military equipment somewhere on the base. Working on the paper, in and of itself, might have subjected a given individual to ugly pressures back at company headquarters, but could not be forbidden outright. The unauthorized use, on the other hand, of an army mimeograph, not to mention involvement with the paper during duty hours or with its distribution on base where it was considered contraband — any of these infractions would have provided the brass with ready grounds for initiating disciplinary action.

Who better than me to get a close-up look of the Strut's operation? — I argued back at CI. Didn't I at least look the part? I was early John Lennon in wire rim glasses with a longish, nonmilitary hair style and my bushy mustaches now regrown. What I chose not to confide to my military mates was that, once inside, I planned to see as little as possible and above all, to keep completely to myself whatever I did observe that might potentially incriminate someone.

Despite these virtuous intentions, carried out to the letter, I could never feel at ease sitting around the Strut. What if someone recognized me and I was accused of being what I was only pretending to be, a spy? The chances were remote; still I avoided conversation; that way, in the worst case, no one could claim that I had been actively gathering information. To pass the time I'd nurse a coke and browse back issues of *Rolling Stone* and the *Village Voice*. Once or twice I'd see or overhear something, and think, wouldn't those buzzards back at CI like to know that! But I was like a browser taking cover in a bookstore, waiting out a rain storm. I was strictly "no sale." Before long I had to stop going to the Strut. I couldn't bear it anymore.

That I might possess the choice of openly siding with the opposition never crossed my mind. My head just wasn't there. I admired the Strut activists and their GI allies, but I didn't identify with them. It wasn't the war; I'd already smelled a rat there for a long time, though why I never bothered to look into it more deeply is still a mystery to me. I guess language study never exposed me to a deeper vision of history. What I didn't get is where these kids got the balls to stand up to an authority as seemingly all-powerful as the army. The fact that they could, and did, however, made it unmistakably clear why their mere presence gave the brass what in the colorful barracks idiom was "a case of the ass."

And that was why, from the moment of its inception, the Oleo Strut was under siege by a host of local authorities demanding this or that permit, or citing some litany of alleged code violations. The two chiefs at CI gleefully kept me abreast of every form of bother and intimidation the command helped direct, with the willing cooperation of Killeen's town fathers, fire department, and police toward these brazen outlanders. In an atmosphere of escalating threats the Strut's front window was smashed one night by vigilantes; in Killeen this meant either the Klan or the "goat ropers," as the teenage rednecks were derisively labeled.

I found news of these attacks upsetting, but at least they were public and tended to neutralize some of the hostility aimed at the young crusaders by the more genteel townsfolk, whose distaste for the native underclass had its own roots and prejudices. And, of course, by bureaucratizing the conflict around issues of legitimate civic concern like food service hygiene or fire safety, the local establishment inadvertently laid a path for compliance which the Strut organizers were quick to follow. Fighting such skirmishes in the open was one thing; but against the clandestine provocations being engineered behind this diversionary smokescreen by various military agencies, including my own, defense was not so certain.

For some time, the command had been keeping an eye on a young enlisted man I will call Specialist Booth, who worked in the mental health clinic as a social worker. One of Booth's duties was to provide counseling for all new arrivals at the Ft. Hood stockade. He was also one of the most active volunteers at the Oleo Strut, quietly at work wherever he was needed, from renovations to counter service. It was strongly alleged, moreover, that Booth was a guiding principal behind *Fatigue Press*.

To the brass Specialist Booth symbolized the worst kind of enemy within. He despised the army, but nonetheless functioned as a model soldier. And while he openly organized against the war on his own time, he was careful to do so without overstepping the narrow bounds of legality imposed by military regulations. The brass hoped to make an example of Booth, to slap him with some violation that ideally would put the man behind bars, or, at the very minimum, deny him the benefits of an honorable discharge. But with only a short time remaining in his service commitment it looked as if Specialist Booth would escape the clutches of his vengeful superiors.

Enter the dastardly CI cabal: I arrived at work one morning to find the two chiefs huddled in their office with a third man hatching a plot they would later describe, without a hint of apprehension for its Freudian transparency, as a "penetration." Beckoned to join their circle with the grave invitation, "Lieutenant, I think you'd better get in on this," what I heard blew my mind. The "third man" was also an agent on loan from an outside command. He was a "plant" about to be *inserted* in the stockade where, in the course of normal in-processing, he would be interviewed by Specialist Booth. The plant would then tell Booth that he wanted to desert, and could Booth help him make contact with a network of resisters known as the underground railway ,who could spirit him safely to Canada?

I had by now developed some small stake in Booth's security. What I'd seen at the Strut — Booth and his cronies loading stacks of the *Fatigue Press* and other antiwar "contraband" into his car for probable circulation on post — was just the kind of trivial evidence the brass needed to trump up charges against Booth and the others. Knowing that Booth was a prime target of official wrath, I had been all the more determined to do any small thing in my power to shield him from pursuit.

Fortunately this required nothing more on my part than keeping my mouth shut. I had by then correctly surmised that the CI honchos hadn't taken my bogus stake-out at the Strut any more seriously than I had. Now I discovered why. It was like in the old Bogart movie, *Treasure of Sierra Madre*, where the rogue *federales* spit out that they "don't need no stinkin' bat-ches" to exercise their authority. Well the two chiefs "didn't need no stinkin' stake-out"; they had the powers of entrapment at their finger tips. All I could do was watch from the sidelines, and hope that Booth was as savvy as I suspected.

Indeed, he was. Booth slipped the trap with ease, whether wittingly or otherwise, I'll never know. Not that it came as any great surprise when I heard that he simply refused to provide self-incriminating information to a perfect stranger who had "agent" written all over him. Having parried their best thrust, Booth ceased to command the attention of Ft. Hood's intelligence hounds. They could not risk a second failure in an operation which required authorization at the highest levels. A month or two afterwards, much to the chagrin of his would-be tormentors, Booth was honorably discharged from the United States Army. But not before a conjuncture of events, quite unrelated to this drama, led to one final and — for me — troubling encounter between us.

❖ ❖ ❖

"So, what's new," I asked Marty, one of two enlisted men assigned to CI, when I found him inside the darkroom on that Thursday morning early in June. "They killed Bobby Kennedy," he replied, visibly shaken. Marty, a pudgy, slightly effeminate, and very decent young guy, was ticking off his four year enlistment in the lower echelons of army intelligence. He and Benson, his peer in rank, handled CI's routine administrative chores; Marty spent hours honing the skills of black and white photography, dipping from the rich trove of materials and equipment the army furnished us, and intended for our professional, not recreational, use. After Marty taught me how to develop and print my own film I signed out a fine old Leica and a Hasselblad, and these became boon companions during my long night in Texas.

News of the assassination hit me hard. At that moment Bobby Kennedy represented the embodiment of my tenuous link to domestic politics. Style, not content, made him the obvious choice over Eugene McCarthy, the other "peace" candidate seeking the Democratic Party presidential nomination — the flamboyant Kennedy sneer over the owlish pedant and countercounterculturalist who wanted kids to look like fifties clones, "clean for Gene," if they wished to associate with his campaign. That and the fact that I nourished a memory of a breezy encounter with the former attorney general.

Back in college in the late spring of 1966 I'd been working in a pub called the Tombs, a popular watering spot for Georgetown undergrads located virtually on campus. Following the lunch rush, another waiter and I decided to take our break on the sidewalk. Parked in the street was a blue Ford convertible, its top down, with a huge black Lab retriever all but overflowing the back seat.

"That's a Kennedy car," J.C. observed casually. Bobby knew some Jebbies — as the Jesuits were called — and he hired students like J.C. to work on the grounds of his Virginia estate, which is where my friend had seen the car. "One of the crew probably over here running some errand," J.C. figured. We crossed to the car and I hopped aboard the rear fender where I sat patting the dog with one hand and puffing on a Pall Mall with the other. Suddenly the door to the main dining room opened, and out sprang Bobby Kennedy making a beeline for the Ford intoning *alto voce*, "I ah-hope the ah-dawg isn't ah BAAAH-thah-ing yew." He was all smiles and charm and we shook his hand in the same high spirits before he slid behind the wheel and peeled out, disappearing around the corner of N Street.

Some part of my psyche doubled over when Marty told me Bobby Kennedy was dead; another blow around the same time struck even deeper. The truest cliché in war, someone wrote, is the *Dear John*, because nearly every soldier seems to get one. The letter from Katie, though long anticipated, had to await the requisite long distance separation between intimates that typically accompanies military service and spices this ritual with its air of irreversibility. And so, with these two events I experienced that sensation many soldiers feel of being marginalized, cut off from ties to the past, and of suddenly becoming, even in one's own eyes, expendable.

A healthy young man under stress, as I was, is thought to be well equipped to fend off life's normal setbacks, to find new avenues of escape and compensation. Gripped by such instincts I made every effort to do so. Having abandoned my naive fantasy of finding a haven in the Oleo Strut, I made frequent trips to Austin only sixty miles away — unique in Texas for its small cosmopolitan enclave centered around the prosperous and diverse University of Texas.

Photography now filled much of my spare time. I'd shoot during the week and haunt the darkroom evenings and weekends blowing up snapshots into glossy 8 × 10s, including one self-portrait where I'm seated on my bed smoking a cigar with a poster of Che Guevara hung on the wall to my rear.

And though I hadn't a clue yet as to what writing was all about, I had the sudden urge to begin jotting down my thoughts and feelings. I purchased a thick spiraled journal, the size of a quality paperback, Masterpiece Notes No. 169. Most of the entries now strike me as painfully glib and sophomoric; a lack of thoughtfulness in the way I snaked around things frustrates my current obsession for documentary certainty. Still, it was a beginning, and at least one passage clearly reflects my self-described dilemma and state of mind at that time:

> I don't want you to think that I go around with a long face at every second, or that I can't cope with my everyday activities. There are some nice people,

Self-portrait taken at Ft. Hood, Texas, summer 1968.

and even one stimulating person. It's just that when I'm depressed, it's just a little too depressed over nothing, and when I'm happy, it's just a little too happy over nothing.

I'm going to San Antonio — with my two cameras and sit by the little canal and drink some wine.

I have to tell somebody. I can't go to a doctor. I look alright on the outside, but my mind is screaming.

I guess I just can't face this type of reality — but is that good or bad — that's the question?

This reads like a letter, but I don't think it was meant for anyone but myself, with perhaps the idea of Katie looking over my shoulder. For she is the only one to whom I would have ever confessed such pain. It was probably not long after making this entry that I did "go the doctor." An appointment was made for me at Mental Hygiene, and as I walked past Specialist Booth to enter the consultation room, I detected an attitude in his expression as his eyes locked into mine. And I thought to myself, "You sonofabitch. I saved your ass. How dare you give me that look." The shrink heard me out, and gave me script for Librium, which I took once and didn't like; it sapped my will, the only source of whatever wiles I still possessed to steady myself under circumstances that were difficult, but hardly unmanageable.

June, July, into early August — the days groaned along, the worst of it being that I had no real function other than my maneuvers to avoid the ideological cross fire. Events continued to occur which filled me with disgust. A Fourth of July "Be-In," one of those mixed political/cultural events that were true artifacts of the sixties, had attracted the participation of some two hundred off-duty GIs at a park in Killeen. Really what you were talking about was a picnic, a momentary window of civilian reality that was too threatening for a tight-assed military command to tolerate.

There'd been some dope smoking. No doubt. Mexico was a hundred miles south, and they didn't call this place "Fort Head" for nothing. (No one in authority, of course, ever asks the question, "Why do people smoke dope?") And there were MP detectives with cameras photographing the kids who'd gathered there. For two weeks thereafter pictures of those GIs circulated between our office and every unit in the command, where company sergeants were told to circle in red the face of any troop they could identify, then write his name on the back of the print. The delight with which the two chiefs at CI took on this task illustrates better than any other single incident I witnessed the boneheaded narrow-mindedness of the career military, and its utter incapacity for grasping, much less adapting to, the tide of change in values and behavior that, by 1973, would all but swamp the American armed forces.

That stool pigeon mentality masquerading as command prerogative is just the kind of antidemocratic virus that breeds among professional soldiers and makes it clear why, in a society wishing to remain free, the military bears watching. This is how I feel today. At the time, I saw those fistfuls of black and white photographs as tokens of foul play, poor sportsmanship, *in loco parental* tyranny, dirty pool, bad form, and — in military parlance — conduct unbecoming. What this bred within me was an allergic reaction to army life, even under privileged circumstances that the average draftee would have killed for.

The Rebellion

One Saturday morning in August the phone rang early at CI, where I'd spent the night as weekend duty officer. My immediate boss, the deputy G-2, was on the line. I'd better get my young ass over to the MP lock-up on the double, the major advised. There'd been a "riot" the night before. Scores of black soldiers had gathered in a parking lot, and many refused a direct order to disperse by no less an authority than the commanding general himself. Over forty arrests had been made. Something to do with Chicago and the men wanting a guarantee that they wouldn't be used there against their "brothers and sisters in the ghetto." The major suspected "outside agitators," and I was to interview several of the "leaders" to find out who was pulling their strings.

The young black man behind the bars of the cell was a study in contradiction. His summer khakis were crisp and embroidered with the evidence of many service achievements. He had three proud stripes, a buck sergeant, and was heavily decorated. Beneath several rows of ribbons he wore the CIB, the combat infantryman's badge of honor (in contrast, my breast pocket sported a single commendation, the National Defense or "everybody medal" they give you just for showing up). Lean and handsome, his was an image off a recruitment poster. But his face was broken with fear.

He made up some tale about having been a victim of mistaken identity, asleep in the back seat of his car and rounded up in an MP dragnet just because his skin was black. "Please, Lieutenant" — I wore my rank in conformity with my assignment as duty officer — "call my company sergeant and have him come and pick me up." It made me sick to have this combat veteran stand before me and beg for help; everything he'd gained in the army, everything he'd given in Vietnam, counted for nothing now. Singled out as a leader of a petty mutiny, he would be court martialed, sent to jail, then, very probably, cashiered from the service in disgrace.

I asked a guard if I could use the phone to ring up the young man's unit. A voice at the other end bellowed, "Company such-and-such, this is Sergeant First Class so-and-so, SIR!" I could hear his heavy breathing as I repeated the prisoner's alibi, telling him he could come and secure the man's release at his convenience. "Now you listen to me, Lieutenant," he spat out, the cadence of his words purposely slow and threatening, "I saw that boy there personally and he can rot in that cell before I'll lift a finger to get him out."

This was not the response I had anticipated. Foolishly I imagined that a call from an intelligence officer assigned to corps headquarters would carry some clout, that I could spring this one forlorn trooper whose courage in refusing to be herded off to Chicago to police urban blacks or protesters deserved — in my eyes — an additional medal for his already resplendent chest. What really disturbed me, however, was that this man had been to war, and this was how his country rewarded him.

I was furious and humiliated when I hung up the phone, and easily defeated. Slinking away, I left that soldier to his despair and returned to my office knowing that my boss, the deputy G-2, would never follow up on this investigation. He was a cracker who'd come up through the ranks; a mustang they called them. I'd been out drinking with him once, and the "Negro question" soon dominated the bar chat, as it often did then when Northern and Southern whites sat down to socialize. After a few stiff Bourbons the major bared his teeth; like that old routine about LBJ being tutored to pronounce the word "Negro," and he'd strain, saying "Negra," "Neeeegra," but it always comes out "nigger" in the end.

The case against these men in the major's mind was open and shut long before he put me on the spot that morning. The young sergeant may have been a scoundrel for all I knew; but he stood condemned, as he and I could both agree, as much for his race and pigmentation as for his actions. Twenty-six of those men known as the Ft. Hood 43 were convicted and sent to prison, the longest for 10 months, a relatively light sentence, the histories reassure us.

Choosing Vietnam

A week-long field exercise brought a break in the tedium. Back in fatigues, loaded down with web gear, steel pot and rifle, I reassumed the outward appearance of a soldier. To arrive at the bivouac area I hitched my first ride in a "slick," a Huey helicopter; it was an exhilarating ordeal that racheted my already considerable acrophobia to a pitch of sweat-soaked hysteria.

Somewhere beyond view tanks rumbled across those scrubby wilds day and night, while back at field HQ we shot the shit and played hearts. Old sign-out sheets from Supply in my own files do confirm a vague memory of having been issued both sections of a "shelter half," so I had a pup tent entirely to myself, and I remember thinking, how could two grown men possibly share these stingy accommodations. At night I read by flashlight, *Ulysses* by James Joyce, my ongoing literary passion.

One significant, fateful conversation did occur during that week in the field. One of my few drinking buddies at Hood, an LT —"El Tee," we said — from personnel, had come out for a day on some inscrutable chore pertaining to his office. It just came up. I asked him how orders come down for Vietnam? Personnel, he explained, received faceless levies from the Department of the Army. Warm bodies were then chosen at random from the various units scattered throughout Ft. Hood, subject to a bit of horse trading as commanders attempted to keep their own outfits at strength, or moved to favor certain individuals over others. Could one initiate this process? Yes, he said. A Request for Orders could flow in the opposite direction from Hood to DA. And flow it did. Soon after returning from the field such a form, dated August 13, 1968, was dispatched at my request.

A week later the orders arrived. Lt. Uhl was to report to the Americal Division in Chu Lai, Republic of Vietnam, no later than the 23rd of November, which meant that, even subtracting for a thirty day leave, I still had two months to twiddle my thumbs in Texas. I'd always sensed I'd end up in Vietnam; now any lingering uncertainties were removed. The surface emotion propelling me to commit this putatively reckless act was one of uncontrollable restlessness; but that was only half the picture. I did not have the need that some men do to prove themselves in battle; my curiosity was of the kind that kills the cat, the kind — as I have later come to understand — that writers have. The great and eccentric jurist Oliver Wendell Holmes expressed it somewhere, that if the central event of one's generation was a war, then that was where you had to be.

❖ ❖ ❖

The weekend just before my new orders came I caught a ride to Dallas to visit my maternal uncle, Bill Cushing, his wife Ponnie and my cousin John, the youngest of their three sons, and the only one still living at home. They were the gypsies in our family, and Bill, the black sheep, a civil engineer in construction temporarily settling his family in Texas by way of Brooklyn, Ohio, and Venezuela, to name the major points along the compass where they'd put down roots. We barely heard from them one year to the next, but the sense of kinship among siblings and cousins remained strong.

Ponnie and Bill were quite odd in some respects compared with their contemporaries in my family, traditionalists to a person. They were drawn to spiritism. A letter they sent to my parents a few days after my visit recounts that "Mike got up at 8 a.m. Saturday and we had a chance to get reacquainted with him. We all talked at once and had a great time." In fact, Bill, a numerologist, did his mumbo jumbo with my numbers, while Ponnie read my aura, she being a devotee of Edgar Cayce. Everything about me, the portents revealed, was special. Their eccentricities awed and fascinated me, and their sons Willy, David, and especially John, I saw as wild men.

But in one critical respect this branch of my family was as conventional as all the others. Of eight male first cousins on both sides of my family, including my younger brother Tom and me, not one — like our fathers before us during World War Two — would make an effort to avoid military service. Age, marital status and disability exempted most of them according to how the rules of the draft were written. But of the three of us who served — John, myself and another cousin on the Cushing side, Doug — all went to Vietnam, a considerably higher percentage than the national average for families of our generation. John, a door gunner, was reputedly a junkie when he came home;

he was killed a year later in a head-on collision on a Texas highway. Doug died relatively young of cancer. War related? Agent Orange? Who can really say?

The real evil Vietnam portended for me, my cousins and tens of thousands like us, was foreshadowed in a friendly but cryptic cautionary tale I heard from Benson, who, aside from Marty and myself, was the only non-lifer in the CI section. I didn't register its true meaning at the time, but the story so impressed me that I copied it clean from a draft version I had quickly scribbled on a paper napkin into my notebook. I think it was that thousand mile stare, and the bloodless, zombie tone he used more than anything he actually said that really got under my skin.

Benson's Tale

This is about Jones, the one man in Vietnam I could not stand. One day Jones stubbed his toe on some makeshift weights I made in Nam. Jones said, get those fuckin' weights out of the way, Benson, or I'll saw them in fuckin' half. I said, if you touch those weights, Jones, I'll blow your head off. I won't fight you, because you're too big and I'd lose. I'll get my .45. I won't give you any warning. I'll just come up behind you and whisper, Jones, and put a bullet in your head. And that will be that.

That slowed him down, Benson told me.

III

Days of War (1)

We are the music makers, and we are the dreamers of
dreams.
                                    — *Arthur O'Shaughnessy*

Late in 1968 a lame duck LBJ still occupied the White House. The war
that cost him his presidency, while no longer always front page news, was stuck
to the body politic like a tar baby. The American troop buildup wouldn't
even peak in Vietnam until March of the following year. Nixon's "secret plan"
to end the war sounded about as credible as his later claim, after Watergate,
"I am not a crook." With its novel assembly line system for conveying replace-
ments to the front one soldier at a time, warfare had begun to occupy a kind
of permanent industrial presence on the American landscape like any other
giant corporation or institution. The afternoon I put my own body on that
line — November 18th — the four parties to the Paris Peace Talks finally agreed
on the shape of the table they would sit around to negotiate; it seemed to me
as if the war might go on forever.

A brief note to my parents begun shortly after touching down in Vietnam provides the bare facts of the journey. I'd left McChord Air Force Base
in Tacoma, Washington, at 5 p.m. on the 19th, and arrived in Cam Ranh Bay
sometime after noon on November 21st — having lost part of a calendar day
while crossing the International Date Line. After a few lines itemizing the
flight's itinerary, the note tails off to be picked up two days later with the
addendum that an "alert" and order for "lights-out" had interrupted my writing, and that I'd finally caught up on my sleep following the exhausting trip
and would soon be en route north to join my unit, the 52nd Military Intelligence Detachment of the Americal Division. "All is well," I hedged.

"All is surreal" would have been closer to the mark. Commercial airlines
flew troops to Vietnam on charters; mine was a Braniff 707 painted purple

and yellow like an Easter egg. Our first stop was Honolulu, where I'd no sooner sat down in the airport bar over an icy Michelob when some prick of a captain ordered me to accompany him back to the runway. An officer with the appropriate security clearance was needed to serve as courier for some "top secret" documents. And, no, I could not "just finish my beer," which was abandoned two-thirds full. For the next two hours I sat alone in the plane with two huge mail bags at my feet.

Ten and a half hours later, sleepless in my case, we landed at Clark Air Base outside Manila in the middle of a clear, starlit night. Someone relieved me of the mail bags and I joined the other GIs in a gigantic hangar, empty except for a long line of collapsible tables where I queued up for a stale powdered donut and a cup of watery, lukewarm coffee.

An hour and a half out of Cam Ranh the chief stewardess announced they had a surprise for us, and handed out hot dogs, one to a man. This was the army's idea of a treat. You'd think someone would have had the sense to lay it on, all you could eat. I mean, forget the sentimental rhetoric about "concern for the welfare of the men." It's just so obvious. Most of the GIs on that plane were kids; hungry, growing boys. Everyone knew it was just more army bullshit. But we all sat there, numb as cods, and took what was coming to us when the bubbly, miniskirted attendants passed around the little cardboard containers. It's silly, I know, but I'm still bitter about that lost beer and that single stingy hot dog.

In-Country

If what happened next sounds as if you've read it before, it's probably because you have. The ritual of the arrival "in-country" has entered the Vietnam literature virtually in the form of a parable. In its interchangeable essentials the experience had been shared and retold by countless veterans of the war.[1]

The heat nearly sucked the breath from my lungs as I stepped into the open air, a proverbial oven. Olive drab buses idled a short distance from the plane's exit ramp. The new arrivals filed aboard as ground personnel barked rapid-fire instructions. I plopped into a front seat and scanned the horizon. No perimeter was visible beyond the airstrip, no hint of the *native* civilization, only the kinds of impermanent structures you'd expect to find on a U.S. military installation overseas. Wide sandy patches, like flattened dunes, separated the footpaths and roadways. The quiet vastness of the place, interrupted now and then by the roar of an aircraft engine, has left me with a strangely permanent shadow of anxiety.

Before we'd driven far I leaned forward to ask the driver why the windows of the vehicle were covered with wire mesh. "It's the gooks," he said, jutting his chin in the direction of an elderly Vietnamese squatted beside the road, filling sand bags. "Grenades," he added, just as the "gook" looked up to watch the bus pass by, his expression hard and ominous. This old guy hates us, I thought. If we aren't safe here, where are we safe?

That in a nutshell is the story of the Vietnam War, as anyone knows who got at all close to the fighting or to the people who lived there. Every memoir, every novel, and much of the poetry written by American veterans over the past thirty years, whatever their author's political slant on the war, relates this elemental truth about the Vietnam experience. Right from day one it was us — the Americans — against them — the Vietnamese, every one of them. And the kernel of that truth appeared to me in the epiphany I describe above only moments after arriving in-country; it was all downhill from there.

Chu Lai

Up in Chu Lai I was called into the office of Major Heinz, who commanded the 52nd MI Detachment. He told me I'd be going south to take charge of an intelligence team attached to the 11th Infantry, one of three brigades that comprised the Americal Division. The brigade base camp was LZ — for "landing zone" — Bronco, which bordered the coastal town of Duc Pho in the lower quadrant of the division's AO — area of operations — between the provincial port towns of Quang Ngai and Qui Nhon.

I copied Heinz's word into the small black leather notebook I carried throughout my tour. His briefing is by far the biggest entry, beginning with the names of the Americans in my new team, then the ARVN (Army of Vietnam) soldiers who were the unit's interpreters and interrogators. Heinz gave me the brigade's strategic profile, the placement with map coordinates of its combat battalions and the fire bases — those outposts fanning deeper into the surrounding countryside — that they garrisoned. There was the 4th Battalion of the 3rd Infantry on Firebase Thunder here, and the 3rd of the 1st on Firebase Liz there, and so on.

Heinz also identified with numerical designations the three "main force" VC (Vietcong) units that normally operated in the brigade AO, the C219th, the C120 Sappers, and the 83rd Mobile Battalion, which I would never hear of again in the field. He became momentarily animated when he talked about information we might come by that even remotely spoke of the sighting of an American prisoner of war. This, he said was to be coded "bright light" and immediately wired to intelligence headquarters in Saigon.

Heinz moved on to housekeeping chores, some procedural information

LZ Bronco, Duc Pho, South Vietnam, base camp of the 11th Infantry Brigade.

on the pay and supervision of Kit Carson scouts who were supposedly former enemy guerrillas who'd rallied to the government of South Vietnam, and were now assigned to guide American infantry companies in the field. Then follows assorted entries on other standing activities, mapping the enemy's "order of battle," maintaining "black lists" on suspects who might pose as scouts or laborers and attempt to infiltrate base security. And finally there's a vague notation with the three initials ICF, a reference to our heavily monitored "intelligence contingency fund," a stock of local currency and premiums like quarts of Jack Daniels and cartons of Marlboros kept on hand to bribe informers who reported the enemy's movements, and, in the most dramatic instances, fingered VCI — Viet Cong Infrastructure, the cadres of the National Liberation Front who moved from hamlet to hamlet performing duties that varied from collecting taxes to conducting political education.

I had to spend three days at division in Chu Lai completing the mandatory "jungle" re-orientation, a rehash in shorthand of all the stuff I'd learned, or failed to learn, at Ft. Benning's Infantry Officers School. Garrison behavior prevailed at Chu Lai, an up-tight attention to the petty military formalities that intensify in direct proportion to one's proximity to "the flagpole," the seat of command. A division base camp in a combat zone, commanded by a two-star general, is top-heavy with brass, every species of staff officer and semiautonomous headquarters for support elements like engineers, transportation, intelligence, artillery, air force liaison and so on. Everyone kissing ass or kicking ass, depending on his spot in the pecking order. Over drinks a couple of disconsolate LTs who shuffled paper at the 52nd, and who weren't career minded lifers, let me know how lucky I was to be leaving for Brigade.

Well, yes and no. In both cases you were on the frontier, the Chu Lai base camp being to Dodge City what LZ Bronco was to Ft. Apache. Either place you could be a sitting duck when the lead or flaming arrows began to fly, but your odds were a lot better at Division, if for no other reason than it was ten times larger, plus there were amenities the brigade base camp lacked. Chu Lai wasn't Saigon or Nha Trang, where men with my counterintelligence training lived like Yankee pashas in their Cho Lon flats or in seaside villas, jollying their concubines and playing secret agent man. But you could get a steak or hamburger and a cold beer seven days a week at Chu Lai, even take a dip in the South China Sea. With the 11th Brigade you lived like a grunt even if you weren't one; while the real grunts lived like ants, holed up in bunkers on fire bases or wandered like game in the bush, bait on the hoof, to lure the enemy into making contact. Still, when the "legs," or infantry soldiers, filed into LZ Bronco every month or so for their periodic stand-downs, it must have felt like they were entering the Emerald City. Like Dante's *Inferno*, the war was a hell with many levels.

I was no grunt, but I hadn't gone to war to parade in garrison or paint rocks, GI lingo for some meaningless chore when there's nothing productive to be done. Staying with the Americal in Chu Lai would have been like being trapped in a giant truck stop for a year on an isolated stretch along the interstate. It was still your culture in some deprived form; it didn't feel like Vietnam.

Duc Pho had an exotic ring to it, and I was more than a little puffed up at having been given command of the unit I was going to. This ego boost would turn sour soon enough as it gradually became clear that oversensitive souls like me do not great leaders make — especially when their health takes a nosedive — as would be my fate — and your body isn't there to prop you up when things go bad.

LZ Bronco—The 1st MIT

When the C-123 prop transport finally touched down at Bronco I wanted to inspect the fuselage to see if the ungodly turbulence we'd bumped through all down the coast had left a single rivet snug in its seams. Real flying, the thrill-seekers call it. On the ground in Vietnam I would expose myself to many risks without a second thought, but in the air — though I would eventually overcome my fear of flying in choppers — I become like the cowards Shakespeare's Caesar spoke of who "die many times before their deaths."

My face drained of color, I squinted through the midday glare at the young man who stood before me smiling warmly. "You must be the new LT," he said, saluting, then offering his hand. "Gray, Sir. Sergeant. Gordan Gray. Welcome to Duc Pho," his grin turning ironic. In lieu of stripes he wore a "U.S." stitched in black on each lapel of his jungle fatigue blouse revealing that, even with a combat unit, counterintelligence agents were not required to display their rank.

First Military Intelligence Team Compound, LZ Bronco.

Gray led me to a Jeep and we drove a short distance to a tidy circle of tent-topped hootches — knock-up constructions of screens and plywood — set behind a timbered portal carved pagoda-style and painted red. This self-contained military intelligence compound was an incredibly good berth as quarters went at Bronco. Earlier tenants had provided for three essential creature comforts that few other outfits as small as this one could boast of: recreation, hygiene, and reasonable safety.

One hootch was the unit's clubhouse. Pains had been taken to decorate the interior with strips of red vinyl and Christmas tree ornaments, and the large commercial cooler behind the shiny plywood bar was almost always filled with cold beer and soda. Nearly every evening after chow team members gathered here to play ping pong and poker. Flanking the club was a luxury whose importance to morale is difficult to exaggerate, a concrete shower stall with an immersion heater powered by a small kerosene engine that dispensed water as hot as you could stand it. Next to the shower stood the team's communal bunker with a thick steel plated roof that lent an extra layer of protection against the ever-present possibility of a direct hit from enemy "incoming," rockets or mortar rounds.

The MI team was divided into three sections, two of which, OB (Order of Battle) and CI (Counterintelligence), had their offices within this compound. The third section, IPW (Interrogation Prisoner of War), was under the supervision of a Lieutenant Patton, whom Gray kept referring to as the "General," and was located in a corner of the camp near a helipad where Vietnamese prisoners, rounded up during infantry sweeps, were ferried daily from the field.

Gray introduced the team members on hand. The lieutenant I would officially replace in two day's time signed over his M-16 rifle and a snub-nosed .38, the regulation side arm for CI types, about as useful in Vietnam as a sling shot. Later I switched this for a heavier .45 semiautomatic, because the heft riding my hip made me feel not only more secure but more officer-like. I took an odd pleasure in going about armed with a loaded gun in a holster, an obvious fulfillment of childhood war play. But I never fired that forty-five nor any other weapon during my tour, not even for target practice.

There was a great trade in firearms in Vietnam, unauthorized but largely overlooked. GIs armed themselves with enemy AK-47s, the Russian model favored over the Chinese sawed-off shotguns; I saw what looked like a Thompson sub-machine gun once — exotic knives and hatchets, brass knuckles. Every man's fantasy about weapons and warfare had its own threshold, which, by and large, could be explored in Vietnam without inhibition.

The man who tended the OB section was "short," a short timer, and would be gone in a few weeks' time. He was not replaced and Order of Battle at the 1st MIT lapsed into an entropic void. Not that it mattered. The brass hats in Saigon, with all the manpower and techno-gizmos at their disposal, couldn't get a fix on the enemy's position; how could one poor schmuck in a backwater like Duc Pho do any better? He had merely marched colored pins across the face of his giant map, based on dubious sightings of enemy units he was being fed by the other two components of our team.

And that was hardly the point; conventional North Vietnamese forces may have passed through the area of operation from time to time, or even with great frequency, but the local guerrillas didn't concentrate. They massed and dissolved according to the mission at hand, which explains the nomadic tactics of our own infantry, the endless humping over the same terrain, the night patrols and ambushes, all geared toward the chance encounter with an enemy gathering for the moment and caught by surprise.

The two other members of the CI section, Sergeants Dick and Stranzo, approached when they saw I had arrived with Gray. The target of choice for CI, they explained with considerable condescension, was the network of civilians and political operatives who supported the guerrillas, not the fighters per se, but the so-called Vietcong Infrastructure — or VCI.

The way these two guys talked to me was gratuitously hostile, like adolescents who feel compelled to challenge an authority figure even when there is no immediate cause for strife. I took umbrage, and, for the five months I was in their company our relations never sweetened. "*We* go into the field," sneered Stranzo, a short, solidly built Italian-American from upstate New York. "First MI has a rep to uphold, the battalion C.O.'s love us," drawled his crony, Dick, a Georgia boy, with a hint of venom behind the facade of an ingratiating smile. "We're combat-ready and they know it," he boasted. "When we got something hot looo-tenent, we CA² right out there with the grunts to whatever it is, weapons, food caches.... Sometimes Victor Charles himself ... we give 'em bodies."

IPW

"Not everyone goes to the field," Gray volunteered as we drove down to IPW. "It's up to the individual." He himself never went, and neither did the "General." Dick and Stranzo were good guys, he added, trying to tidy up their bad impression, but they were really *into* the war. What about me, he asked, did I think I'd go out? I didn't think so, I replied, as we pulled to a stop before a long, low building painted white with a row of windows stretched along the wall facing the road.

I remember pausing before going in, taking in Bronco's layout and environs, more noticeable from this less cluttered end of the camp. The LZ was oblong, like a race track, and looked to cover no more than a few hundred barren acres studded with hootches and sheds of varying dimensions. A long, wide airstrip occupied the infield. Dominating the boundary of the base camp's eastern straightaway was the foot of a massive hill rising to approximately 400 feet, over which a thin veneer of vegetation spread. Beyond this, some two kilometers to windward, was the sea. A number of similar stand-alone, but natural, mounds appeared in random isolation at several points along the immediate horizon, and the ground was sandy as you would expect near the shore.

Stepping inside the interrogation center I saw a short, compact man with curly dark hair and horn rimmed glasses perched at the tip of his nose, who paced the floor like a mad impresario delivering — to no one in particular — a tirade aimed *in absentia* at one Major Crud, the Brigade S-2, or staff intelligence chief. Five or six desks lined the windowed wall, each occupied by a pair of soldiers, one American, the other Vietnamese, who berated and cajoled the prisoners seated on folding chairs before them.

Patton tried to ignore our arrival at first, and I found myself watching as a wiry young interpreter with a cowlick of black hair that made him look like an Asian Tin Tin, rapped the head of one detainee with the eraser-end of his pencil. With each flick the old man winced and cried, "*khong biet, khong biet.*" "Don't give us that 'cum bic' shit," his American partner bellowed. "We *know* you know. Ask him again, Hung, 'who honcho Farmer Association your ville?'" But before the Asian Tin Tin could frame the question, the GI leaned into the man's face and screamed, "*Ong VC, ong cac-a-dao,*" which is to say,"you're dead meat commie." The old man froze in terror; he understood all too well the foreigner's fractured pidgin.

Gray finally spoke up. "John ... Lieutenant Patton, this is Lieutenant Uhl, the new team chief." Patton turned on his heels and spied the two intruders warily from over the top of his glasses. He didn't mean to appear comedic; nor was he completely blind to the effect his mannered eccentricities had on those around him. The nickname "General" really suggested something Chaplinesque, beyond the coincidental reference to his notorious namesake. On occasion, though rarely, my excitable subaltern would even demonstrate the capacity to laugh at himself. Not on this day, however, as he approached me like a boxer moving toward center-ring to tap gloves with his opponent. I was the new "first john," and he was still second fiddle.

In fact my promotion to first lieutenant had come while I was still in Chu Lai, and, like a cub scout initiate, I felt relieved to pass from Webelo to Wolf. Patton suffered from similar insecurities; as a result, we would spend our months together in one clash of wills and wits after another, a rivalry more intellectual than hierarchical, almost sibling in its intensity. Yet we were companionable in many ways as well, and since our day-to-day military duties occupied different realms, work itself was seldom a source of dispute.

Patton offered a wan handshake, showed me around the premises, and introduced his men. As Gray and I were about to leave, I asked Patton what was behind a closed door at one end of the building. He obliged my curiosity by leading us into a windowless compartment — a Conex ship container that had been adapted as an extension — where an unattached field telephone sat on a blanket-covered table, and, with a solitary chair, provided the room's only furnishings. It was, in effect, the torture chamber. Here, Patton explained, recalcitrant prisoners with potentially vital information were "rung up," subjected to electrical shocks caused by turning the phone's signal crank when the bared ends of the wires were attached to the suspect's fingers.

The revelation of this illegal practice was completely matter-of-fact. Patton said it wasn't used very often. It hurt like hell, of course, but did no lasting damage. To confirm this he once attached the wires to his own fingers and had someone turn the crank. Would I like to try it? he sheepishly inquired. There was then a moment of amusement at my expense as I was quick to decline. Patton's prankish tone broke the ice a bit.

Duc Pho

Gray had offered to show me Duc Pho. And the moment we left IPW I ceased to reflect on what I had just seen and learned. The sight of ordinary American boys bullying what appeared to be ordinary Vietnamese, a few young women, but mostly middle aged and elderly men and women, had not registered on some level. As for the instrument of torture, I imagined an uncomfortable shock from a poorly grounded outlet. Apparently my deeply internalized assumption of America's right to dominate other peoples remained, as yet, unexamined below the baseline of my own moral conscience. This assumption remained sheltered, and temporarily reinforced, by my unexpected stumble into a small position of power.

Then, as if the Vietnamese world I was about to discover in Duc Pho was on a different planet from the scene I'd just left behind, I breezed off in a Jeep like a character in a wartime sitcom to ogle the natives. Psychologically I was probably returning to my undergraduate adventures in Brazil, my only prior exposure to a Third World culture where visual exotica and underdevelopment struck untutored, privileged eyes as some inexorable meld.

We drove past the airstrip and out Bronco's main gate along a rough access road that led to the nearby village. For security reasons the roadside had been cleared of ground cover and structures. But a Catholic church and orphanage stood there still to one side, and on the other, a complex of lean-tos, partially obscured behind scores of jungle fatigues billowing in the open air, suggesting what an army-navy store might look like in an oriental bazaar. This Gray identified as a private laundry that served the entire base camp.

"Downtown" Duc Pho stretched a half-kilometer in either direction from where this access lane to Bronco intersected with Highway 1, Vietnam's main north/south artery that GIs dubbed the Red Ball, unpaved at that time beyond the outskirts of all but the largest cities. It was the lunchtime siesta and the town was quiet. What appeared to be a few shops in front rooms on the ground floors of the most prominent stucco buildings showed no sign of commercial life. Pointing to one of these, Gray said it belonged to a jeweler with suspected VC ties. I naively wondered at the time how such a presence could be tolerated, uninitiated as I was to the social and political complexities of the Vietnamese resistance.

At opposite ends of the road were the town's two bike shops, like filling stations. You'd almost always see activity in these shops, mechanics bent over in repairs of Vietnam's principal mode of overland transport for goods as well as people. The flow of bicycles up and down Highway 1 was constant; otherwise traffic was confined to military vehicles, and an occasional Vespa bus which carried locals from one town to the next. A dozen or more Vietnamese would routinely compress themselves into the rear compartment of one of these wobbly three-wheeled contraptions, roughly half the size of a VW van. The sight never ceased to elicit mirth and mockery from the foreign invaders who observed them.

Duc Pho, as a district capital, was under the direct authority of a military chief appointed by Saigon, whose fortified compound in the middle of the village also housed a MACV[3] team of U.S. advisers. Across the road was the home and office of the police chief, also a government official. The 1st MIT, our intelligence team, explained Gray, maintained almost daily contact with both these entities. *LAY-ah-zon*, he called it, a diversion providing a ready antidote to base camp boredom, hinted Gray. Unlike the infantry and other support troops, MI had *carte blanche* to go between the *ville* and Bronco at any time from dawn to darkness, after which the night belonged to the enemy. Of course the vast majority of those on the American LZ, officers and EM alike, didn't necessarily share the perception that daily contact with the locals was a form of privileged dispensation.

The Colonel's Mess

The next day I appeared at the 11th Brigade commander's mess at noon to join my brother officers for Thanksgiving. On the back of a generic menu printed with the brigade's insignia and motto, "Swift and True," I wrote a brief note home:

> This is a copy of our Thanksgiving menu. Each setting had one of these menus, plus other propaganda from the base chaplain & Gen. Abrams.

We were served every course of the middlebrow menu from shrimp cocktail to fruit and nuts, with turkey and trimmings in between. And there was wine, but I don't recall if it was good or bad. The turkey tablecloths and napkins were incongruous, if not bizarre. My note continued:

> I am forced to eat in the Colonel's mess due to my "lofty" position, i.e. chief of the Bde. MI Team. It's very formal, air conditioned, good food. [?] ... but will take up too much of my time. I have a new section to shape up, and countless things I myself must pick up — rapidly.

Some junior officers, more well-adjusted than I, would have looked upon entry to the Colonel's mess as a boon, a shunt to the inside track. For me the company of career officers left much to be desired. Conversation was stiff in the presence of the C.O., a West Point traditionalist named John Donaldson, and mouthed in the "tough guy" idiom of the infantry. The lieutenant colonels who commanded battalions or occupied key staff positions were like parodies of themselves, stumpy cigar butts clenched in their teeth, grunting "Outstanding, Sir!" every time the old man favored them with a comment or question. I suspected they were the kind of men who turned maudlin when they had the liquor in them; sober, they were guarded, mute and focused on the hunt. In retrospect, they make me think of dim, arrogant jocks with four year scholarships; you can almost hear some Hollywood general demurring, "but they were damn good soldiers." That too is debatable.

It wasn't long before I began to hear the rumors about Donaldson. He and the S-2, the aforementioned Major Crud who was my *de facto* boss at the 11th, had the reputation of being gook hunters. The way I heard it the pair flew around in the colonel's chopper with a crate of grenades, "frags" they were called, and popped them in the rice fields over the "dinks" who would attempt to run for cover when the chopper swooped down to chase them. Whether or not this account was true, it circulated widely. I never saw them do it; but in 1971 Donaldson was under investigation for similar allegations brought by the very man who served in Vietnam as his pilot. That was the end of his promising career.

Donaldson was different from the other bird colonels I'd encountered in the service, haughty, more image conscious. He lacked the avuncular quality, however stern, I'd come to associate with men of this rank which demanded executive competence, not field command machismo. Maybe Donaldson's advancement had been too swift. Certainly his matinee idol good looks hadn't hurt him there; if a movie were ever done on Donaldson's life, a critic could not complain that the actor cast to play him was uncharacteristically too handsome. But handsome is as handsome does, as Forrest Gump would say.[4]

It soon became clear that I would not be forced to eat at Donaldson's mess; I don't think I went there more than three or four times. And I doubt if my absence was even registered, much less resented. Quite the opposite. I might sometimes struggle to keep my highbrow opinions to myself, but my very demeanor betrayed me. None of those guys wore a mustache and wire rimmed glasses, for example. The incompatibility was entirely mutual.

Modus Operandi

Anyway, the MI team's nexus to the brigade was operational; we weren't linked organically to its chain of command. Sergeants Dick and Stranzo, as leaders of the team's war faction, covered my flank with Major Crud and the other staff-infantry types, who were quite content to deal with them directly without the slightest reference to my existence. The interrogation unit was the only component of the team that the S-2 shop kept close tabs on, and

Patton would prove a thorn to them with such increasing frequency that he was eventually relieved. The only man I had to satisfy, Major Heinz, was stationed fifty miles north at Division. Heinz wanted paper, and that was what I gave him. Every contact CI made with a source had to be documented with an AR, an agent report. A low-energy task, but it proved like pulling teeth to get the action figures of the counterintelligence, Dick and Stranzo, or even Gray, to file them.

Gray was easy going, well-liked and, if not lazy, completely indifferent to the team's mission. This was not an unreasonable attitude, yet he at least acknowledged the practical merits of my argument, that it required so minimal an effort to keep Heinz off our backs by simply maintaining the paper flow, filing ARs in a timely fashion. If you talked to the police chief or a district official in Duc Pho, you filed an AR; if a source came to our shop with alleged information on whatever, you pushed an AR up to Heinz. This wasn't deathless prose, you just plugged your data into the prescribed format; took all of five or ten minutes. At the end you attached an evaluation code, always the same — I think it was C-6: "usually reliable source; information impossible to verify." Copies to Heinz, the brigade S-2, artillery liaison officer, and the CI file cabinet.

To this day I can't unravel exactly why this issue provoked such conflict between me and the two CI commandos. It's true I have a foreman's blood in me and I could be unyielding if I felt my righteous word was being challenged. But it's hard to imagine that things could have gone differently. I would come to see Dick and Stranzo as versions of those boys in *Lord of the Flies* who'd reverted to barbarism; they would have been difficult to control under any circumstances — especially in Vietnam where barbarism was condoned, even encouraged, by American military practices.

A kind of honeymoon atmosphere extended over my first month at Bronco, during which the general pattern for my tour was established by the day-to-day routines I duly reported in my shallow, newsy letters home. There was the office work, debriefing and paying off the informers who wandered into the CI hootch almost daily; liaison flights up or down the coast to meet with counterparts in adjacent military fiefdoms; the occasional trips to Chu Lai; coping with the two prevailing modes of weather, endless rain or stifling heat; the almost daily visits to Duc Pho, if only to the open market for fresh produce or ping pong balls; the MI club and the late night gambling; scrounging to make improvements within the MI compound; accounts on the progress of my gardens; beer runs to Qui Nhon; complaints about the starchy food in the common mess; and interminable appeals for care packages of canned goods, which, along with C-rations and freeze dried packets, provisioned the lion's share of our diet.

The darker side of our experiences, and the inner turmoil I suffered almost from the beginning, are all but missing in those letters home; these more unpleasant verities about the war I documented loosely in my notebook and in the daily diary I would begin on the first of January. Duly noted therein are the fact that we lived in constant anticipation, if not fear, of the next enemy offensive, or waited with considerable resignation for the war to show its more familiar face in the form of booby traps, snipers' bullets and incoming bombardments; the relentless, unnerving thunder of our own outgoing artillery, nightly fire missions called H&I, harassment and interdiction, some of which were aimed at unverifiable coordinates we'd provided that same day in our agent reports; the bickering and morale problems plaguing our team and my obsessive preoccupation with the stresses and loneliness of leadership; the self-conscious commentaries, bordering on compulsive nihilism, on the literature I immersed myself in most evenings after duty hours, Gide, Hesse, Joyce, Wilde, Kafka; and the steady deterioration of my physical health, which, in the end, proved my salvation.

Duc Pho open market, early 1969.

Torture

As to the many horrors I witnessed which led to a conviction that our hostilities were directed substantially toward the civilian population of South

Vietnam, and which later formed the basis of my public opposition to the war, these I seldom committed to writing. Or if I did, most references are so oblique that only I can decipher their true significance. The first such incident occurred barely a week after my arrival. Dated December 11, the following entry appears in my Masterpiece Notes:

> Tonight — as if awakened from the dream of a past life — or an earlier year — I am in the war. The fantasies of a child cowboy/soldier with a stick gun are fulfilled in the reality of one second's thought. But the reality fades — it doesn't linger. It is only a link with the past. The present is the fantasy of the future. It is the indifference of the war that frightens me almost as much as the indifference within my own cold heart.

This convoluted reflection masks an actual incident of torture, the first of many I was to witness. During those initial weeks I would drop into IPW fairly frequently, a practice I soon abandoned. On the day in question I arrived just as a girl, perhaps in her early twenties, was being led into the back room. There seems little doubt that the vast majority of those dragnetted into IPW by the infantry were indeed sympathetic to the cause of liberation. This was Quang Ngai Province, after all, a hotbed of national resistance since the days of the French when Duc Pho itself had served Viet Minh fighters as a place to rest and recuperate.

But this girl, the IPW team fervently believed, was an actual VC of some stature; the allegation had apparently sharpened during her preliminary interrogation. Maybe someone fingered her. Possessed of the same solemn purpose and absolute sense of right that inquisitors must have demonstrated when confronting heretics and dissenters, the interrogation team attached the field telephone wires to the girl's tiny fingers. At each denial the crank was turned, and the suspect screamed in agony to the weird accompaniment of the phone's bell which rang with every revolution. Almost immediately blood began to pour down her leg, staining her black peasant trousers and dripping to the floor. The girl had begun to menstruate violently. In horror, Patton ordered the wires removed and the girl was placed under the protection of an old woman.

The words *indifference* and *cold heart* in my notebook suggest a mood of self-indictment, a recognition that, at least intellectually, I registered this brutal act as morally depraved. Yet the deep feeling of shame that attended this knowledge was almost immediately displaced as my moral compass shifted imperceptibly to accommodate behavior that, prior to Vietnam and without a moment's hesitation, I would have recognized as abhorrent. If I had felt constrained to hold my tongue at Fort Hood, the added instinct for survival in Vietnam moved to anesthetize my ambivalence even more completely. It would take a far more sensational incident two weeks later to establish for me the unmistakable line in warfare between right and wrong.

Booty

In the meantime a most unusual communication led to one of those Catch-22 episodes that can only take place in the culture of war. The land line in our office rang infrequently, so when one morning I picked up the receiver and one of the battalion commanders spoke from the other end, that in itself might have been the landmark event of a slow day. Say, he began, almost apologetically, one of my companies uncovered a tunnel with a shit load of bicycle parts. I can't use then, but I thought maybe you intelligence guys could. Sir, I said, we'll be right over.

Grabbing Hieu, the CI interpreter, I hopped a Jeep and sped to the sector where the battalion was in stand-down. What went through my mind as I surveyed the mound of frames, wheels, tires, sockets, pedals, and what have you was not how exciting it was that we had put such a large dent into the enemy's logistics, rather that blind fortune had disgorged a cornucopia of booty I could imagine many uses for, none of which had anything to do with military intelligence.

I had Hieu accompany me because I'd already thought the matter through to its next logical move — a visit to the bike shops in Duc Pho — and I needed someone to help me haggle a deal. Hieu seemed to know one of the owners. Over cups of green tea and raunchy Vietnamese smokes we came to terms. Missing from the cache — something on the order of fifty disassembled units — were two critical parts, ball bearings and brake cables. The man said he would provide these and furnish fifteen bicycles, fully assembled, in exchange for the remaining stock. Hieu thought this sounded fair and I readily agreed.

A week later I informed Major Heinz of our windfall and offered to ship a half-dozen bikes to Chu Lai in the team's only large truck, officially stripped from our motor pool when the unit was reduced in size, but as yet unreturned to division. Heinz reacted like a kid in a toy store; he was thrilled. I suspect he was responding to the sheer novelty of possessing a Vietcong bicycle, much as I had, though the exercise in entrepreneurship was the true spice of my satisfaction. The decision to cut him in was calculated. I knew full well I couldn't get along with any commander for a whole year, much less some guy I already despised. I was in his good graces for the moment, but this was insurance to forestall my inevitable fall.

With the exception of two bikes, one the shop owner had customized for me as a gift and another I gave to Norm Edwards, the brigade Red Cross representative — which on occasion he and I would use to ride around the perimeter at Bronco — I traded the remaining lot for such extravagances as a box of fresh steaks, spare parts for our remaining vehicles, and building materials that added to the morale and comfort of the team.

I have since wondered if Hieu himself somehow profited from this transaction. But that question did not occur at the time, because I could barely see the culture that surrounded me as having a reality beyond its subjugation to American power. Western chauvinism distorted the perceptions of most Americans in Vietnam, and I was no exception. Hieu's English was poor, and his value as an interpreter limited. But he was a very agreeable fellow, a favorite around the team and a fiend at table tennis.

My Vietcong bicycle.

As a soldier he made a good impression, and, unlike most of the ARVN or militia troops who languished on the grounds around the district office, Hieu seemed to actually be ideologically engaged, a fact attributable perhaps to his being a devout Catholic. In the five months we spent together this was the only fact I learned about his life, not his full name, not even his real rank, though we always called him "Sergeant."

Collection

Hieu was involved as well in an event that occurred three days after Christmas, the antithesis in spirit of the bike escapade, and, for me, the defining moment of the war. In fact it was Hieu who ran into the CI tent that morning to announce the arrival of D-7, one of twelve registered sub-agents CI carried on its payroll. There was a thin dossier on each of these characters in our files, and their bonafides were supposed to have been certified at the highest reaches of counterintelligence in the manner prescribed by regulations. Obviously you wanted some modest reassurances that the recruited and compensated agents were working for you and not the other guy.

It was not cynicism that caused me to doubt that these Duc Pho irregulars had been properly vetted; few Americans possessed the language skills —

the most obvious of our cross-cultural deficits — few South Vietnamese the resources or motivation, to conduct the extensive background investigations required to fulfill even the minimal criteria for a collection operation, the spy versus spy stuff that attracts the real adventurers. All I'd seen so far, walking in and out of the CI office day after day, were a few local farmers or fishermen who'd been enlisted as warm bodies to simulate the modus operandi of genuine collection.

We didn't recruit a single agent the time I was there; I inherited the net as constituted, and had almost no faith in the information we were being given, most of which seemed innocuous, if not fabulous. As noted earlier, what these drop-ins unwittingly provided most regularly was fodder for the nightly artillery blitzes, despite our less than ringing endorsements that the information could not be substantiated. Every night I heard the howitzers expel their rounds; only years later would I allow myself to imagine that they actually landed somewhere.[5]

The collection drill was simple. Agent D-3, say, would appear late one afternoon after a day emptying his crab traps. We'd march him into the back room and sit around a table covered with a map under a sheet of clear acetate. He'd spin some cock-'n-bull about VC troop movements and point to a place in the bush west of Duc Pho, which we'd mark with a grease pencil to record the coordinates. Maybe his in-law's ancestral hamlet for all we knew. Next we'd open the treasure trove. What'll it be today pal, Dewars or Johnny Walker Black? Then the guy would depart for town and get home with his quart of booze just in time for cocktail hour.

I'd actually been to this chap's hootch on the outskirts of Duc Pho a week or so before, to a party he'd given in honor of our departing Order of Battle man. D-3's real name was Phao, a tiny man with a craggy fisherman's face and the blush of an alcoholic's sly grin. I recorded in a letter home an inventory of possessions in the spacious one-room thatched dwelling he shared with his wife and six kids: two big beds, several hammocks, a table and chair set, a radio, a stereo, and a bogus bronze star citation from the U.S. Army. Phao was a kulak, a man of means by local standards, and a generous host serving us roast duck — scrawny like the natives — sauteed crabs with *nuc mam* — my first exposure to that addictive native condiment made from fermented fish-heads — plenty of beer, and, of course, some very good scotch.

D-7, however, was a horse of a different color, a fact driven home immediately when I saw Stranzo all but cartwheel out the flap of the CI hootch, whooping like a Warner Brothers Indian, to greet the man whose sudden appearance had lit Hieu's usually placid expression with a high beam of excitement. I followed closely in their wake. Astride a Honda-90, still revving its engine which echoed loudly inside the canyon of tents formed by the MI compound, was an imposing figure who stepped from his machine the instant he saw Stranzo and Hieu approach. The man's lip curled slightly into a mock smile of recognition without disturbing a single tendril of his remarkable reserve. Taller than the average Vietnamese and dressed in the uniform *de rigueur* of Third World bureaucrats — dark trousers and a tailored white shirt — D-7 came armed with a 9mm pistol and two M-26 baseball-type grenades which hung ominously from his dark thin belt. He nodded a curt greeting and spoke a few words.

Me at entrance to the counterintelligence hooch.

"Sonofabitch, what's he saying, Hieu?" demanded Stranzo, almost frothing.

"Good 'tuff, Tran-Tso, you see, you see," chirped Hieu, greatly amused by the American's display of impatience.

The whole delegation then trooped to the debriefing map and D-7 began his tale, which Hieu passed on to us in spurts. Three VC cadres would be paying a visit to a certain hamlet later that afternoon. At the edge of the settlement is a spider hole where they can hide should American soldiers approach the area. A resident of the hamlet in the employ of D-7 will place pieces of red cloth near the mouth of the hole to alert us to its general location. But we must move quickly, D-7 urged, or they'll be gone.

I couldn't believe what I was hearing. Talk about cloak and dagger melodrama. But that's not the way Stranzo read it. In a flash he made contact with the firebase in whose territory the hamlet lay. The colonel wants a briefing on this — personally, he gushed with a disarming enthusiasm that dispelled momentarily his constitutional sullenness. He's sending his Charley-Charley to pick us up in zero zero one zero.[6] Stranzo's "Want to come along, lieutenant?" amounted to an almost friendly invitation.

Without a second's hesitation I responded in the affirmative, joining the others on the run to retrieve my rifle and combat gear. Patton had come back to the compound for lunch, and when Gray told him that the team chief was going to the field, the two men exchanged looks that implied, well, we've lost another one.

The slick coming in just as we pulled up to the helipad never touched the ground while the four of us — Hieu, D-7, Stranzo and myself— clambered aboard. In seconds the pilot dropped the chopper's nose and plowed forward for takeoff, then banked sharply to starboard, rising in the direction of the firebase. The battalion S-2, a Captain Nett, was there to greet us. He steered us under the prop wash and right into the colonel's TOC — an underground dugout that served as the battalion tactical operations center. In the antechamber a radio operator hunched over a squawking console, and we brushed past him through a curtain of blankets to the inner sanctum.

Behind a desk sat another of those cookie-cutter field commanders, a lieutenant colonel chomping his cheap panatella who'd probably been to the Army War College, where he'd majored in Sergeant Rock comics and minored in intimidation. My role was the Woody Allen character who'd stumbled onto the wrong sound stage, or at least that's how it felt on the inside. With ill-concealed contempt the colonel slapped a pointer in my hand, indicated the huge map on the wall and barked, "Now, what's this all about, looo-tenant." Somehow I stuttered through, providing the essential outline, before he cut me off dismissively and turned to his S-2 to solicit, in the most fatherly of tones, the opinion of a brother infantryman. Nett was quick to respond with enthusiasm that the track record of the 1st MIT was, "Outstanding, Sir!"

Things being slow all over, I guess, the colonel decided to take a flyer on what still struck me as a most improbable venture. He told Nett to round up the headquarter's squad — a half dozen seasoned grunts who'd paid their dues in combat and now served in relative safety as the colonel's Praetorian Guard. They would accompany us by chopper to rendezvous with a mechanized recon platoon currently only a few clicks,[7] the radio operator confirmed, from our target hamlet. Nett asked, and received, permission to tag along.

Airborne once more, we soon spotted the four armored vehicles crashing through the tall elephant grass, and radioed our descent to a spot that seemed suitable. Five feet above the ground the squad scrambled from the Huey to secure the landing zone, followed by Nett and the rest of us when the struts touched the grass a couple of feet closer to terra firma. The APCs rumbled forward, preceded on foot by their commander, a rare black lieutenant who saluted Nett and shook my hand. Stranzo began to run the show from this moment on. He pointed to our destination on the recon LT's map, and suggested that D-7 ride the lead vehicle and serve as our guide. I climbed up beside him, my feet dangling over the front, as if we were going on a hay ride.

We rode for some time, thirty minutes or more, when a shout from Hieu punctured my reverie; the slow, lunging pace of the APCs, the heat, the bucolic splendor of the surroundings, had caused my mind to drift — underscoring the wisdom of someone in the Pentagon who'd prevented me from ever becoming a small unit commander. The initial order to halt had actually come from D-7, who was already on the ground eyeing suspiciously a thicket of viney growth only a meter to our front which the driver had planned to ride right through. Smelling the ideal setting for a booby trap, D-7 convinced us to back off and go around.

Booby traps — often fashioned from one of our own dud artillery rounds — were the low-tech means the VC had devised to kill and maim a plurality of GIs who fell in Vietnam. Americans had the gall to characterize this ingenuity as devious, but got back at the enemy and their whole population in spades with *our* favorite means of slaughter, saturation bombing and endless barrages of artillery. In any event I paid a bit more attention when our march resumed.

Before long D-7 again called the column to a halt, this time at the edge of a fair sized grove, beyond which a few thatched roofs could be seen adjacent to a broad patchwork of dikes and paddies. This, he informed Hieu, was the place. The recon lieutenant instantly ordered his troops and the headquarters squad to form a *cordon sanitaire* and ring the tree line for security. D-7, Hieu, and Stranzo scampered off like bloodhounds in search of the telltale signs, while the three officers stood aside making small talk, seemingly redundant to the proceedings, and, certainly in my case, more than a little incredulous as well.

It was Hieu who discovered the bits of red paper — not cloth as D-7 had forecast. Then Stranzo uncovered the mouth of a hole that seemed too small for a rabbit to squeeze through. His mood switched from intense to manic as he stood above this tiny aperture and emptied a clip from his M-16 into the ground. Hieu's demeanor also harshened as he shouted something in Vietnamese, a command to *chieu hoi*, I think, to rally to the arms of those currently assailing them. Before a response was even possible Stranzo dropped a grenade down the hole, which exploded with a resounding thwang; and then a second one as Hieu and D-7 kept up their high pitched chorus.

When the smoke cleared the other officers and I rose from the ground some thirty feet away where we had been observing Stranzo's one-man fire fight. An eery silence reigned, broken by the string of profanities Stranzo began to mutter loudly. He asked the recon LT for a fucking claymore — a lethal fragmentation mine — and a detonator, which one of the troops brought forward and Stranzo quickly assembled, then lowered through the mouth of the opening, the face of which had not been appreciably altered by the assault thus far. As Stranzo backed off some distance from the hole, so did we, ducking behind a slight depression in the terrain. The explosion was deafening, but caused no obvious change in the balance of forces. It was still Stranzo versus what was now a ragged mound of dirt where the rabbit hole had been.

In consultation with Hieu and D-7, Stranzo resolved on one final onslaught. A large tree stood some ten feet from the original opening, and Stranzo called for a block of C-4 plastique and some det-cord — a booster — to ignite it. The explosive was secured to the hump of a fat root at a point where it surfaced from the earth. There was a coy exchange of eye-rolling between the other officers and myself, but we kept quiet and retreated once more to safety, with me thinking that Stranzo, his aggression near the boiling point, was himself about to erupt. At the command — Fire in the hole! — the charge was blown, leaving a dusty mist in the air that reeked of a burnt offering, while excavating a new cavity measuring roughly two feet in diameter at ground level.

Rolling up his sleeves D-7 leapt in, and, to my amazement, instantly disappeared from view. Five seconds later he shouted something and Hieu told us he wanted a skein of commo wire, which was promptly relayed down to him. With the wire tied around his waist for leverage, D-7 emerged, blackened by dirt and sweating profusely. He motioned for Hieu and Stranzo to join him, and the three men strained with all their combined force until finally, the body of a middle aged man, one leg violently amputated, was pulled to the surface. Again D-7 went down with the wire, and the missing leg was retrieved on the next pull. In rapid succession, two more bodies were recovered from what had been a tiny hollow beneath the root system of the giant tree, where the three men had been packed back-to-belly with not an inch to spare.

For the next five minutes the scene took on the frenzy of a victory celebration. One by one the grunts made their way from their cordon on the perimeter to witness the kill. Each man seemed to carry a Kodak Instamatic in his rucksack, and the popping of many flashes caused a strobe-effect under which the leering smiles and back-slapping of the principals, posed by the corpses like great white hunters, appeared especially grotesque. I watched this spectacle as if from a vortex, like a mind outside its shell. When Captain Nett began to pump my hand, I snapped to rights, and it was only then I noticed that he wore a ring from the United States Military Academy.

Suddenly someone yelled, "That dink's alive! His chest is rising" — pointing at the last body to be pulled out, a boy in his late teens. The celebrating and the picture-taking stopped. Stranzo moved quickly to reassume command. Squatting behind the body, he grabbed a shock of thick black hair and wrenched the senseless head a few inches off the ground, using his free hand to jam the barrel of a .38 into the boy's right temple. Purposely, slowly, Stranzo surveyed the faces of his three superiors, and said, "We don't take prisoners, right?" For a few seconds, everyone's eyes made the rounds of everyone else's until Nett turned to me and shrugged — It's your show, Mike.

Sensing from the hard look I shot him that the "show" was over, an edge of panic crept into Stranzo's eyes. "If we don't do him now, Lieutenant, he'll be back out there in two days planting booby traps that'll kill more GIs," he argued. It's not so much that I didn't buy Stranzo's argument, I wouldn't even hear it. The sap of righteousness rose up in me, that stern certainty of the preacher who marks the narrow trail above the slippery slope. My sermon, hardly calculated, was crisp, inelegant and sincere: "Maybe what we've done here today is justifiable as an act of war. I don't know. But I will not stand here and allow you to commit premeditated murder."

Purple with rage, Stranzo twisted his weapon fast against the boy's head. Checked, not yet mated, he cursed me, swore he'd never go to the field again with some green lieutenant. The others, fifteen to twenty in all, stared ahead like glaze-eyed mannequins, immobilized, unstirred by my abstractions. Yet their indifference would condemn that boy. By intuition I shifted to my salesman's voice. "The guy may have valuable intel," I improvised with no great conviction. "We've got to get him to the rear and interrogate him. That's what's gonna save GIs."

This appeal to concrete military practicality animated Nett, restored his sense of proportion. "That's right, Mike," Nett affirmed, placing a hand on my forearm and motioning for Stranzo to back off. "Get a medic over here NOW," he commanded. The recon lieutenant took the cue and shouted, "Doc, up front. Plasma!" And to his radioman, "Get a dust-off in here pronto." From laid-back American boys who'd been responding to a combat death ritual as if the home team had just scored the winning touchdown, the men reverted to a cog-like state that reflected the ideal of our training, and the schizophrenia of our human condition.

I heard the medevac land off beyond the grove. Two corpsmen with a stretcher trotted in and whisked the boy away. I barely noticed, having turned my attention to the personal effects we'd stripped from the three VC, some photographs of loved ones, a letter or a poem, and a few rumbled piasters which probably ended up in the MI team's slush fund to purchase decks of cards and ping pong balls. Stranzo stopped sulking and the incident was soon forgotten; he had, after all, brought home the bacon, and Nett remained ecstatic in his praise. D-7 must have faded into the surroundings; I never saw him again, nor anyone else from that operation except Hieu and Stranzo. It was dusk when we returned to Bronco, and Colonel Donaldson was there to greet us personally and shake our hands.

At exactly 2110, ten minutes past nine that evening, I made another of those cryptic entries in my notebook:

So that you may remember that it was not a moral issue — but a life experience: 2 Dinks KIA, 1 WIA. War is a human absurdity.[8]

I must have been desperate to distance my heart from what I'd witnessed, and to again realign my conscience and behavior to some degree with that of my comrades. It never even crossed my mind to raise a hue and cry. Survival instinct again warned me to adapt. I had eleven long months to go. But I was, and to some extent remain, genuinely perplexed as to why the moral choice so obvious to me was so ambiguous to everyone else. Does this mean that all the others would have countenanced murder if I had failed to object? That was certainly my impression.

But how could such an act be justified? There had been no heat to this battle. We took no casualties, did not run the risks that sometimes led GIs to take a soldier's revenge on a wounded enemy, or on civilians at random whom they held responsible for not revealing the presence of a sniper or a booby trap.

Was it just that I was green, as Stranzo had charged, naive about the realities of war, or at least about the rules governing this particular war, which, in time, experience would correct as had been the case for himself and the others? If the foot soldiers who'd witnessed this had been made callous toward all Vietnamese because they'd seen too many buddies blown to bits, and too few enemy faces to put the blame on — that was a rationale for cruelty I could grapple with. The land itself, every stone and every blade of grass, was against them, and most didn't have the time or the luxury to figure out why. In the end, if they survived and stepped aboard that Freedom Bird to take them back to the World, they might turn to some sidekick and ask that question with their eyes. And what could he say? That's Vietnam, Jake. And he'd be right.

But Stranzo could profess no such mitigation. It's true he exposed himself to constant peril, but nothing on the scale of the typical grunt, who didn't just go to the field; he was in it and of it, and any other preposition you can slot in that phrase to express the teleological bond between the substance and symbol of such a relationship. Stranzo was a hit man, pure and simple, his blood lust detached and pathological. These were qualities he brought with him, and which the nature of the war allowed him to express with minimal restraint; the others may have stood aside and let him execute that boy, but I don't believe that most would themselves have been able to pull the trigger. There is no question that, had I not prevented him, Stranzo would have done just that.

It's not that he was out of control. From his point of view the third VC represented a bonafide kill; that he was still breathing was a mere formality. Stranzo was pissed because he'd been forced to settle for two scalps that afternoon instead of three. He didn't give a shit about the well-being of other GIs. Body count was everything, and he was simply out to pad his own statistics. His pique was based on greed. I'd been greedy for bicycles; he was greedy for bodies.

As to the spinelessness of Captain Nett and the other lieutenant, this had been enlightening to me. It would not be the last time I would witness officers senior to myself play Pontius Pilate in the presence of American atrocities. These are the men who ran the army in the postwar years, right until the run-up to the Iraq War now in progress as this is written, including men like Colin Powell, who was a major at that time on the Americal Division staff and had to know the score, but chose career over honor.[9]

As for my own actions, I have little to pat myself on the back about. I did stand up to the mob and turn its course. I'll never have a nightmare over that. But my true moral fiber didn't run quite so deep as I imagined. I gave no thought to the other two men we killed — though I've never doubted for an instant that they were cadres of the NLF, and thus fair game in as much as we, foreign invaders or otherwise, were an army in the field pitted against an adversary. I can't pretend that they were given a sporting chance to surrender; but I can live with the fact that "shoot first and ask questions later" is an ethos of warfare rooted in self-preservation.

As for the one I saved, he was out of mind the moment he was out of sight. I never followed up, even professionally, to find out if he'd survived, much less revealed anything of value under interrogation. Only years later did I entertain the not-so-improbable thought that he was hurled from that chopper long before it made it back to the rear. But the real blot on my conscience is that I felt pride when Donaldson shook my hand; I welcomed his recognition for a job well done, and accepted my share of credit for what we'd done that day. And that's how the war began for me.

IV

Days of War (2)

Don't be alarmed, she told me, the telegram said, but Mrs.
Brown your son is dead.
— *"Vietnam," a song by Jimmy Cliff*

Began ... and ended. That, I vowed, was the last time I'd ever go to the
field. And I believed it, for just under two weeks. Had there been more to
occupy me at Bronco I might have kept that promise. But official duties
absorbed barely two hours each day, chiefly make-work at that. Other distractions were at a premium. Ideally I'd have snuck away more often to Qui
Nhon — or on some other liaison run — but I couldn't be sure just how closely
the brigade S-2 monitored my movements on behalf of Major Heinz, the MI
chief up at Chu Lai. I wasn't about to raise my profile and jeopardize that
weekly escape by having my name appear on the courier manifests more frequently than it already did.

The dilemma lay in filling up the other six days when I couldn't fly off
on some sightseeing excursion. I designed stratagems for foiling the monot-
ony, little projects completely irrelevant to the war, a vegetable garden, a
screened-in patio for the club house. If you could get through the daylight
hours, evenings weren't so bad. We had volleyball, the occasional barbecue
when a rare spirit of harmony descended amongst us, card games and bull
sessions. The usual campground fare. On days when nothing stilled the
heebie-jeebies, that overflow of energy is what caused me to soldier when I
didn't have to.

Around New Year, a week after that first trip to the field, the monsoon
struck with a fury; penetrating dampness and chill replaced the steamy,
suffocating heat. The team was driven indoors for days on end, interpersonal
tensions neared the point of combustion. I holed up with *The Immoralist* and
The Picture of Dorian Gray, then, like a straw, siphoned their dark moods onto

the pages of my diary, complaining of "melancholia." On January 7th — now 1969 — I wrote: "It has rained steadily for almost twenty-four hours. The rain kept me confined to the office ... like a caged animal."

Next day the skies began to clear. I joined Stranzo, Hieu and one of our paid informants on a long patrol. There had been a tip, something out there we wanted to find, probably a weapons or rice cache, I don't recall exactly what, nor did I write it down. Presumably Stranzo and I had shelved our differences. My relations with him — the whole crew for that matter — never steadied; I constantly stumbled between unacceptable extremes, like the parent of a teenage boy, now father, now fiend.

Even assuming that a state of nervous restlessness provided the main impulse, I have tried to remember what specific circumstances led me not simply to place myself in harm's way so soon after that initial misadventure, but to do so in the company of my despised nemesis. The record comes up empty. I can only say that such behavior was not atypical; humors within the unit shifted as regularly as the flow of tides.

I did write down that a few days prior to this second patrol Stranzo went off on a beer run. In this monthly ritual, two team members hopped aboard our pickup — three-quarter ton in army lingo — and joined a convoy heading south, then, a day or two later, returned with a *mat* of beer — in the vicinity of a hundred cases, Mabel's Black Label on this particular occasion.[1] Special orders were filled for individuals, for me, a quart of Canadian Club, some cigars and a couple of bottles of red wine. Maybe Stranzo got his ashes hauled at the House of Madam K and came back from Qui Nhon feeling mellow; a change in the weather certainly improved the collective disposition around the compound; but the most telling factor was undoubtedly my ingrained craving for a dose of the war, like the weekend junkie between fixes who takes his connections as they come.

What I do remember vividly are the twisted dividends of that day: an unforgettable trek in the countryside sullied by more episodes of American cruelty. We walked Indian-file over kilometers of grasslands bordered by hamlets and rice fields, and watched as a great dark curtain hanging between earth and sky along the horizon galloped speedily in our direction. Soon it overtook our march and a downpour, the intensity of which I have never witnessed before or since, soaked us to the core almost instantly. It took only minutes for the storm to pass; then the sun returned as strongly as before, and steamed us dry before we walked another thousand meters.

Wherever I turned that day, scenes of peasants working their crops stood in relief against the sky. Toward late afternoon we entered a *ville* and discovered diagrams on a blackboard in a one-room school, impossible to say how, if at all, this cipher was linked to the hostilities. A shot rang out; maybe a sniper, maybe not. The usual suspects were rounded up and beaten, then we returned to Bronco empty handed and ignored.

To this day I'm not comfortable speaking to myself through the medium of a journal; thirty years ago, just beginning to write, my prose was painfully self-conscious. The exercise served more to plot my mood swings, hope one day, despair the next, than to detail an account of what occurred around me. There are some notable exceptions: the entry for January 8th is inexplicably direct. Rereading the diary brought back the event; I'd long forgotten the part about villagers being "beaten." My memory chose to sanitize the occasion, recalling the beauty of the landscape and power of the rain, rather than the dark side I recorded only hours after returning from the field:

> The people's faces in that hamlet — full of fear — and for good reason. S really beat that one woman. I didn't flinch, nor was I repulsed — but I rather doubt I should be able to do the same thing. This whole business is such a nightmare that the atrocities don't stand out in the least.

Not repulsed? There's an admission I might have censored, but didn't since the conviction that our mere presence in Vietnam constituted an atrocity had already formed on me like an ineradicable moss. Everywhere the land fell thrall to schoolyard bullies. Day in, day out, on the base camp and beyond, one observed these perverse interactions between GIs and the Vietnamese, whom we patronized, cursed, and ridiculed, pushed around and rounded up; in extreme cases they were beaten, tortured and "wasted." Totally apart from the anonymous terrors wreaked by American saturation bombing and artillery bombardments, these depredations involved face-to-face encounters with common folk whose greatest offense was often inseparable from their very existence. Those we considered good Vietnamese, and treated with a modicum of civility, were a small minority, our servants, or the mandarins and upper echelons among our Saigon allies.[2]

The stilted phrasing in that diary entry, that "I rather doubt," reveals how quickly and how passively I had become acclimated to this ubiquitous brutality as the norm. This and the fact that I was reading too many novels written or translated by Englishmen. It was as if one had been wired to filter the war through a kind of moral schizophrenia, embellished, in my case, by a strong measure of bookish romanticism. I have often had recourse to reflect since then on whether the sin of *doing* is only slightly more repugnant, if at all, from the sin of merely *seeing*. Yet mine was a heart divided against itself. The deep empathy I felt for our victims was no less genuine, and a good deal easier to live with, than whatever aloofness and detachment my crippled emotional circuitry simultaneously allowed.

Two days later, the mental imprint of those people's faces already erased,

I tried to capture the idyllic, poignant scene of that patrol in the first real poem I ever wrote.[3]

> Black silks, black mud, knee deep they work
>> the rice
> Bamboo plow furrows through the rows, a black
>> wake behind
> Simple thoughts and lives — the targets of
>> our progress
> "Let me till my rice
> this is my only plea
> I trade my fragile body for this
>> fragile plant
> And when black night comes
>> my thatched hut
> Calls me to an island hamlet."

Another comment — quite offhand — in that same January 8th diary entry reads, "I'm amazed how fast I tire," and strikes what would soon become a thematic drumbeat punctuating nearly every page of my chronicle. In the meantime, my letters home continued on a smoother track, a rote inventory of care-packages requested and care-packages received. "Send lots of canned chili, it goes good with rice" — which by now my hootch maid, Ba Hue, served me most days at the noontime meal.

Once or twice I commented judiciously in those letters on the latest family drama involving my kid brother Tom, whose clandestine marriage and impending fatherhood at nineteen threatened to end his enrollment at the New York State Maritime Academy, where, by regulation, cadets were obliged to remain single. Of dispatches from the front, I reported mostly on the progress of my several gardens.

The Constant Gardener

I had been contemplating the unused ground between various hootches for some time, and decided to fill it with growing things. Hieu once again was my principal support; he played chief steward to my baronial whims. "Hmmm," I mused, "sandy soil means tomatoes, right?," vaguely recalling an axiom of the Long Island backyard gardener. Hieu allowed that tomatoes would do fine there. And bite-sized hot peppers like the one he'd offered me as an initiation prank a day or two after my arrival; it had barely touched my lips yet all but incinerated the inside of my mouth. "Peppers sound good," I nodded, "for you dinks." His smile was all innocence, beatific. "Peanut like dis ert," he added, and he spoke the Vietnamese name for that green herb used to flavor almost every dish and soup in Vietnam, cilantro or coriander, a taste I initially loathed but soon acquired.

Oscar and Melvin, the MI team's two laborers, were enlisted to procure manure from their neighbors and prepare the site. Hieu and I went shopping for seedlings in a shady lane just outside Duc Pho where a cultured Francophile from the *ancien regime* kept a greenhouse. Next day I supervised Hieu, who supervised Oscar and Melvin, who laid the seeds and tiny plants in their neat, short rows, affording me, in the process, one additional distraction from the wheel of time and another neutral topic for my letters home.

Shit Burners and Hootch Maids

Oscar and Melvin were shit-burners; their number one chore was to clean out MI's two-seater each morning and cremate the night soil. They also policed the grounds, raked the sand, and planted the occasional banana tree — another of my pet projects — more touches of green, a bit of shade and, ultimately, fresh fruit at hand to ward off the institutional maladies: Captain Bly had his breadfruit; I had my bananas.

Oscar and Melvin displayed a bit more style than the average day-laborers, especially Oscar, ever a sly foil like the servant in an opera buffa. Sporting a mile-wide grin that reminded me of Joe E. Brown, Oscar proclaimed his endless desire for things with an alphabet of facial expressions that a master pantomime would have envied. He had a junk dealer's passion for scavenging and by day's end on more than a few occasions he'd cajole some team member into carting a truck load of pickings from the LZ dump, anything from scraps of lumber to broken office equipment, to his shanty in Duc Pho.

This native division of labor within our little compound was replicated throughout the LZ; every unit had its shit burners and hootch maids. By seven each morning the locals lined up at the gate and began to enter the base camp single file, showing identity cards listing the organization that employed them, and submitting to searches on demand — though these occurred more at night when they reversed the procedure to return home.

I was called down there once to rescue Ba Hue, reduced to tears as an MP stood over her in triumph holding a bar of soap he'd found in her possession. Poor Ba Hue, she was scrupulously honest, and always asked before taking even the most trivial item. "You-souvenir-me Truong Huy (First Lieutenant)," she screeched over and over, her head bent in abject humiliation. It was true, but I'd neglected to give her a note authorizing the gift.

The traffic in soap we could monitor; information was something else. The MI team shared responsibility for base security with the office of the provost marshal. The more demanding lot of physical security fell to the MPs; MI's province, more elusive, concerned the infiltration of enemy agents and the leakage of intelligence the other side might find of value — our brigade order of battle, for example. But this was an impossible mission. The mere fact that literally hundreds of Vietnamese poured into LZ Bronco each day catering to the petty domestic needs of all and sundry, from the lowest ranking private on up, gave *de facto* sanction to the very info gathering efforts on the part of the enemy that MI was tasked with obstructing.

The place was a sieve from a counterintelligence point of view, and it was only natural to assume that any member of this labor force might be in the employ of the NLF — a point gleefully confirmed by former guerrillas I met on returning to Duc Pho a quarter of a century later. Just once before my tour ended in 1969 did MI get involved in a security case. An old man was caught placing a mirror on a tin can near the airstrip. Was it a signal to target our choppers for incoming VC mortar rounds, or a quiet place to take a shave as he insisted? We never found out.

Return to Duc Pho, summer 1994.

Friendly Fire

On January 15th, a Wednesday, the MI team sent nine men to the field for three separate operations. My group unearthed a rice cache and got another pat on the back from Donaldson, who'd swooped down in his command chopper for a quick inspection of the booty. We'd had a helluva time finding the spot, sloshing through the paddies for hours, getting the predictable blank stares and "no savvies" from the local toilers. At one point a dozen villagers ignored our shouts of *lai de, lai de,* to hustle over to where we were standing a hundred yards away. When they didn't budge, I took out that snub nosed .38 I still carried at the time and waved it menacingly in their direction.

I'd played officer hard-on before. Back in Texas I ordered some enlisted guy in a bus station to button his blouse — jacket — and tighten his tie. He's seen me enter and had given me a "fuck-you" look, so I jumped all over his shit. Now I was going off on a few ragged dinks who didn't *di-di* fast enough to suit my mood. Instantly, on both occasions, I'd felt like a horse's ass, penance enough, I suppose, under the circumstances, since I was all steam and no fire. But I have to recognize that the bully was in me too, this reflex to apply coercion when one's own authority was shaky, derived, not from any true legitimacy but from some accident of caste.

I was already back at the clubhouse after that patrol nursing a beer when in strolled Dick and Stranzo, waving their M-16s like braves returning from a war party. They'd had a good day, they said, all gaiety and smiles, which meant no good for somebody. And, oh, by the way, Stanley R. got hit. He's been medevac'd to Qui Nhon.

Stanley was one of Patton's interrogators, a lean nineteen year old with a shock of blond hair draped perpetually over his forehead. Why Stanley even went out that day is still a mystery to me; the IPW guys almost never left Bronco, and certainly didn't go to the field. That was an extravagance of the CI section. But Stanley had gotten the bug, I guess, and now he was a statistic, WIA — wounded in action — shot pretty badly, though expected to recover, Major Heinz informed us later that night.

Most team members were shaken by the news, but in a day or two the impact wore thin, and Stanley's name came up less and less frequently. The mental fragmentation one suffered in Vietnam went well beyond the callow self-absorption that puts a normal limit on youthful empathy. We all shut down emotionally, though everyone made the right noises about getting down to Qui Nhon to visit Stanley. And some of us did. Only when I approached his bed in the hospital ward nearly two weeks later did the reality of the situation unleash some recognizable human response in me, and that was embarrassment.

I had arrived just as a medic was struggling to insert a catheter into his patient's urethra. Seeing that Stanley took the procedure in stride offered some relief, and, over all, for a man who'd just had his spleen and a segment of his small intestines ripped out by machine gun fire (or was it a "friendly" rocket from one of our gun ships? as I was told informally), he seemed in good spirits and well on the mend.

That night, for the first and only time in Vietnam, the tone I struck in my diary was consistent with the account I wrote home the following day, January 27th. Reed's misfortune was "senseless," I recorded for myself, an "absurdity." Once again I vowed to abstain from this war ... until — adding cynically — I change my mind. I already understood that the horror I associated with what had befallen Stanley Reed would not sustain this latest impulse to resist the war any more than it had before on the heels of the equally shocking events I'd already witnessed.

I now wince when reading the prose of the letter home, so full of posture.

> One of my men was severely wounded ten days ago. I went to see him over the weekend in Qui Nhon. As I gazed around the ward at the mangled human forms, my only thoughts, besides pity, were "for what reason?"

Switching topics with an almost indecent lack of transition — inserting what I believed was the requisite false note of optimism to soften the bad news, I added lamely, "You should see our garden."

Tet

Tet was now approaching. Celebration of the Lunar New Year would occupy virtually all Vietnamese, North and South, for the better part of a week in February. To GIs this meant the strong probability of an enemy offensive. The suspension of popular routines on such a scale provided ideal cover for an intensification of hostilities by the liberation forces. Two months had passed since I'd arrived, and Bronco had yet to receive any consequential in-coming fire.

That a sustained bombardment was overdue at Bronco, no one seemed to doubt. And when it came, if the past was any guide, it would be in the form of a heavy barrage of mortar rounds and rocket fire. GIs often referred to Duc Pho as "the rocket pocket." These were highly mobile weapons, not bulky artillery pieces hard to conceal and move about. To set their tubes, a guerrilla team moved rapidly within range of the base camp, fired a volley or two, moved to another position, fired again, and so on; finally, they'd evaporate into the hills just as American gun ships were hovering overhead, and long before our own artillery could calibrate where exactly to aim its retaliatory fire.

Retaliation was always in grotesque disproportion to the duration or intensity of the attack on us. And, of course, given the rapid withdrawal tactics of the enemy fire team, someone other than they would inevitably bear the wrath of the American response. Even assuming that most VC teams were not so cruel or stupid as to mount their assault from a populated zone, the radius of American destructiveness would often far oversweep the patch of real estate from which the enemy projectiles had been initially launched.

Time weighed less heavily during these pre-Tet days, and contacts with the Vietnamese ran far more smoothly than was usual. One sensed in the people of Duc Pho a slight leavening in the communal mood, a turning, like flowers to the sun, toward those few anticipated days of Tet when, if the battlefield were quiet, they could shut out the war, even indulge a glint of hope in the promise of renewal that each new year is believed to bring forth.

For me personally this was a period of intense immersion within the local culture, highlighted by daily meals, lunch and dinner, in Duc Pho's only restaurant, the enterprising brainchild of a Vietnamese member of our team. Mr. Hinh was said to have taught mathematics at the university in Hue before being drafted; it was certainly not English. Although he spoke excellent French, Hinh had but a smattering of English, and was by far the poorest of all Lieutenant Patton's interpreters. He was an intelligent, unassuming man, however, and well liked. And somehow he had managed to have his wife and children join him in Duc Pho. Shortly thereafter, a few tables appeared at roadside under the overhang of a small storefront, and Hinh's restaurant was open for business.

My first meal there one afternoon in mid–January was not promising. Mrs. Hinh served a bowl of chicken soup with a pair of hen's feet floating above the noodles. This delicacy, she said by way of Hieu, was in my honor. It was a case of too much authenticity too soon for someone whose tastes in food were as culture-bound as mine, not to mention that I was still turned off by the overpowering flavor of fresh cilantro, the herb of preference in much of Vietnamese cooking, especially the soups.

The next night the American members of the team held a party at Hinh's place for the MI interpreters, and Mrs. Hinh, a vivacious woman in her early thirties, produced a round robin of stir-fries and spring rolls, mixing vegetables with chunks of chicken, shrimp, duck, and pork, that converted me on the spot. From that night on I became a regular, fully emancipated at last from the greasy slop that passed for food at the brigade mess hall, though I'd still slip in on mornings when SOS — shit-on-a-shingle, more commonly known as creamed chipped beef on toast — was on the breakfast menu.

Understandably, the Vietnamese took kindly to my attentions and curiosity about their way of life. These were happy interludes for all of us, I think, the lanky young American known about town as First Lieutenant Moustache, and the circle of smiling Asians, mostly soldiers, who pulled their chairs around his table, jousting each other for the dubious honor of teaching him the proper use of chopsticks; or to correct his pronunciation so that a word he might utter came out as "horse" instead of "whore." Or maybe it was the other way around, which only added to the general air of camaraderie and amusement. Naturally, they were quick to teach him how to curse, beginning with that oddly universal epithet of misogyny, "motherfucker,"[4] "*do ma,*" the second word spoken in a flat bleating tone like the "baaa" of a goat.

It was during one of these exchanges that someone casually let me know that the VC had a price on my head, a plausible assertion considering the degree of havoc the intelligence apparatus caused in proportion to our meager numbers. But I never took this much to heart, feeling that somehow correct relations with the Vietnamese would lessen my vulnerability despite the frequency and predictability of my appearances around Duc Pho. The warning, if such it amounted to, didn't cause any change in my routine, since the alternative — being trapped day and night on LZ Bronco — was even less appealing than being shot at. After that I did find myself looking over my shoulder more often, especially when cruising in a Jeep near the densely vegetated but thinly populated edges of the *ville*.

The time spent on Bronco now followed a relatively natural cycle. The mornings were devoted to paperwork, including the onerous chore of bookkeeping for the ICF fund, passed to my plate after Gray had made a complete hash of the job — though I was hardly blessed with any greater facility for numbers than he. Following a leisurely lunch, I would roam the base camp scrounging materials to complete the various renovation projects under way within the MI compound. The most elaborate of these was a screened-in patio behind the clubhouse, the work of three native carpenters who mortised every joint in their sturdy bamboo frame and erected the entire structure without a single metal fastener. I also tended my gardens, and planned and planted new ones.

Each evening before dusk I worked out, jogging the dusty base camp roads, then lifting weights with a barbell fabricated — in the manner of my Fort Hood crony, Benson — from large vegetable cans filled with concrete and a bar cut from the metal ribbing of an old canvas Jeep top. Once or twice the Red Cross rep, Norm Edwards, and I rode our bikes — mine with fancy red handlebar grips — around the perimeter just inside the bunker line like two curates on a country lane, totally oblivious to how ridiculous we must have appeared. Many nights, following dinner, Patton, Gray, Edwards and myself would make a foursome for bridge. The conversation was strangely light, seldom concerned with the war.

Before going to bed I'd sit beside my bunk under a naked lightbulb and scribble in my diary, all in all a depressing read after almost forty years. Half to three-quarters of every entry chronicles those pitiful complaints about the loneliness of leadership, while masking the deep, and at the time unacknowledged, conflict in myself between a need to be liked and a need to be listened to, or taken seriously. After putting aside the diary, I'd spend an hour dosing my appetite for great literature before crawling under the mosquito netting, my reading during these weeks having shifted from prose to the plays of Chekhov, Strindberg, and Ibsen.

What did these bouts with inner demons represent? Was I still, underneath it all, the scruple-filled and dutiful Catholic boy who could not reconcile the ideals of Christlike selflessness with the natural pulls of self-interest? I saw the power at my disposal — whether in dictating the actions of others or hoarding a few petty pleasures and forms of escape that added to my personal comfort — as corruption, pure and simple. I was afflicted by personal guilt and did not perceive, as yet, the larger forces in the world that conspired to cloud my judgments and rub my emotions raw. Instead, I dwelt obsessively on my own small melodrama and bribed an aching conscience with all manner of self-flagellating and infantile reflections.

Between the 5th and the 13th of February, we — members of the MI team in various combinations — attended five end-of-the-year parties, all but one hosted by our Vietnamese counterparts and associates. That exception we enacted ourselves, a walk-thru affair, part hospitality suite, part buffet. Gonadal expectations ran high on this occasion as I recall, because someone — one of our rakish interpreters no doubt — had procured RSVPs from five upper school-aged lovelies who appeared, coolly ate their fill in fifteen minutes, then wisely made their exit. They faced no overt danger, but the boys all reeked of homesickness and lust, an intimidating brew that these sensible and desirable *co dep*,[5] draped in graceful *ao dais*, wanted no taste of.[6]

The other Tet parties were relatively buoyant, except for Mr. Toan's. Toan, Duc Pho's chief of police, was a handsome mandarin with a cold, hard countenance. His wife, Mrs. Toan, was herself a figure around the town, a fairy princess in her poise and good looks, but as icy as her husband, a true dragon lady as seen through Western eyes long blurred by the usual stereotypes: is there no evil so vile as oriental evil? The Toans made a striking pair, a living index of every haughty, authoritarian trait and gesture that seemed to mark the henchmen of the Saigon regime from the common folk.

Tet Celebration, February 1969.

In spirit Toan's party also differed from the other celebrations we'd attended among the more provincial locals, where some measure of unfeigned good will and hospitality was in evidence. Toan's feast had a competitive edge, a drinking bout between East and West, with the chief ladling out the whisky four to six fingers at a time, making sure no one's glass was ever empty. The officers sat at a long table all along one side, a dais really, with me hanging on to the corner at one end. Toward the center, where the power lay, you could hear the gruff and bluster of the talk between the ranking dignitaries, conversation as contact sport, a kind of verbal rugby match. I remember Toan, sloppy in his cups, speechifying like a rabid warlord and backslapping the American brass, who must have been thinking behind those steel trap smiles, "He's a vicious sonofabitch, but, by God, he's ours."

A Brutal Beating

Before, during, and for some time after Tet, we waited for the enemy offensive that seemed would never come. As we waited, we made the lives I am describing here. And in MI, some of us still went to the field when the information seemed propitious. At some point not terribly distant from Duc Pho center, whatever the direction, a GI would cross into Indian Country, a hardhat zone. Out there the stray bullet and the booby trap kept our forces in trim, and you'd best trade that jaunty jungle cap you wore back at the firebase for your GI Joe steel pot. There was this too, I guess; the romance, the thrill of danger, the blissful ignorance of life and mortality. There were these reasons for climbing aboard that chopper, armed to the teeth, taking to the chase. Or maybe I just needed to show Dick and Stranzo that I didn't prize my skin any more than they prized theirs.

I didn't understand my thing with those two guys then, and I know even less about it more than three decades later. It was not love-hate, though, that much I can tell you. All-hate would be more like it. And not just because I saw them as monsters of American normalcy, ignorant who'd probably be right at home today at some big league ballpark getting soused and pelting outfielders from the visiting team with flashlight batteries.

Those two pricks made my existence miserable back at the MI compound, so openly insubordinate that I came to see the only resolution as me or them. Things might have come to a head if other forces didn't finally intervene. But by mid–February the worst was yet to come, and for the life of me, I can't reconstruct a single specific of how I came to be in the field again, not with just one, but both of them, unless it was simply another case of being led blindly by my obsessive and reckless curiosity.

We went out to locate a tunnel complex that we'd learned about from an informant. There were a few troops along, including a tunnel rat and a couple of majors, both combat engineers, accompanied by a small demolitions team. It hadn't taken long for the tunnel rat, a wiry American flyweight, to reemerge and inform the war party that the place was cobwebbed, long abandoned. This bit of news pissed off the two MI bad boys no end. Just then an old man and a young boy leading a water buffalo appeared on the trail, and Dick and Stranzo decided to detain them.

Stranzo secured the frail and ancient man, and Dick laid on with a will, pistol whipping the poor bastard with the barrel end of his .38. The two majors, having arrived in their own chopper, lingered nearby waiting for their men to blow the tunnel so they could depart. They might have been a pair of duffers on the fairway pontificating on their golf games for all they seemed to take notice of this sorry spectacle only a few yards from where they stood. It was horrible to see the terror on the old man's swollen, bloody face, and listen to his and the boy's screams for pity.

I only remember that I protested, and somehow the beating stopped before the man was knocked unconscious, and that neither he nor the boy would betray the whereabouts of any Vietcong, whether from loyalty or fear, it's hard to know; though I would prefer to believe the former, so impressed had I become by these acts of non-compliance. Better to die at the hands of the Americans, I guess, if your number was up, than suffer a humiliating death as a traitor at the hands of your own.

After that I tried to avoid Stranzo and Dick as much as possible, and they returned the courtesy. "I'll leave the weapons and dinks to *S & D*," I wrote that night. At the same time, Major Heinz, our boss back at division, all but ordered us to stop sending CI operatives to the field; he'd been shaken by what had happened to Stanley R. We were to just pump our net for intel on the whereabouts of VC infrastructure, Heinz insisted, then let the grunts go after the quarry. But the two MI killers had the blessing of Colonel Donaldson and his infantry brass, so they continued to run their own operation over Heinz's muted objections. And I ran mine, perpetuating the fiction of leadership as best I could and pushing paper up the line to keep Division at bay.

In-Coming

While mental anguish over interpersonal relations within the team dominated my private reflections, by mid–February those tag lines on my health now appeared with ever increasing urgency. "I feel sluggish, instead of more robust, despite my nightly workouts." "Lethargic today — don't know why. Even had trouble chewing my gum," reads another. "Bad cold. Must sleep early." "My cold is making me feel extremely depressed. Feel sick, weak, these

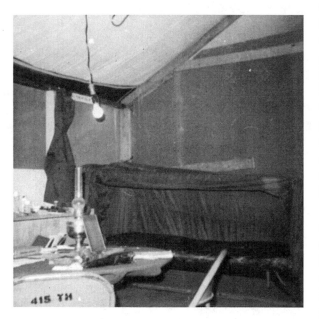

My bunk.

days." "A minor cold has me by the gonads and doesn't wish to release its grip." "My coughing has been so bad lately that it's beginning to worry me. Of course, I wouldn't mind a 'slight' case of TB or some similar respiratory ailment just to get the fuck out of Nam." This last on February 28th.

Just as suddenly, these expressions of concern over my health vanished, returning only toward the middle of March about the time I took leave for R&R. In the interim, there were more immediate threats to con-

tend with: a month long bombardment of incoming fire, the much anticipated offensive.

We'd actually had a preview of how this particular combat experience felt on the 11th of February at dawn, when a friendly 105 Howitzer round fell way short of its target and exploded quite nearby. We spent an hour picking shrapnel from our sandy volleyball pit before the nightly game against the LRRPs could get under way. This six-man Long Range Reconnaissance Patrol team occupied a hootch that bordered one corner of the MI compound. Each of these guys affected a wild, unkempt appearance, modeled on a collage of images from the American frontier with trappings of the counterculture; of the hundreds of troops one saw every day, infantry and support elements alike, only the LRRPs approximated how GIs are portrayed generally in the genre films of Vietnam combat produced by Hollywood, including the self-indulgent, inflated sagas of Oliver Stone, notwithstanding the fact that he himself is a veteran of the war. The LRRPs had a look that was truly forbidding, especially when you watched them clean their arsenal of exotic weapons or spend hours throwing knives, bayonets and hatchets at the various makeshift targets set up outside their single dwelling. But they were total klutzes when it came to organized sports, at least in hoops and volleyball.

The 11th was a day I documented in some detail, beginning with an account of my new herb garden planted with dill, basil, marjoram, borage, sage and anise. Twice that evening — match and rematch — we beat the LRRPs in volley ball. Poor apes, left with their tails between their legs, I wrote with considerable condescension. Later, Norm of the Red Cross hosted a cocktail party for his MI bridge buddies — whipping up Bloody Marys from a brew he'd manufactured out of catsup and god knows what, serving as canapés sardines nested in a bed of mustard on saltines. But the point is that the real shit didn't begin to rain on us until a week later, on February 22nd.

At 3 a.m. — actually the 23rd — we were awakened by what appeared to be mortar rounds. Sirens followed, a yellow alert. "No sweat thus far. It [the shelling] all seems to be going out now." An hour later, I added these amendments: "Wrong again. 4:30 a.m. all hell broke loose. Sounded like about twenty incoming to me. 4:50. Up again dammit. Three more real close. Hit the floor for number two. Sharks are out west doing their thing."

Sharks, Puff the Magic Dragon, Arc Lights — these were the *sons et lumieres* of modern warfare, American-style, that blazoned the night sky with open-air pyrotechnics to entertain GIs all over Vietnam, no matter how remote or civilized their billets. For us at Bronco the show was never more intense than over this three week span when we came under heavy fire. The drill became routine: awaken to an explosion, hightail it for the bunker, wait out the barrage, move to the bunker roof and watch the show.

First up were the Sharks, Huey gun ships rigged with extra firepower, then the Cobras, sleek and lethal, the new generation of dedicated helicopter gunships, not something adapted like the Huey from troop carriers. Soon Puff, a converted DC-3, would enter the amphitheater, so slow it seemed to hover on the near horizon like the Goodyear blimp, tattooing the countryside below with small caliber canon fire from its loud and multiple Gatling guns, every third round or so a tracer glowing in a phosphorescent yellowgreen.

If Puff lulled the numbed minds of GIs into macabre associations with benign explosives, like fireworks on the Fourth of July, an Arc Light provided no such shade of ambiguity. When the B-52s went to work and carpeted a distant place with thousand pound bombs, the edge of the sky lit from pole to pole in a pulsating arc of industrial fluorescence, conjuring visions of Alamogordo. And while the thundering retorts traveled many miles to reach our ears, the ripple of gentle shock waves washing over us was evidence by grim extrapolation of the terrible fury these bombers unleashed on the land and population beneath their sights.

No weapon in the American arsenal took so great a toll in Vietnamese lives — combatants and civilians alike — nor so terrorized the souls of those who lived to record their experiences — as these B-52 raids, crewed by a caste of elite flyboys quartered safely back in Okinawa, Guam or Thailand[7] — who dropped their ordnance from 30,000 feet and never heard the screams of their legions of victims, nor even, one imagines, experienced the half-spent turbulence that reached American units like ours so many miles from the killing ground.

What had begun as a lark, the long expected baptism by fire, ended in a mood of fatalism, where every horror including one's own death became imaginable, even, in the worst moments, a desired end, if it would only still the pounding on the nerves and inner ear of the relentless incoming and outgoing explosions. "Duc Pho looked like a ghost town," I wrote one evening. "Went with Hieu to a little hamlet south of town — he saying, why not?, you believe in fate."

It was not fate, but target selection that set the odds, however. And more and more rounds fell perilously close when the enemy overshot his principal objective — the airfield which had one margin a mere road's width across from where we huddled in our shelter. In fact I had my one really close call when leaving the mess tent — to which I'd been obliged to return during much of the offensive — carrying a hot meal in a metal tray. I heard the loud whistle of an incoming rocket, followed by a resounding KABLAM fifty yards away just a few palpable and memorable seconds before my body reacted by diving under a truck into a double portion of mashed potatoes and gravy. This was in the first few days, before the bombardment had gotten old and unbearable, "just like a World War Two land-on-the-beach movie," I all but gushed in my journal.

Work went on under a schedule of staggered hours. Awake till dawn, most everyone now slept in till at least eleven. The interrogation section maintained a skeleton crew during normal hours to receive and process detainees from the daily transports of the grunts, which had slowed but not ceased. The counterintelligence section functioned on three tracks. I myself puttered around the compound when possible, seeking the usual distractions in a variety of domestic chores, or sat around the office authoring thin agent reports, pure fictions, on the whereabouts and strength of the enemy; Gray loafed; Dick and Stranzo sifted through the arrivals at IPW for fresh meat. Their daily lamb in tow, they'd slap her or him around, rehearsing the standard interrogation drill, then drag them off to where Mr. Toan's police provided a more discreet sanctuary for the torture orgies they would later describe and brag about.

My response to their barbarism was hardly praiseworthy; I pickled my brain in a brine of existential drivel and pseudo Eastern philosophizing that, nonetheless, is painfully self-revealing.

February 25. Clear. I admit my desire for experience, whether it be good or evil, lofty or sordid. Gray, Patton and I await to see if Dick and Stranzo will get positive results using their "interrogation techniques"—with diverse motives. They say theirs is pure curiosity. (I don't believe them.) Mine is much more sadistic and I am not forced to dirty my own hands. I just make the Pilate scene.

Who was that masked man? Did I think I was some bloody Rascolnikov? Was I "just following orders?" Clearly, by this time, I had layered an added thickness of amorality over my truer sensibilities, but deep within the beast was rattling his cage with a fury that can only spring forth when a strong will is confronted at last with its own impotence.

Two days later, around four in the afternoon on the 27th, a rocket attack struck the outskirts of Duc Pho, and we learned soon after when one of the interpreters rushed back from town that three of our agent D-2's children had been killed. Several of us went out to inspect the damage, and console the family, bearing trivial compensations in the form of C-rations, smokes, and half-worn fatigues. A snapshot in my possession shows two MI team members walking into the smoldering ruin, and the face of a man, D-2, collapsed in grief. Late that same night rockets hit a medics' hootch killing at least three, just across the tarmac, the length of a football field away.

The enemy did not strike on the 28th. I must

Rocket attack in Duc Pho, March 1969.

have slept through the night, despite feeling so poorly, because when the phone rang around 7:30 on March 1st, I was already at my desk. The longest passage in my diary documents that conversation:

> "Stanley R. is dead," said Major Heinz in a voice barely audible over the poor land-line connection. As it had been dropped on me, so did I drop the bomb on the rest of the team. All of us felt the shock for probably the very same motives and reasons. One, R. was here — we could identify with him. He was young and strong and very much alive. Now he is gone. Two, it brings the reality of each man's individual death a little bit closer. So we all reflect — if him, then why not me? We are all afraid....
>
> Most of us will probably spend the night in the bunker — which is a silly, futile act really.[8]

Anything but futile, as it turned out. I counted some fifty incoming rounds after midnight when the barrage began, bringing a temporary halt to our cramped all-night poker game. Stanley's name did not come up; a soldier's taboo, I guess, to speak of those who crossed so recently into the spirit world. Fear, though, was very much abroad; you could read it on each man's face. It was an anguished night for all of us, the worst of the lot.

By the time the show came to be dominated by *our* firepower, scattering the VC mortar crews to bunkers of their own, the MI guys had mellowed out. Many of them took to the shadows to smoke reefer. The sweet clouds of marijuana floated through the air and into my nostrils from every corner of the compound. But I did not indulge; it was the kind of infraction no officer wanted to be caught at. There was no drug epidemic yet among American troops in Vietnam, and the use of pot I witnessed, though regular, was discreet. That it remain so was my only concern.

The local installment of the 1969 Tet Offensive ended on March 10th with a final double pounding of Duc Pho and Bronco. During the melee CI was summoned to the Brigade Evacuation Hospital where three NVA soldiers, slightly wounded and in uniform, had been medevac'd from the field following their capture. It was a rare occasion to be face to face with our elusive counterparts, boys, like most GIs, no more than twenty, and frightened out of their wits by rough treatment at the hands of the Brigade S-2, Major Crud and some of the other higher ranking commanders and staff members who snarled and circled them like maddened wolves.

As bonafide POWs, armed and uniformed — unlike most VC guerrillas — they needn't have feared for their safety. These were rare prizes to be showcased in the rear and scrupulously afforded protection under the conventions of war. But under fire and still in the passions of the fray, what with all the brass screaming in their faces, grabbing their tunics, and poking their wounds, the atmosphere at the evac hospital was hardly conducive to gathering information from the prisoners that might have yielded any immediate benefit.

Nonetheless, the rumor circulated widely that NVA units were entrenching themselves throughout the brigade AO, and a real donnybrook was in the offing. While nothing came of this, our sense of well-being and security were now capable of being shattered even by the sound of our own guns. "Our outgoing artillery," I noted in my diary, "is so frequent and so close that its presence has almost the same effect on people as the incoming rounds."

I was scheduled to leave for R&R in Bangkok on the 18th. During the preceding week, judging from my recorded chronology, I was too sick to work. Bitter complaints appear daily, and the return of the monsoon with its wet, cold winds just made my life all the more wretched. I took to my hootch. Despite — perhaps because of — my sagging spirits, my mind now craved escape in literature more than ever, and I used the time to indulge this obsession. I suffered, I believed, from chronic bronchitis, an ailment which had plagued me since adolescence. In fancy I identified with a character from my readings, writing on March 12, "I spent most of today inside in bed. Felt just run down. Rain for the first time in weeks, damp, chilly. Altogether miserable and against my condition. I feel like Michel in Gide's Immoralist," an allusion, I suppose, to the protagonist's bout with consumption.[9]

Amidst these morbid meditations is a single stark description of the symptoms I now experienced nightly.

> About 3 or 4, I wake up drowning in sweat and change my underwear. Get back into the wet sheets and begin to sweat again. Wake up about 7:30 with the feeling that I am lying naked in the dew-drenched grass at dawn.

Such attempts at imagery were suggested, no doubt, by the literary works I consumed in that week of confinement, *The Immoralist*, Solzhenitsyn's *One Day in the Life of Ivan Denisovich*, Chaucer's *Canterbury Tales*, and *The Castle*, by Franz Kafka.

Patton Strikes Back

A running commentary on these books also threads through my entries for this week, bracketing an unrelated account of a curious outburst by Patton, who was himself nearing the end of his emotional rope. To counter some point of mine during the endless carping that substituted for conversation between us, Patton blurted out, "Clivus says you use big words to impress us." Privately, I took great delight in the fact that Patton now resorted to such weak stratagems to buttress his authority: Uhl isn't such a hotshot liberal after all; one of my interrogators, a slow talking, gawky black kid, doesn't like him.

Lt. Patton, a high strung type, impressed the more prosaic blokes in the officer corps as a flake, brainy but volatile. Turns out Patton had a set of balls to match his eccentricities. Three days before the cessation of the VC barrage Patton struck back at the S2, who not only ridiculed him tirelessly, but pressured the IPW unit to classify large numbers of detained Vietnamese as civil defendants rather than innocent civilians. A civil defendant was someone the interrogators suspected of being a law breaker, a draft dodger, or a hamlet-level political cadre. It was one of those quantitative categories peculiar to the insurgent warfare of Vietnam that American forces substituted for the more traditional measure of success in combat, the taking and occupation of ground; like a body count, the number of CDs, civil defendants, added its perverse luster to the Brigade's official claims of glory.

Patton, despite his penchant for contradicting authority, was no rebel. He was inclined in his interrogation duties to follow the book. And the book clearly specified which criteria were required for tagging some dink a civil defendant, conditions which, in the overwhelming majority of instances, were seldom satisfied. If Patton had had his way, the MI interrogation center would have been a revolving gate; the infantry hauling in chopper-loads of peasants from its sweeps of the countryside, Patton, lacking evidence to the contrary, stamping their tickets "innocent civilian," and setting them loose in Duc Pho to get home as best they could.

Under constant scrutiny by the brigade S2, Patton was compelled to compromise his standards, classifying many detainees as CDs based on hearsay or on evidence fabricated outright by one of his interpreters or interrogators. This ongoing row with his tormentor provided much of the emotional back-drop, if not the exact cause, of Patton's downfall.

For one reason or another it was not always possible to identify the full name of an absent third person being referred to during interrogation; perhaps owing to the passage of time, some of the older folk did not remember their neighbors' full names; more likely they chose not to remember. If the given name of an individual could not be determined, she might appear in the IPW report as, for example, Nguyen Thi FNU—first name unknown; or in the case of the family name, last name unknown— LNU. Patton began to beard the S2 around this time, listing certain potential civil defendants to be reported to the South Vietnamese police as FNU LNU — which, when voiced, rendered the comical nonsense string, fa–New la–New.

Crud was not amused. When the clash came, Patton stood his ground like Ensign Pulver confronting the tyrannical naval captain in *Mr. Roberts*. But in Patton's drama, the S2 was a major, and majors are the bully boys of the army, a staff rank for the most part, not in command. Since command is everything in the army,[10] majors must gain through intimidation what captains at the company level and lieutenant colonels at battalion with the power to discipline may demand by fiat. Patton, moreover, was not officially within the 11th Brigade chain of command; operationally, MI took orders from Brigade, but we could only be disciplined by Division.

When Patton failed to wither under a torrent of intimidating threats, citing regulations as his defense, the S2 could only rend his garments and bitch up the line to Chu Lai. After this, while I never said as much, I now held Patton in some esteem and saw him potentially as a brother-in-arms against the Vietnam insanity. Our friendship, unfortunately, was not destined to grow. Patton's days at Bronco were numbered.

My last recollection of him in Duc Pho was on March 17th, the night before I left for Chu Lai en route to Bangkok and R&R, when our bridge game at Norm's Red Cross hootch was somehow transformed into a round of charades. If I have a single happy memory of my time in Vietnam, it was that evening when Patton, Gray, and I all let down our defenses and momentarily recaptured the common ground of silliness that is the special province of small boys and lunatics.

R&R

Nothing moved in the army without one being forced to take due recognition of the institution's fundamental commitment to aggressive inertia; "hurry up and wait" was the order of the day. To transport a single man — myself — from Duc Pho to Bangkok took nearly four full days. It was not the fickle intervention of nature that slowed my progress; the weather could not have been more favorable to travel by air. Nor, obviously, were the logistical and technical means of transportation lacking or deficient in any way. Humans may have a knack for efficiency, but we often lack the will to employ it, especially where, as with the expeditionary forces of the U.S. Army in Vietnam, nine-tenths of those you met didn't want to be in uniform in the first place. Every GI in those days was a potential saboteur, primed to poke his wrench into the Green Machine whenever the spirit moved him.

What made this delay in gratifying my escapist fantasy of whoring in Thailand especially intolerable was being required to spend the night at headquarters in Chu Lai, where parade ground etiquette pinched like a tight shoe. Here one was expected to maintain appearances. Admittedly, I was going to seed. My fatigues were rumpled and my hair un-officer-like, a tad too long; the paint brush mustaches I sported now drooped well below my lower lip.

I'd no sooner reported my presence when a pissy Major Heinz threatened an Article 15 — non-judicial punishment amounting to a fine — if I didn't

clean up my act. This stung me doubly, because Heinz had recently made
much of the fact that he'd rated me above all his young lieutenants in the
annual officer evaluations. Out of sight I could manipulate their game. But
in the flesh, as I humbly came to grasp, my disdain for the military was transparent. Slinking from the tent when my wrathful CO finished reading me the
riot act, I didn't walk a hundred yards before some other low-life major actually crossed a road to scream at me for walking with my hands in my pockets. Could the black major who accompanied him — and kept his cool — have
been Colin Powell, then a staff officer at the Americal?

The rest of the day I hid out in the MI enlisted men's bar. Around ten,
when the featured porno flick of the evening, *The Golden Shower*, flashed on
the screen — the gist of which I will leave to the reader's imagination — I
crawled off to find a spare cot, fighting a dark and dejected mood.

It was not until two in the afternoon of the 21st that my flight, via an
obligatory stopover at Cam Ranh Bay, finally touched down in Bangkok.
Then, following a series of inane orientation lectures that lasted till four, we
were at last free to find a hotel and shop for sex. The women sat bare breasted
behind a large glass window, holding numbered cards which you referred to
when making your selection. I was so sick that night that I could barely get
it up. The next morning, I went on sick call, brimming with self-pity at having to waste these precious moments of R&R waiting in an army aid station.

The RN chirped encouragingly that someday I'd find the right antihis-
tamine and all my symptoms would disappear; in the meantime she gave me
powerful turpenhydrate — GI gin — to suppress my chronic cough. Even in
this frail state I passed a wonderful five days in Bangkok, choosing the companionship of one girl after two false starts; it wasn't so much sex I needed as
female company, some illusion of the familiar and the normal to weigh against
my inevitable return to the asylum on LZ Bronco.

Bangkok was a doable and orderly town in March of 1969, and my driver,
a decent, cheerful fellow, designed just the kind of cultural itinerary I found
most satisfying, bouncing between museums and open markets, glittering
temples and back alley bistros where urban Thais took their meals. On the
last day my two Thai companions and I drove to a university on the outskirts
of the city and chatted all afternoon with students.

En route to the airport, my girl took me home, a sturdy cabin built of
teak, and introduced me to her family. Indeed I did not see her as a whore,
but as a kind of working girl, someone you'd meet and spend time with for
a brief spell while passing through town. Two souvenirs of R&R have stayed
close to me all these years: a sarong she gave me, which I still wear on occasion
after showering; and a postcard featuring a sculpture in wood of an emaciated
Buddha before enlightenment, stapled to the inside cover of my war diary.

End Game

"Here I am — back in reality," was my entry for March 28th, on return to Duc Pho. The mail had piled up in my absence, and I opened two letters from institutions of higher learning. One denied me financial aid to New York University grad school — where I'd already been accepted by the Portuguese Department for the coming fall — assuming my request for an early discharge was granted, normally a formality when one was returning to school. The other came from Bank Street College, rejecting my application for a poverty-oriented master's program the school was running up in Harlem — because, it read, they gave priority to Negroes and Puerto Ricans. "Don't let the whites in where they have to be to learn," I naively scribbled in my chronicle.

The next day I was back on sick call. The doc on duty, a hard-ass captain, affected the élan of the infantry. His mission was to maintain troop strength, not practice medicine in the interest of his patients. Insisting that the X-rays were negative and my blood count near normal, he condescendingly dismissed all legitimate fears for my health and prescribed Librium. This was the second time in my brief army career that this elemental antidepressant had been recommended to help me resist the apostasies of mood that ill adapted me to military life. Again, I can't recall if I took the pills or not; probably not, because my mood certainly showed no signs of improvement.

Nothing in the letters or diary entries I wrote in the days immediately after returning from Bangkok suggests the slightest presentiment that I would soon be gone from Vietnam. In the wake of this latest medical brush-off, I simply went back, even more demoralized and confused than before, to business as usual. But after five months of routine with the same faces, the arithmetic of the troop rotation system, adding and subtracting one replacement at a time, was gradually reconfiguring the roster at the 1st MIT.

Patton was finally replaced and exiled to some desk job at another brigade to finish out his tour; he was one burr Heinz certainly didn't want under his saddle at Division. Another lieutenant arrived, a lifer with more time in grade than I, and he assumed the role of officer-in-charge. I too, it seems, had been relieved, the one objective change I can cite to confirm that a deterioration in my performance had been, somewhere, officially registered.

Nonetheless, on good mornings and bad, I would drag my weary carcass into the CI section and go through the motions of doing a half-day's work, not merely to keep up appearances, but because the distraction provided a partial antidote to my condition. Otherwise I continued to come and go as I pleased, managing a visit to Hinh's in town some days, but mostly retreating to the isolation of my hootch where I lay, collapsed, on my bunk for hours.

I'd shaved my upper lip in Thailand, a change that roused near universal disapproval from the MI team, and, quite unexpectedly, stirred the consternation of many casual acquaintances in Duc Pho as well. Some of the
reaction, I suppose, was simply shock. I can see how ghostly I appeared in a
few old photos, skin and bones, down from 190 to 160 pounds; the hidden
truth of my decline now exposed in a profile of sunken features.

The war was visibly wasting me within and without, and I had become
a grim and disquieting presence. Years later, I can also see in this flurry of
mild public reproaches directed at my decision to shave, an element of flattery,
an expression of familiarity from unexpected quarters. Even at the time, the
attention pleased me, and I was aware of an accompanying emotion, self-
serving though it may be, of having passed some basic test of acceptance.

If some guilt lingers over having exploited for my own comfort the
authority and mystique that attaches to the intelligence operative, there is a
more than compensating relief in knowing that, in the process, I generally
avoided doing harm to others. At the same time, I can not claim my aprons
were entirely stain free. Evil, like, say, radiation, accumulates internally with
each exposure. We are, after all, only human. My conflicted response to the
war was just that, conflicted. When every sense, including the instinct for
survival, is under constant assault, one can hardly be expected to sort out in
each instance of thought or action the rational from the irrational.

By late March — to cite the distortion most conspicuous in my decline —
I'd developed a mild, but entrenched, case of xenophobia; the dinks were getting on my nerves. The strangeness of the place and people that but a month
before had struck me as charming or exotic, was now a constant source of
irritation. Fortunately I could still distinguish between the Vietnamese in my
own circle and the vexing masses, for whom — without the slightest justification beyond the burden of my own woes — I now harbored such disdain.
It's possible for me now from the distance of over thirty years to imagine that
the horrors of Vietnam might eventually have engaged me in a far more direct,
destructive way, had a sudden shift of fortune not cut short my tour in the
war zone.

That, at least, is one interpretation I can plausibly tease from the final
war story I will add to this account. I mentioned above an old man we'd
caught in the apparent act of assembling a signaling device — a reflector powered, if memory serves, by a candle — and who claimed his only intention was
to take a twilight shave. It seemed an open and shut case. He'd been collared
in flagrante, and the gut consensus on the team was that his alibi, while clever
in its simplicity, was an obvious crock.

Did this bird think we were stupid, I asked through Hieu? The man,
sixty-something, with a wispy long goatee à la Uncle Ho, quivered with ter-

ror and babbled the usual disclaimers, to which I took offense. The little bastard, thinks I, gets caught in the act trying to put the hurt on us with a renewed rocket or mortar barrage, then has the vinegar to piss in our faces with this transparently fraudulent protest of innocence?

Still, something didn't add up. The old fool came across in all respects as a typical bumpkin, not a cadre type. But that was neither here nor there; any good actor could pull off that ruse. It was the alibi, lame as it appeared, that intrigued me. Could he possibly be speaking the truth? The element of doubt drew me in, and I decided to supervise his interrogation personally.

This was the rationale that I contrived to make some old papasan's life, if not hell, then damned uncomfortable over the next forty-eight hours. His suffering proved perversely salutary to me, releasing the kind of energy I now associate with organizing a political event or a theatrical undertaking. As the director of this Vietnam farce, I had little taste for physical abuse; the script, at least initially, hinged on the psychological. We would convince the man that great agony, death perhaps, would follow, should he fail to confess the truth and betray his local handlers. We ran the classic Mutt and Jeff routine, the good cop/bad cop fandango.

The prisoner was ensconced in the torture cell down at IPW, our dungeon for this stage set. Gray and I, with one of the interpreters, probably Hieu, began the inquisition, with Gray acting the mensch, struggling to keep me from beating the old man to a pulp. I'd feign rage, grab him by the shoulders and shake him till he wept; Gray would hold me back, calm me down, suggest I step outside for a second; maybe he could reason with the guy....

I didn't really give a rat's ass whether the poor old geezer was guilty or not. How could I begrudge the Vietnamese their resistance to our cruelties and terror? American actions so condemned us in my eyes by then that I no longer imagined for an instant that ours was the side of right. But I was sick and desperate, maybe a little shell shocked. In my diary I find a second reference during this period to how the din of outgoing artillery was driving me mad. "The time grows heavy," I darkly noted, and engineered this one-acter to hasten the clock.

I repressed all empathy or pity for the man, convincing myself that he had, after all, been setting us up for a deadly blitz. For a day or two we toyed with our quarry, but the man clung to his tale and never broke. He had to prevent Gray and me, at least, from resolving our doubts; and I guess he did. Or we just lost interest. It's like threatening a child; when he figures out you're bluffing, you get ignored for your pains.

I remember feeling surprised that Hieu believed this scraggly compatriot, and actually favored setting him free. If any Vietnamese I met was a genuine anti-communist, it was our young ARVN interpreter, a Diem-style Catholic with a choirboy face. Not that Gray and I ever really entertained the choice of hurting the old man ourselves; but we might let the South Vietnamese do it for us by exercising option two, sending him over to the police.

The whole CI section debated the old man's fate. Gray had gone soft on the guy, and I just didn't want any trouble. Dick and Stranzo huffed and puffed at the suggestion, even from their beloved pals, Gray and Hieu, that the old man might be simply sprung without prejudice. Why didn't *they*, crooned the silky Dick, just slip on down to the cell, and have a go at the prey themselves; a plan I vetoed immediately.

Four days earlier, on March 30th, the provost marshal had been in my face screaming, literally, that a doc from the A&D had just filed a verbal complaint about some dink who'd been brought in with a broken arm, sustained, allegedly, during his interrogation by CI's fearsome twosome. "I don't care what the fuck you do outside the gates," he menaced, "but keep it off the base." From this I gathered, with considerable relief, that the 11th Brigade's head cop meant for the incident to go no further, and I toadied him with meek assurances that it wouldn't happen again, Sir.

In turn I reamed out the two killers, and made them fear, with perhaps a bit too much zeal, that, if the incident went higher, their asses, not mine, would be in the hot seat. A night or two following that very heated confrontation, which buoyed my own spirits enormously, I awoke to a muffled explosion. A smoke grenade had been popped right under my hootch, an unmistakable warning that, in this lawless American world of warfare, you didn't blow the whistle on your mates, no matter how much you loathed them. I had no doubt about the origins of this message. At the same time, I knew the boys understood that it was hardly in my interests to make a stink to Heinz or anyone else. They didn't scare, so much as force, me into a resolve at last that something had to be done to get them out of my hair once and for all. And that's what happened, not through confrontation, but by default.

For a week or so my bronchial symptoms had been relatively stable. Now they flared up. On the morning of April 8th I vomited. "The pain in my chest got so bad," I wrote, "that I was forced to visit A&D again." But the hard charging pro-war medico had gone on R&R; in his place was a new doc, a nice Jewish boy from New York who'd come down from Division to fill in. "Your X-rays show many clouds," he told me, voicing some genuine expression of concern. "I think you have TB." Several days later I lay on a stretcher in a giant hospital plane en route to Japan, and within a fortnight, I was back in the USA.

BOOK TWO

V. Days of Reckoning

V

Days of Reckoning

Anyone can consider ... what he knew twenty years ago, and
can see ... he was striving toward something which he can
only now understand — if he is fortunate.
— *Noam Chomsky (debate with Michel Foucault, 1974)*[1]

---

1. Days of Reckoning

Early Saturday morning, March the 21st, 1970, I heard the doorbell ring.
In the threshold stood a short, well built young man in a safari hat, Sam-
sonite briefcase in one hand, bulky reel-to-reel recorder in the other. I'm
Jeremy, he announced, flashing what I would later recognize as his most coy
and playful smile. I'd been roused from bed after a late night of student philosophizing at the White Horse Tavern, but Jeremy's arrival was not unexpected.

Earlier that week I'd attended a rally at New York University to build
for the spring offensive of the antiwar movement. Someone handed me a flyer
as I crossed one morning from my apartment to the student union on the
opposite side of Washington Square Park. What caught my eye was the featured discussion for the evening: U.S. War Crimes in Vietnam.

This was probably the first teach-in I'd ever been to. NYU's law school
auditorium was packed, and a succession of speakers pumped up our enthusiasm for the next big demo. At one point someone asked if any Vietnam vets
were present. Two activists from a group they called the Citizens' Commission of Inquiry wished to see all Vietnam vets after the meeting.[2]

It was late, but I listened to their rap that CCI, they called it, was organizing vets to expose the truth about what was happening in Vietnam. I remem-

New underline{evidence}:

"war crimes in vietnam"

* CAPT. BOB JOHNSON | former US Army Captain
West Pt. graduate. Vietnam veteran. Co-ordi-
nator - Citizens' ~~Commission of Inquiry~~

* . . . TAPES & SLIDES   of the Commission of Inquiry

* CONRAD LYNN   attorney

* "THE WAR & NYU"   reports on ROTC and the war
machine by Student Mobilization Committee

* CHAIRMAN: Kai Neilsen, Prof. of Philosophy, NYU

THIS MEETING WILL document the truth about genocidal massacre of the civilian population of South Vietnam. CITIZENS' COMMISSIONS OF INQUIRY are being organized to give returning GI's, newsmen, scholars and others a place to provide further evidence of War Crimes in Vietnam. At N.Y.U. four faculty members have formed a committee to hear such information; they may be contacted by calling (212) 598-2761. SMC and other groups have been working on "THE WAR & NYU", a report on what's happening right here. This meeting supports the campaign to remove ROTC from campus. This is the first in a series of activities in the Spring Offensive against the War.

FUNDS & ASSISTANCE ARE NEEDED.
ALL OUT FOR THE SPRING OFFENSIVE! ALL U.S. FORCES OUT OF VIETNAM NOW!

TISHMAN AUDITORIUM
NYU Law School
Washington Square * NYC

TUES. MARCH 17   8 pm
(St. Patrick's Day!)

Sponsors: NYU Committee to End the War in Vietnam * Student Mobilization Committee
(partial list)

For Information: Call (212) 777-5675/ Write NYU Committee to End the War in
Vietnam * 2 Washington Square North * New York City * NY *

"War Crimes in Vietnam." Flyer announcing teach-in at NYU, March 1970.

ber thinking, these guys don't look — or was it *feel* — like vets, so maybe I hung back a little, didn't really engage them. But I gave my name and phone number to Arthur, or maybe it was Jan — who was indeed a vet — without a clue that they were the very emissaries I'd been waiting for with my hand delivered invitation to the movement; they told me someone would be in touch.[3]

An eager Jeremy Rifkin called the very next day, and we made the arrangements that now brought him to my door. I would see and work with Jeremy during practically every day over the next two years, forming a political collaboration and friendship that began in a coffee shop on lower Broadway, as he listened to — and taped — my testimony almost a year since I'd been evacuated from the war zone.

With Mom just after arriving at Valley Forge Army Hospital, April 1969.

Coming Home

The previous year's journey leading to this encounter with Jeremy had been quietly eventful:

After leaving Duc Pho, I spend a day in the Division _evac_ hospital at Chu Lai. From behind a screen at the end of the ward, far from the other patients, you can hear me picking out chords for _I've Got Sunshine on a Cloudy Day_ on a borrowed Red Cross guitar. It's April 14th, my twenty-fifth birthday. Out of nowhere three guys from my old unit show up. It's Gray, and, maybe Patton, and another kid, an interrogator, I think, and they produce a split of Korbel Brut for this unanticipated ceremonial farewell. I am touched.

I then remain a week in the American hospital at Camp Zama, Japan, isolated in a private room, awaiting the diagnosis of TB to be confirmed. On the morning after my arrival, April 16th, 1969, it actually snows an inch or two; by midday all sign of this post-wintry dusting has melted away. Two snap shots taken from my hospital window, _before_ and _after_, memorialize what had for some reason struck me as this freakish, unfriendly display of local weather.

On April 21st I am once more strapped on a stretcher for a last ride in a medivac helicopter, which flies above a strangely familiar, yet surreal, back street scene in Tokyo. The avenue is lined with automobile junkyards like you'd see in South Brooklyn, while mostly men — Japanese men — wearing London Fog–style trench coats and gripping black bumber-shoots to their sides, rush along heads down in the light drizzle. They all look so Brooks Brothers....

For the second time that month I am loaded aboard a jumbo medical transport, bound for distant Edwards Air Force Base, near Washington and home. My disease is highly communicable. The nurses order the stretcher spaces above and below me left unoccupied; across the aisle a boy in a body cast moans the entire flight, while attendants add and subtract clumps of gauze from a crevice in his plaster armor to stem the flow of blood.

Our single stopover is Anchorage, Alaska. Red Cross volunteers swarm aboard and distribute the same species of weak coffee and stale donuts that the army had laid out at Clark Air Force Base in Manila on my way over, which is a kind of parable, if you think about it, on the banality of good.

Two days later I enter a TB ward in the large army hospital at Valley Forge, Pennsylvania. Powder blue pajamas are the uniform *de rigueur* throughout the institution; TB patients wear black, a nice twist, which not only places us in the ranks of repugnant medical outcasts like lepers, but aligns us symbolically with the Viet Cong, whose standard apparel resembles what is now our own.[4]

Within three months I begin to regain my physical strength; the record notes a mental slide, however, a personality change. There is an incident. I'd taken French leave one afternoon with a fellow inmate, and am sighted in a local tavern hooking rounds of Pennsylvania brew; heavily medicated and long on the mend, the doctor has assured me that the chance of my disease being spreadable is next to nil. Predictably, the chief pulmonary officer, a colonel, is outraged; he calls me in, speaks abusively, makes threats. I listen, returning fire, both barrels blasting on verbal automatic.[5]

That confrontation was one of those emancipatory moments that mark a critical transition in a person's life: not simply, as in this instance, a redemptive return to civilian status from the nightmare of war and an oppressive, authoritarian military. The outburst was a jump start to my confidence for the political struggles that lay before me. A week later, I was honorably retired from the active ranks and transferred to a VA hospital quite wonderfully located in New York City on Manhattan's east side. I rated a temporary disability of 100%, and a tax-free income of $400 a month.

New York Summer, 1969

It was now early July. New York summer was in full flower. For the next three weeks, I remained — officially — confined to a ward for the length of time it would take for lab reports to certify that the active tuberculin bacilli no longer infiltrated my sputum. Every day I boldly snuck away through the hospital's front entrance onto First Avenue.

My ruse was simple, and, if ever suspected, never challenged. In a shopping bag next to my bed was a change of clothes. Early each morning I'd walk to a private bathroom on the floor below, get dressed, and stuff my hospital garb into the same bag. Then, I'd schlep through the streets like any other New York denizen on his daily round of the shops and markets.

On most of these outings I had no special destination. My great pleasure was to wander the city streets, forging a habit I retain to this day of walking distractedly about New York (or any other large city) for miles on end whenever I'm in town. During one of those escapes I'd arranged to meet my old girl friend Katie in the park at Madison Square. I'd heard nothing from her all those months in Vietnam, nor at Valley Forge. Suddenly, Katie'd gotten in touch. She was still living in the city, going with the guy she'd eventually marry. There wasn't much to say, but our definitive ending as a potential couple did not occur for several months.

Another morning I walked into the graduate department of linguistics at New York University. The chairman, Lew Levine, a World War Two vet, admitted me to the program before even seeing my transcript from Georgetown on the strength of our shared experience with war. Lew saw in me a potential ally in the anti–Chomsky rearguard action he was waging within the department. This miscalculation on his part exemplifies the vast gap in worldview that typically separated vets from Lew's generation and my own — especially at a time when the Vietnam nightmare raged on, and some of its worst excesses were still to come.[6]

I've mentioned elsewhere that when I left Georgetown in the summer of 1967, virtually no one, among students at least, at the Institute of Linguistics had even heard of Noam Chomsky. By 1969, you couldn't imagine entering linguistics as an undergrad, much less a grad student, outside the framework that the young MIT professor had created to revolutionize the discipline. Levine's academic niche was sociolinguistics, a particularly anecdotal branch of the mumbo-jumbo school that had dominated linguistic research during the preceding half century. Poor Lew, he was fighting a losing battle; then his hoped-for relief column, yours truly, quickly defected to the opposing side.

Studying Chomsky's transformational grammar was the hardest intellectual work I'd ever taken on. Rooted in genuine scientific inquiry and methodologically complex, Chomsky's system was leagues more intimidating than the pseudoscience version of the field I'd been exposed to at Georgetown, which, to be honest, I'd found difficult enough. The most daunting task, quite simply, was learning how to think. Even at the tender age of 25, such a leap demands some considerable rewiring of the mind, not unlike, I imagine, what stroke victims must undergo to regain lost speech or motor function.

I threw myself wholeheartedly into doctoral studies that September, sweating blood while sorting through the tangled world of abstraction in which Chomsky designed and debated his theories. I'd sit at my carrel in the student center late into the night, reading and rereading a single paragraph from one of Chomsky's two formative texts, *Syntactic Structures* or *Aspects of a Theory of Syntax*, until some glimmer of his deeper meaning dawned on me. With each breakthrough, however modest, I experienced an indescribably exhilarating emotion, much more of a jolt than I'd ever suspected any form of work, much less scholarship, could provide.[7]

Many a morning around 3 a.m. I'd be strolling across the park toward home, my mind totally given over to some Chomskian conundrum. On one occasion, this distraction nearly cost me dearly. A young black man fashionably turned out in a full length leather coat emerged from the shadows. He pulled an eight inch stiletto from a bamboo sheath and demanded all my money. With my long scraggly hair and army field jacket, I looked about as prosperous as an unmade bed in a flophouse, and in fact, I had all of three dollars in my wallet; I also had a vial with a few tabs of synthetic mescaline.

During an instant of immobility which lasted a lifetime, when anything, including the worst, might have happened, we stood at opposites, frozen in the terrifying intimacy which binds victim to assailant. Instead of reacting from fear at the menacing way he waved his blade in my eyes, I began to rap about Vietnam. We walked and the youngster just listened. By the time we reached the subway stop at Lafayette and Astor Place, he concluded that I was not a suitable prey; he refused my three dollars, and had less interest in my stash of pills. We parted — what? — with some compact of understanding unspoken between us. I watched as he descended toward the train, having resolved, at my admittedly perverse urging, that the pickings on the Upper East Side might be more fruitful.

Choosing Sides

In those first months after Vietnam, many remnants of the attitudes that fastened me to the immediate past began to dissolve. I started living in a manner that suited me, urban life, a free agent — thanks to my VA subsidy — drawn to everything radical in the city's intellectual and cultural circles. New York in the seventies was the existential proving ground of the spirit of the sixties. For all its deep provincial underpinnings, the city was, after all, the undisputed seat of the American imperium, whose privileged citizenry now warred among themselves over the merits of a military adventure carried on in their names halfway around the globe.

An ambience of antiwar sentiment dominated life at NYU, and Vietnam was the topic *du jour* on campus, every day. Manifestations of student activism could not be ignored, though, no doubt, the majority of those enrolled were not, or were only marginally, involved in the protest movement. You couldn't walk ten feet without someone thrusting a leaflet in your hand; just for my own amusement I made a random collection of handouts I received crossing the park from October through April. These cultural artifacts, approximately eighty in number, are still in my possession, and, with only a few exceptions, each is related to the war.

I'd been caught up in the rank and file of the protests from the start of the semester. Without affiliation, I boarded one of the buses NYU's antiwar coalition charted on November 15th, 1969, and, around dawn, departed for the big mobilization scheduled for Washington that same day. Most of my crowd those first months at NYU were seniors, undergrads in clinical psychology. For reasons now obscure, none of them was going to DC, and I traveled in the company of several hippie friends. After a few hours we blew off the demo — a bummer, my companions whined, while the crowds simply made me uncomfortable — and took a Greyhound to Baltimore, where my old friend from college, the flamenco guitarist, was playing lead guitar at a local rock club.

In the men's room of the Baltimore bus station one of my companions dispensed tabs of sunshine; within seconds of swallowing mine, I stood crouched over the toilet retching violently. Soon recovered, feeling no pain, my first and only acid trip had begun. Of that exploit just the bus ride home is even remotely clear in memory, a milk run making all the local stops as it perambulated up the coast toward New York. Stuck bolt upright by a window, fully alert, the passage of time ceased to oppress me; outside a one-dimensional world swept by in ribbons of color. Despite what was unarguably a fundamental distortion of normal consciousness, I can testify that, overall, the disorientation, bordering on euphoria, was entirely satisfying. That trip, I figured, would be hard to duplicate; so I never tried.

In bed shortly after dawn the next day, I lay on my back till noon while showers of light and color played across the insides of my eyelids. John, my roommate, feared for my life, and I tried to reassure him that, if this was death, I was content to make the most of it.

I'd first met John during one of those early visits from the VA hospital to the linguistics department. He was sitting on the stoop of a brownstone bent over a much crumpled *Village Voice*, pondering the apartment listings. We made some small talk, and then, with a spontaneity totally out of character, I suggested that he and I go hunt for digs together; in an hour we found two rooms half a block from what serves NYU as one of the more lively "main quads" of any campus in the country, Washington Square Park.

John was a first year grad student in English lit, passionately fond of the Romantic poets Wordsworth and Coleridge.[8] That first term John was also a near basket case. The draft, just then being reformed along more democratic lines, and soon to reemerge as a lottery, was breathing down his neck. By December 1969 John would learn that his lottery number was just above the cutoff beyond which anyone was likely to be called into service. His fears had not been irrational. Despite Nixon's plan for a phased withdrawal, and for "winding down" the war, half a million U.S. troops remained mired in Vietnam that fall, and a draftee might yet find himself in the thick of the fray at any time over the next two years.

John was a sweet guy, and I think we would have remained friends under other circumstances. But he didn't care a fig for politics, while I was cautiously inching toward the Left, looking for some point of entree to connect with the movement. Two or three times that fall, having jotted down an address from a flyer or alternative newspaper — *The Guardian*, perhaps, or *Liberation News*— I'd walked to a vintage high-rise off Union Square and banged on a green metal door, behind which the antiwar vets were supposed to have their offices. No one ever answered.

Despite the by-then well-established contact within the antiwar movement between activists and GIs, the mobilization on any scale of veterans opposed to the war was still a good half year in the making. A few dedicated Vietnam vets had been appearing at antiwar demos for several years, but their presence in late 1969 remained sparse, consisting of small contingents organized by the disciplined Left or those who'd come as individuals, bearing witness.

Groups like the original Vets for Peace were holdovers from the Old Left and the Big War and Korea, and therefore of marginal appeal to Vietnam vets, barely past twenty, many from minority or underclass backgrounds, but mostly from the working class, and who generally saw the movement as student-based and socially elite. Vietnam Veterans Against the War (VVAW) would become the organizational vehicle many recent returnees from "Nam" eventually embraced to channel their radical commitment to stop the war, but VVAW — though founded two years before — remained in late 1969 an entity on paper. It would not explode in membership and prominence until midsummer of 1970.[9]

CCI and the Antiwar Vets

The CCI — the Citizens' Commission of Inquiry — would play a catalytic role in building this unprecedented formation of antiwar veterans by framing an issue around war crimes that the former soldiers could address and legitimize with reference to their own experiences on the battlefield. And no one knew better, from the inside out, what was wrong with Vietnam than the troops who'd fought there. What made this mobilization of antiwar vets all the more astounding was that the war was still far from over. Moreover, the vets who were eventually filtered — directly or indirectly — through CCI into Vietnam Veterans Against the War, already possessed strong needs to communicate their disillusionment to the Middle American communities from which they sprang: these same folk who President Nixon caricatured as the silent majority, a great blob of drones and tongue-tied patriots, among whom, nonetheless, the message and style of the antiwar movement played with such little sympathy.

It was in linking Vietnam veterans to the powerful antiwar forces already in existence by means of a highly publicized campaign to denounce U.S. war crimes throughout Indochina that CCI's two principal coordinators, Jeremy Rifkin and Tod Ensign, made their considerable contribution — though largely overlooked in accounts of the times — to organized antiwar opposition during its later stages from 1970 through 1971.

2. Tod & Jeremy

Tod Ensign and Jeremy Rifkin may not have been the original "odd couple," but their partnership was cut to that mold. The one, Jeremy, was a day person, TV addict, up early and in bed by nine; the other, Tod, would seldom bloom till after midnight when he roamed the downtown bars and jazz dives. Tod ran hot, and seemed to thrive on human conflict; not that Jeremy shrank from controversy, but the thicker things got, the cooler and more detached he became from any charge of emotion that one might legitimately associate with such moments. Jeremy, of Russian Jewish stock, was something of a tennis jock; Tod, an Episcopalian, his roots in old Anglo-Teutonic America, harbored a deep abhorrence for the smells and sounds of the locker room.

In appearance, despite a few outward accommodations to the eccentricities of the counterculture — a safari hat that was his trademark, for example — Jeremy remained essentially clean cut; while Tod, with straight brown hair reaching well down his back, wore electric bright shirts and tight pants tucked into calf-high boots, and festooned himself in exotic scarves and African jewelry. Tod, though, was no hippie — a breed of cat he viewed contemptuously as "apolitical" — his costumes were unique, even for the times. With his swarthy complexion, there was something about Tod oddly suggestive of the nineteenth century native American, the colorful chap familiar from old daguerreotypes who mixed and matched his outfit willy-nilly from the white man's wardrobe.

But the similarities between the two activists were equally striking. Both were Midwesterners — Jeremy from Chicago's South Side, Tod from Battle Creek, Michigan — brought up in households dominated by strong and doting mothers, outnumbered by sisters. Each was spoiled in those ways that transform favored only-sons into "golden boys" within the hierarchy of the sexes. Both came from backgrounds sustained in material comfort, though hardly of the first rank, by emotionally distant fathers more or less successful in private business. From this mixture of savvy paternal entrepreneurship and unstinting maternal encouragement, each man developed a kind of slick vitality and competence that didn't always go over well within the more ascetic ranks of the New Left.

It was under circumstances typical for radicals of the times that Rifkin and Ensign came together in New York City, where both were living by 1969. Tod, a lawyer, had ridden out the draft a few years earlier by taking a degree in graduate law at NYU, and then found work in nearby New Jersey with that relic of LBJ's Great Society, the Office of Economic Opportunity, known popularly as the Poverty Program.

As a boy, Tod had been exposed to a limited panorama of left-liberal politics through his father's association with organized labor as printer for certain local AFL-CIO materials. "My dad had one friend, a skilled worker, who started bringing me his used *Progressives* when I was thirteen or fourteen," Tod mentioned once, and he himself had been involved with progressive causes since his undergraduate days at Michigan State. At Wayne State School of Law in the early to mid-sixties, Tod was active in both the civil rights and antiwar movements.

Just months before joining forces with Jeremy, Tod experienced a dramatic epiphany in West Africa, weeping uncontrollably while standing on a wharf at Goree, an island off the coast of Dakar, Senegal, where slaves had once been stacked like cordwood into ships bound for the middle passage. Returning home, he quit his job at OEO, abandoned plans to take a PhD in urban planning at Rutgers, and pondered an uncertain future.

Jeremy was a BMOC — a big man on campus — at Penn, where, as president of his graduating class he too had organized against the war; he was now wrapping up a tour in VISTA, a tactical ploy to put off, and possibly avoid, military service. Jeremy had done his master's work at Tufts' Fletcher School of Diplomacy, where a fascination with Hitler and horror of the Holocaust led him to research and write about eugenics and genocide. Jeremy, too, had experienced conversion the summer before landing in New York. On a European tour he stopped at Dachau, and suddenly, in mind's eye, saw swastikas plastered all over American policy in Vietnam.

After settling in New York, Jeremy gravitated in his spare time toward solidarity work on behalf of the Black Panthers and had been attending meetings of a Left coalition called NCCF — the National Committee to Combat Fascism. The committee was coordinating public support for the Panther 21, victims of a concerted campaign of government repression called Cointelpro,[10] whose trial for conspiracy was just then getting under way. This repression, in Jeremy's way of seeing, was evidence of the fascist potential built into any highly centralized corporate state, including the U.S.

Tod had also begun to frequent these NCCF meetings at the behest of a small Maoist collective of public health workers he had befriended, which included several nurses, a surgeon and a psychiatrist, all living communally on Staten Island.[11] They too, like so many of the radicalized young people from privileged backgrounds in those times, were as focused on domestic racial injustices as on the U.S. imperial mission in Vietnam. The Staten Island folk wanted Tod's help with some legal matters for one of their black community projects, but Tod had no patience for the practice of law. He found it boring and confining. He was looking for something more exciting. How, he asked himself around this time, do people like Dave Dellinger and Abbie Hoffman do that? How do they get to go around every day and be activists?

The Brothers

Tod got part of his answer on an early December night in 1969 while he and the rest of the crowd at the NCCF meeting waited restlessly for the black leadership which ran the show to make its appearance. To Tod's amazement, this young, good looking Jewish guy suddenly got tired of waiting and took the podium. "He and a couple of others," Tod recalled nearly thirty years later, "began to lead the meeting. This went on for maybe a half hour. Then, Tod says chuckling, the brothers came in the door, Brother Zaid Shakur and four or five others ... all wearing the obligatory black leather ... really ominous looks on their faces. They went up to the front and basically said, What the motherfuck are you fuckers doing? Get the fuck off that podium. Motherfucker! After which Brother Zaid treated them to a twenty minute peroration on democratic centralist leadership. And how these usurpers — these *white* usurpers — had to accept the condemnation of the group, blah, blah, blah. I liked that about Jeremy right from the start," Tod recalled, "it was a cheeky thing to do."[12] It also meant that Jeremy would thenceforth be seeking other arenas for his political involvement.

Enter CCI

The *New York Times*, ironically, pointed the way for both Tod and Jeremy. Jeremy, who seldom availed himself of public transportation, offered Tod a ride in his beat-up Malibu convertible to the East Village, where both men had their shabby flats. On the way Jeremy mentioned reading this blurb in the *Times* about a war crimes initiative in the U.S. similar to the Russell Tribunals, and would Tod like to join him at a meeting he'd set up with the group's founder, Ralph Schoenman, who told Jeremy that he was looking for field organizers.[13]

❖   ❖   ❖

From day one, the Schoenman/Felberbaum axis, which was launching the CCI enterprise, and the Rifkin/Ensign axis, which — according to Tod and Jeremy's recollections — had been somewhat ambiguously welcomed into its ranks as very junior partners, did not see eye to eye on how to move the issue. Here too, as with the NCCF affair, the organizational orthodoxy of the Old Left clashed with the free-wheeling, individual style of the New Left.

A split soon occurred. There's something comic in the scenes of confrontation as recalled by Tod. He describes how, when he and Jeremy submitted their field proposal for organizing

> Arthur immediately starts picking holes in it, making obscure political comments, finding political deviation or error, that kind of thing.... And Jeremy and I were looking at each other ... what's with this guy? He was really into some kind of retro-thirties mind set that probably was the style in the SWP [Socialist Workers Party] when he was a member. A very hectoring, lecturing style. At that point I realized I couldn't work with him. And I'm pretty certain Jeremy had the same feeling.[14]

It was, in Jeremy's memory, a difference in organizing approach.

> We wanted to go ... around the country, and go into the bars in the neighborhoods, and talk to Vietnam veterans. Enlist their support, and see if we could encourage them to speak out in their communities in front of the press and the media about their experiences in Vietnam. To build public awareness of the nature of the war, and hopefully, to bring people into the Antiwar Movement from those parts of the population that had not been involved.[15]

This grassroots emphasis was viewed by Ralph and Arthur, according to Tod, as a big mistake. "What the hell do you want to go out to these obscure places for," Tod says they demanded of his and Jeremy's proposal to hold commissions throughout the heartland. Many on the Left seemed to fear a certain truth behind Nixon's faith that Middle America represented homogenous support for the war, right or wrong. Ensign and Rifkin, with their own formative and emotional links to life in the provinces, thought otherwise.

The First Commission

Ralph, says Tod, wanted him and Jeremy to focus on the media centers, which in practice meant New York and Washington. And that's just what Schoenman attempted with CCI's first public meeting on a Thursday evening, December 11, 1969, at New York City's Diplomat Hotel. Keep in mind that the catastrophic event which made it reasonable to suggest that a domestic political campaign around U.S. war crimes might even be plausible had only occurred in late November, less than a month before — that was the shocking revelation in the U.S. press of the My Lai massacre.[16]

A window had been opened in the mainstream media, and Americans — like it or not — were going to be treated to more and more unpleasant facts over the next two years on how their war in Vietnam was being fought. Rifkin and Ensign assimilated more quickly than most how critical it had become to mobilize the voices of vets who had returned home disaffected from the war.

It's vintage Tod when he describes that meeting at the Diplomat,

> one of those places built in the twenties ... where a thousand Elk Lodge annual ceremonies have been held, ne'er-do-well weddings and bar mitzvahs of the less prosperous Jewish families. It was a run down, dumpy place, foot worn rugs, smell of antiseptic.

Then with the unique gusto Tod reserves for such foibles of the human kind, he goes on to parody the Stalinoid atmosphere that night, the hard-backed folding chairs in which an audience of seventy-five, all true believers, sat braced before the stormy harangues on U.S. imperialism being delivered from the podium. It wasn't that Tod or Jeremy disagreed so much with the content of the message, they just thought it was being delivered to the wrong audience by the wrong messengers.[17]

❖ ❖ ❖

The two young activists began their work in earnest during one of the most charged moments of civil unrest that the United States had ever seen, on a scale greater than the mass workers' strikes of the thirties and the civil rights movement of the recent past. Within days of Tod and Jeremy's launching of the vet road show they would mount over the next year to promote their organizing strategy, Vietnam had struck home with an embittering brutality. Students who'd joined the protest movement were suddenly being gunned down by American police and National Guardsmen — not on foreign soil, but in Ohio and Mississippi. Kent State and Jackson State gave their martyrs to the cause.[18] Blood was spilt, and a spirit of taking revenge on a tyrannical state and its governing creatures filled the raps and rhetoric of radicals across the splintered landscape of the Left, releasing a new impetus for unity of action, a deeper resolve amongst thousands to fulfill their activist commitments.[19]

3. The Commissions

Toronto

Tod and Jeremy's first attempt to incorporate flesh and blood former combatants into a political event around the issue of U.S. war crimes was a press conference CCI hosted on March 4, 1970—three days before Kent State—at the Four Seasons Motor Hotel in Toronto.[20] There, contacts from the Canadian Left, probably the CP,[21] had produced three Vietnam veterans, one, a Canadian ex–U.S. Marine, the other two, American army deserters now seeking official immigrant status; also present was a highly articulate former army major, psychiatrist Dr. Gordon Livingston,[22] who had accompanied Tod while Jeremy remained at work in New York.

A reporter for the *Toronto Daily Star* filed a story of some length for the next morning's edition, leading with CCI's quoted aim to "prove that the alleged massacre at My Lai ... was not an isolated incident." The bulk of the article is given to the vets' gruesome descriptions of the Vietnam battlefield, the seemingly systematic torture and murder of prisoners of war, the mutilation of Viet Cong corpses, which accounts were, the veterans insisted, based on personal experience. A man identified as Larry from California, formerly with the 173rd Brigade (Airmobile) said his unit "took souvenirs ... such as an ear, eyes, scalp." Tod still talks about having suffered horrible nightmares that night after the press conference. "Fortunately, it never happened again," Tod reflected many years later referring to the disturbed dreams, "or I simply would not have been able to continue that work."[23]

Mau Mauing the Press

It's probably important to acknowledge from the outset that Jeremy Rifkin and Tod Ensign were inveterate newshounds, a predilection I would rapidly assimilate in the months to come. Feeding the media with eyewitness accounts by Vietnam vets of atrocities they themselves had witnessed or committed, was, from the start, the essential vehicle for CCI's effort to attract the average American's attention to this issue within the pages of his or her own daily newspaper, or on the local installment of their TV evening news.

But media impact also became a critical measure of the group's credibility in its quest for funding to support the campaign. The actual organizing of antiwar veterans from CCI's internal point of view was a desirable by-product of these efforts, but one entirely independent of how we, as activists, saw our role within the division of forces mobilized against the war. CCI sustained its perpetually fragile existence as publicist of American atrocities with contributions from radical and liberal donors whom we provided with reprints of our ever-increasing clipping file.

It was Jeremy who had actually garnered the organization's inaugural press clip, a brief notice in the *New York Post* appearing St. Valentine's Day, February 14, 1970, three weeks before the event in Toronto. The *Post* was a liberal rag in those days, not the Rupert Murdoch right-leaning scandal sheet it has since become. As New York's afternoon tabloid, it was reasonably popular with straphangers on their homeward-bound commutes. "The committee will examine U.S. military policy in Vietnam," the story quoted Jeremy explaining, "and inquire into whether specific policies now in effect are in fact war crimes."

There is an open-endedness to Jeremy's tone that would soon disappear from CCI's official pronouncements; no one associated with CCI harbored the slightest doubt about the atrocity producing[24] nature of the Vietnam War, nor of the claim that American war crimes, witting or otherwise, had been, and continued to be, committed on an enormous scale in that battle scarred nation. My Lai, as we repeated so often it became our mantra, was just the tip of the iceberg.

Integrating Vets at CCI

The next news account of CCI's activities appeared in Washington's *Evening Star* on the eve of an upcoming initiative in nearby Annapolis.[25] Tod and Jeremy had been laying the groundwork since February for a hearing in Annapolis centered around the testimony of Robert Bowie Johnson, a 1965 West Point graduate and All-American lacrosse player who lived there.

Bob Johnson had attended an open forum on Capitol Hill in January 1970 sponsored by ten liberal members of Congress, where public concerns over widespread rumors of American atrocities in Vietnam were explored. Mark Sacaroff, a professor of English at Temple University and a member of CCI's National Coordinating Committee, was at the meeting and alerted

Ralph Schoenman to Bob Johnson's participation. Ensign and Rifkin followed up, traveling to Annapolis where Johnson, about to retire from the army after a tour in Vietnam as an infantry captain, was soon recruited to the CCI team.[26]

Johnson would join two other Vietnam vets who were already affiliated with CCI. Peter Martinsen, a Californian long acquainted with Ralph Schoenman, may have been the very first rank and file vet to denounce American war crimes publicly, having testified in Denmark at the Russell Tribunal in December of 1967; Jerry Samuels was the *nom de guerre* of an American army deserter living in Canada who had participated at the Toronto press conference.

Annapolis established the CCI format preferred by Tod: a public meeting with participation and cosponsorship of local individuals and groups — in this case, the Baltimore chapter of the old Vets for Peace. The Annapolis meeting — spread over two consecutive evenings — was more elaborate than any event CCI would ever produce, with the important exceptions of the group's grand finale in December 1970 and a series of rump hearings on Capitol Hill in April 1971. A story in the Annapolis paper reported that "Photographs, motion pictures and slides of dead and maimed children were used last night to convey the horror of the Vietnamese War to an audience of some 100 persons at the ... Unitarian Church."[27]

The Baltimore Afro-American quoted Peter Martinsen, a former U.S. Army prisoner of war interrogator: "One technique I saw used to get prisoners to talk was to wire them around the ears with field phones and 'ring' them up. Sometimes they would have burn marks on their ears from the electric shock." Many vets, including myself, would come forward over the coming months with corroborating accounts of Americans torturing Vietnamese detainees or prisoners using similar techniques.[28]

Behind the scenes in Annapolis Tod remembers Ralph Schoenman lobbying a CCI supporter who'd been invited to attend, Herb Magidson, representing the California-based Business Executives for Peace, in an effort to attract some real funding for CCI's fieldwork. Tod says the conversation between the two men went like this: "'Well, Herb, you know we've got a plan here. We need ten other cities. And then we need fifteen more.' And Herb just said, 'No, Ralph, No. I've talked around. No go. Can't do it.' So that is my recollection of the end of Ralph's real interest," Tod concludes. He went back to New York. Herb went back to LA. And that was the end of it.[29]

Exit Ralph

And no doubt, Ralph's decision to abandon his campaign around publicizing American war crimes in Vietnam was likewise hastened by the fallout from a brief notice that had appeared nearly three months earlier in the *New York Times* on December 9, 1969, under the head, "Russell Disavows American Ex-Aid." The story reported that Lord Bertrand Russell "had tried unsuccessfully to get from Mr. Schoenman an undertaking 'that he will not use my name in any way whatsoever to suggest that I am associated with his activities or he with mine.'" Ralph's disgrace, some say, resulted from the jealousy of rivals within Russell's Peace Foundation who exploited Schoenman's reputation as an overbearing egocentric to turn Lord Bertie against his former secretary. Whatever the truth, Ralph Schoenman, a ubiquitous presence on the American Left throughout the sixties, and a player of some importance in the anti–Vietnam War movement, is a man who is unlikely to ever receive his due in the histories of these times.[30]

4. How I Grew

By late March I was already coming into the CCI office with Jeremy most mornings, continuing to study in the evening, when my classes were scheduled. Tod didn't take to me initially, nor I to him. I was, so to speak, Jeremy's new sidekick. Tod, who can intimidate like few humans I've ever known, played the heavy for a week or so. But he quickly saw my value to the group. CCI had three vet activists, all out of town; they needed someone in house. Besides, Tod's and my personalities, far from clashing, quickly proved compatible. I got as close to Jeremy as I'd ever get in that first year; it would be a year or more before Tod and I became really close friends.

Yet, from the start, we worked extremely well together. An eager intern, I looked to Tod, as well as Jeremy, as my political mentors and was fascinated by their seamless collaboration, their invention, moment by moment, of CCI's organizational and programmatic realities; the virtuoso improvisations of two precocious fifties brats and know-it-alls.

This was the movement berth I'd been looking for. But I didn't move in all at once; I brought my baggage piece by piece over a period of months. The world of grad school still filled many needs, including confidence-building for bulking up on the kind of intellectual muscle that would in time allow me to function alongside Tod and Jeremy, not merely in the client status of a representative vet, but as a partner among equals, a transition occurring over the best part of a year. In the meantime, downtown Bohemian life remained a novelty, and a distraction in those early months of 1970, from a full-time commitment to politics.

For a while I was something of an urban tourist, almost as if I had to begin my sojourn in the city at the same point where I'd first entered years ago on that eighth grade expedition to buy fire crackers. I hit the familiar Greenwich — or West — Village dives, the White Horse, the Lion's Head, from time to time dipping into the club scene on Bleecker Street, overrun with out-of-towners on the weekends, to catch some headliner, like John Sebastian, at the Bitter End. East of NYU was a stretch of old immigrant New York which, by the late sixties, most locals referred to as the East Village. In those first few months, I never went east, though; some atavistic fear of the ghetto and the gutter steered me toward the more domesticated aesthetic of the West Side.

Something else remained from the past, some unfinished business with Katie; we'd been seeing each other all fall, casual and friendly, nothing physical. Then, out of the blue she broke off with her intended and wanted to get back together. I've never quite figured that one out. Fact was, I didn't know it wasn't what I wanted until we were making out furiously on my bed, and she didn't want to go the distance. So I kicked her out. We stayed friends, but that was that. The sexual melodrama masked a distortion of my true feelings. Suddenly, after carrying this person in my heart for eight long adolescent years, I finally accepted that our worlds had become irreconcilably detached. From my view, her world hadn't changed much, but that's where she needed to be. Mine had, and I could never go back.

Besides, I wasn't looking to women for solace and commitment just then. I was falling in love with ideas and politics, and I'd actually lost considerable ground in *affaires de coeur*. But it was Vietnam, not Katie, that had stomped all over my heart.[31] And in this new world of mine, what men and women were, or could be, to each other was not as clear as it had once seemed.

I had a girl friend, a succession of girl friends, but I was too brittle emotionally to connect with any of them, and while sex became more and more frequent, it was less than memorable — certainly nothing like I'd experienced with Katie in our good years. The companionship of women on platonic terms had always been more interesting to me than the company of most men; and that attraction hadn't changed. But the women I was now being drawn to were themselves undergoing many changes. And I credit, in particular, Tod's steady Pamela Booth[32] as my most important guide to these transformations. In Pamela's view, women's liberation was quickly understood, not as the advent of something new, but the latest wave of historical feminism's struggle for equality now taking new forms appropriate to its era. In early 1970 that meant women's consciousness raising groups, which absorbed much of the free time among the women of our circle.

Seeing Tod and Pam together was to witness the pure antithesis of the idealized American couple of the fifties, Ozzie and Harriet. Supercharged with thunderclaps of Wagnerian volatility, Tod and Pam acted out the battle of the sexes whenever some untoward word or action by one seemed to link the other to the now despised gender models that echoed our corrupt and bourgeois pasts. Depending on the issue at hand, either Tod or Pam could take the high or low road at a given moment; but seldom did the contest ever appear quite so clear cut from an outsider's view.

I first met Pam one afternoon late in March when she rode into CCI on the whirlwind of some powerful agenda, demanding Tod's immediate and total attention. Pam was small and thin, but curvy, a pretty woman around thirty, who wore dress-up, a trendy mini-skirt over dark tights and boots that reached just below her knees. To me this marked her as a career girl in contrast to most women I circulated with at NYU, who'd already traded in their pre–Vietnam wardrobes for the costumes of the counter culture.

Jeremy and I retreated to one corner as Tod and Pam stood toe-to-toe, their phrases tough and clipped. But the confrontation proved benign, and the negotiations for that evening's plans were soon agreed upon to mutual satisfaction; it could have gone otherwise, as I would observe not infrequently in the years to come. Then the fur would fly, and it was even money on which one would get the best of it.

5. The Commissions (bis...)

Springfield

In the next month the transition cementing my alliance with CCI was dazzlingly quick. I moved east and now lived alone in a tiny cube of tenement rooms on East 5th Street. Around the corner Tod and Jeremy's apartments were separated only by the wall that divided their two neighboring buildings on First Avenue and East 4th Street.

I attended my first CCI affair, a fund-raiser in Springfield, Mass., following the highly visible coverage of a public commission CCI conducted there on April 6. A story appeared in the *New York Times*— the ultimate in U.S. press legitimacy, as any savvy publicist understands.

THE SPRINGFIELD UNION, SPRINGFIELD, MASS., TUESDAY, APRIL 7, 1970

PAGE 1

U. S. Army Veteran Alleges Vietnamese Civilians Slain

A 22-year-old Vietnam War veteran from Springfield has accused his former commanding officer of killing 33 South Vietnamese men, women and children in a Vietnam rice paddy in 1967.

Shot From Helicopter

David Bressem, former U. S. Army warrant officer, now of Gateway Apartments, 1150 Wilbraham Rd., alleged Col. Lewis Beasley of the 1st Air Calvary Division of the Ninth Calvary, saw the group of Vietnamese in the field, pursued them in his helicopter, and shot them.

Speaking at a public hearing on U. S. War Crimes in Vietnam in the Stonehaven Motor Inn, sponsored by the Veteran's Coalition of Springfield and the Citizen's Commission of Inquiry, Bressem said that, while he did not witness the "mass murder," he heard radio conversations between Col. Beasley and his helicopter co-pilot, T. W. Beckwith, as it allegedly was taking place. He said he later saw the

bodies during an Army body count. "We found only one carbine and a few hand grenades with the bodies," Bressem said. "One boy was still holding onto the halter of a cow."

Bressem was one of three Vietnam war veterans to describe "atrocities" in the war.

"Death March"

Peter Fossell of Amherst, a former U. S. Marine Corps rifleman described an enforced "death march" of approximately 200 Vietnamese civilians in late 1966, while Robert B. ohnson, a 1965 West Point graduate, and former U. S. Army Captain, said "irrational acts," of servicemen in Vietnam are traceable to the "irrational policy of the United States in Vietnam."

The three men, were dressed conservatively in sports jackets and ties, and their presentation, made in a question and answer format, was articulate, dignified and moving. Approximately 50 young men and women heard the testimony.

The hearing was the third conducted by the Citizen's Commission of Inquiry on "serious injustices in Pentagon policy," Jeremy Rifkin, one of the moderators said.

Bressem told the group murder" of Vietnamese civilians occurred in late July or early August of 1967 in the Central Highlands, north of Dak To. He said that the civilians were shot because they were "taking evasive action."

Conduct 'War Crimes' Hearing

Former U.S. Army Captain Robert B. Johnson, center, a graduate of West Point and a Vietnam war veteran, urges the United States to "stop the insanity" in Vietnam, during testimony before the anti-war Citizens' Commission of Inquiry in Springfield Monday. Moderating are, Jeremy Rifkin, left, and Tod Ensign, right, of New York City CCI's national co-ordinators.

Article in the *Springfield Union*, April 7, 1970. Courtesy of *The Springfield Republican*.

The big splash in Springfield highlighted former helicopter pilot David Bressem's account of having seen the results of a massacre by U.S. forces of more than thirty Vietnamese civilians in the central highlands north of Dak To in late July or early August 1967. Later that afternoon, the impact of Bressem's and another vet's presence in the newsroom of the *Springfield Daily News* was to become part of the news story. The reporter wrote that

> The two men [Bressem and CCI's Bob Johnson] were there to talk about Vietnam, about soldiers' experiences there, and about what they hope is a growing anti-war sentiment on the part of veterans who saw action.
> After the interview, one office worker walked up to the interviewer: "You couldn't exactly call me a dove. But it's hard to fight a man who's actually been there and knows what it's all about. What can you say," he said.[33]

This was precisely the reaction Jeremy and Tod had predicted for their strategy. If they could hook a *cynical* reporter from a mainstream provincial daily, the way forward seemed promising. Even the *New York Times* condescended to provide a rare view in its pages from the trenches of the Left.[34] Correspondent Douglas Robinson reported that "former Army Capt. Robert Bowie Johnson ... said that individual soldiers should not be blamed for any atrocities they may have committed.... It's a barbaric policy we're dealing with rather than barbaric Americans," Johnson had emphasized.

One day later a United Press International wire story reported that the Department of Defense "has begun an investigation into the alleged slaying of 33 Vietnamese civilians about 30 miles from My Lai and six months earlier."[35]

Making It

Springfield brought a degree of media recognition which Tod and Jeremy were able to parlay though some urgent pleading with a few well-heeled sympathizers into enough ready cash to pay the rent and the phone bill, and to purchase an occasional bus or plane ticket; the two activists also wished to pay themselves forty bucks apiece each week, the kitty permitting. You could live on that in the East Village in those days. As a newcomer on the East Side, my rent was a whopping $75 monthly; Tod and Jeremy each paid thirty bucks less.

As for food, you could also dine out on subsistence wages if, like Jeremy, you ate at the same cheap restaurant every night, the Ruby Khan, just down from his apartment on First Avenue. Most evenings that spring I'd join him there. The place was a hotbed of Bangladeshi separatism, and, in 1970, one of only three so-called Indian restaurants in a neighborhood that would soon became saturated with the cuisine of the subcontinent, lining E. 6th Street, where you'd swear they all served meals from a common trough behind the buildings.

Tod also seemed to get by fine on his wages, and I had my own relatively comfortable disability pension. So, Tod's question about how to live as an activist was being answered with each modest organizing success. Politically, moreover, we did more than survive, we thrived. A unique CCI style and analytical framework began to emerge almost immediately.

The notion, for example, that individual soldiers should not be blamed for atrocities stemming from barbaric policies not of their creation, and the litany of the repetitive naming of actual tactical field policies in question — search and destroy, free fire zones, carpet bombing, body counts, forced relocations — these were the components increasingly woven into CCI rhetoric during each publicized showcase.

With our line of thinking focused on policies, not individuals, we concluded it would be incorrect, however tempting in terms of potential impact, to name the names, including superior officers, of those whose actions, however barbaric and despicable, were being described in the testimony of our voluntary eyewitness vets, who themselves represented, by contrast, the antithesis of anonymity.

Thus CCI also refused to cooperate with the criminal investigation divisions of the various military branches whose gumshoes dogged our tracks at all our early press events and tried unsuccessfully to question our witnesses. Names, they wanted names, which our witnesses constantly refused them, not taking the bait to scapegoat one individual and avoid any discussion of the policies that each individual was expected to carry out, routinely and without question. In time the military cops stopped showing up. Under the circumstances, they could only come off as heavies.

When challenged on this particular evasion by reporters, we argued strongly that military investigators would either attempt to intimidate our witnesses with threats of personal prosecution, or would channel any energies we might lend to these authorities in a spirit of cooperation toward an ultimate whitewash of the issue.

This refusal by CCI to name names was in no way mixed with sympathy for the perpetrators of gross criminal acts on the battlefield, and despite the obvious echo, had nothing to do with the anti-communist hysteria of the McCarthy era when certain turncoats of the Left ratted on their friends to save their own skins. The issue sprang from an emerging philosophy that emphasized a hierarchy of blame. If, CCI reasoned, we must consider individual responsibility, let's begin at the top of the political and military structures where policies leading to these atrocities are designed and managed.

❖   ❖   ❖

By early 1970, I was already quite clear about Vietnam, and ready to tell anyone willing to listen. Suddenly I'd been given a forum in the company of some prime time heavyweights. CCI's national board was like an All-Star selection of the American liberal left, representing at least some of its most prestigious institutional and academic branches. Several of these big names would actually call the office, or readily take calls from either Tod or Jeremy to arrange meetings, discuss strategy, or to be hit-up for a quick fifty or a hundred bucks.

I couldn't believe I was really getting to meet Noam Chomsky at a fundraiser in Springfield. It was a cocktail party and Professor Chomsky was already a major draw for every manner of Left-oriented confab, including the funding circuit. Chomsky was one of those CCI national board members who never said no, when Jeremy hit him up every few weeks to spring for an emergency donation.[36]

And now, me, a lowly grad student struggling to grasp the most elemental concepts of his revolutionary linguistics, would be standing toe-to-toe with the Maestro, chatting politics. Naturally, I made an ass of myself. The few moments I had Chomsky's ear, I challenged him about playing a more direct leadership role in the movement; he smiled good-naturedly and replied, I'm just a good researcher.

New York and Los Angeles

It had only been a fortnight since I'd joined up, but my integration within CCI was so complete in spirit that I lived a short lifetime in those first two weeks. By the eleventh of April, I myself had become part of the road show, taking on the group's least desirable speaking gig, an invitation from Clarkson College of Technology in remote Potsdam, the virtual tundra of upstate New York and about as far from the action as a think tank on the moon. I jumped at the opportunity with a relish that ignored the crippling stage fright that had plagued me since childhood whenever called upon to address even small gatherings in my own voice.

A week later I made another debut with several other vets who had also served in Vietnam as intelligence operatives. CCI held simultaneous press conferences in New York and Los Angeles on April 14th, my twenty-sixth birthday — one year to the day since I'd left the war zone. Each vet testified that he had tortured or witnessed the torturing of Vietnamese prisoners by other Americans. My personal account follows pretty much what I have written here in an earlier chapter. The press coverage was hardly overwhelming.

I now dimly recall the cramped but formal room we'd rented at the Overseas Press Club in Manhattan. A lot of milling around, waiting to see who, if anyone, from the media would show. Two or three film crews appeared, and started moving their equipment around. It was twenty minutes past curtain. Presence of the press corps was light, but we could delay no longer. The only vets in New York were me and Ed Murphy from Staten Island, a special agent who'd served with the army's 4th Infantry Division out of Pleiku. At the last moment, Gordon Gray, my old comrade from the 11th Brigade in Duc Pho, reneged and stayed home in Silver Spring, Maryland. But he'd already given his testimony to a reporter, which appeared in the *New York Post*.[37]

The post mortem for this and every subsequent CCI activity involved Tod and Jeremy in endless detailed discussion, with serious input coming from a few key vets — at this point Bob Johnson and myself in particular. And we, in turn, educated our political mentors, Tod and Jeremy, not only about conditions in Vietnam, but about the military life in general. I myself began to shape a few ideas and issues by applying to my military experiences analytical skills that were being constantly sharpened by graduate studies.

In my talk at Potsdam, I had stressed the point that stated or official military policy could be used to cover up what was really going on, what we were calling *de facto* policy in Vietnam. At the same time, CCI relentlessly maintained that atrocities, like indiscriminate killings of civilians and torture of prisoners, resulted from standard operating procedures; while the Pentagon characterized such incidents as the aberrant behavior of a few bad apples.[38]

With Springfield, and now New York/Los Angeles, CCI had begun a modest political dialogue with the Pentagon, brokered by a media which was struggling to define its own line on the issue of American atrocities. Back East, so far, the media had been neutral; in a few cases, sympathetic. In Los Angeles, however, Tod and his witnesses were confronted for the first time by a hostile press, which, Tod later told me, spooked the vets.[39]

The concept of one vet corroborating another also emerged from this set of press conferences, by offering testimony of vets who'd served together in the same unit — like myself and Gordon Gray. But this was difficult in most cases, where, instead, we would bundle the testimony of those who'd served in similar kinds of units. The decision to present only intelligence operatives at this latest CCI commission had the deliberate intention of providing a profile of torture techniques employed primarily on civilians by U.S. interrogators throughout Vietnam, not only to demonstrate their widespread occurrence, but to confirm their status as routine SOPs, standard operating procedures.

CCI also moved quickly to refine its position on the Pentagon's promise to probe our group's mounting list of allegations. "It's absurd for the Pentagon to investigate itself for war crimes ... that are a matter of Pentagon policy," Jeremy told *New York Post* reporter Tim Ferris. Instead, we vaguely proposed an investigation of the Pentagon to be carried out by some independent agency. That Congress itself was not specified for this role underscored what was felt by each of us then as an irreconcilable rupture of faith in the capacity of America's vaunted governing institutions to carry out an impartial investigation of a very real and ugly truth, the widespread commission of war crimes by American troops in Vietnam.

Nuremberg at Tufts

Boston would be next on CCI's press itinerary, a liberal city where we hoped for a more receptive hearing on our allegations that, among these atrocities, were systematic acts of torture. This was essentially Jeremy's show. Through VVAW's Jan Barry Crumb, he'd made contact with a vet named Larry Rottmann[40] who lived in greater Boston, and, once again, Noam Chomsky was invited to lend his authority to the occasion, a no frills morning press conference in a downtown Boston hotel.

This time the charges received much greater coverage. Rottmann and I had both given accounts of U.S. torture techniques and practices, and these were reported locally in the Boston papers. The UPI picked up on a charge Rottmann made about American troops operating in Cambodia, which to the home folk here was as yet a secret war. But, torture — and the horrible image of American boys performing such acts — was the castor oil of the war crimes medicine show which Jeremy and Tod hoped to spoon out across middle America.[41]

For me the trip to Boston was exciting and memorable. We'd packed the room with press, then squeezed in some political schmoozing with Chomsky back at MIT in his stark Quonset hut-like quarters.[42] But an unanticipated denouement occurred that evening when Jeremy Rifkin returned to Tufts University, scene of his recent studies, and caused a near riot at the student/faculty teach-in he'd been invited to address.[43]

I remember having to whisk Jeremy off the stage that night, rushing for the exit with the mob at our heels. He'd gone a bit too far. A potentially eloquent speaker on any occasion, for a while Jeremy held the entire hall in rapt attention as he sketched the inevitable construction of war crimes from the syntax of American combat policies.

You could actually see the pieces being put together on the faces of people in the audience; they were getting it, and it was not a pleasant sight. Then, for the first and only time that I ever witnessed, Jeremy crossed the line from overblown New Left oratory to outright demagoguery. He turned and faced the administrators of Tufts' Fletcher School of Diplomacy seated near him on the stage — many of whom had served in government, and at least one of whom, the director I recall, held ambassadorial rank. Indeed, their lordly presence inside the communion rail smacked of high church elitism. "And these men," Jeremy thundered, pointing an accusing finger and resurrecting the imagery of Nuremberg, "...these men are the true war criminals, not the low ranking GIs in the field." And here, the ruling estates were flung from their thrones into the docket, as each of the accused, as god is my witness, actually hung his head on cue.

It was *coup de theatre* such as I have seen only rarely since. The crowd sat stunned. Then, one by one, voices shouted opposition to having this forum for the exchange of opposing views by reasonable men transformed into a terrible *auto-da-fé*. Fortunately, Jeremy caught the mood change quickly and emerged from his trance; as we sped into the night, we laughed our asses off. Neither of us could remember an evening for ever so long when we'd had this much fun.

Accused

I never cried in Vietnam, though I broke down several times in the TB ward at Valley Forge, sobbing uncontrollably to purge dark moments, which, in others, I could meet with empathy, but which in myself became, not merely repressed feelings, but the facts of despair. But that night at Tod's place, where he and Jeremy confronted me with a rumor they'd heard, I cried the righteous tears of one falsely accused.

The drama opened after an Upper West Side writer with good liberal credentials had expressed in some transmittable form the assumption that any former intelligence operative, like me, must still be treated as a spy. Since the liberal viewpoint tends to ignore such powerful tools of social analysis as, say, class distinction, this person might have had some misguided notions about who actually went into the military — and why — during the Vietnam War. How economic and social forces act, generally, on consciousness formation in the working class, or shape and limit certain options available to its members, are concepts strangely unavailable to social elites — especially liberals — who turn a blind eye to their own sources of privilege.[44]

The star chamber staged by my two new comrades, whose approval and respect I then wanted more than anything, was hurtful and unnerving. But, in regaining their trust, I never resented the ordeal, and could understand, given the stakes with which CCI was playing, why it was necessary — even unavoidable. This crossover between American war veterans and the Left — on the scale Vietnam had created — was virgin territory, and the Man, as we all knew, had his informers everywhere. It could have been me, but it wasn't. Later that night, still very upset, I overcame my sense of awe, and placed a call to Noam Chomsky, telling him what had transpired and asking his intervention with the writer in question. He obliged, as I recall, and that was that.[45]

6. A Grand Tour

The grad school semester ended in late May. By the first week of June I was on a plane headed for Europe with a letter of introduction from CCI. Jeremy had wanted me to forgo the trip, stay home, and organize. Whether it was because I was not fully integrated within the group, or I had some vague misgivings about not having a role commensurate to my ambitions, I'm not sure. I do know that I was not cut out to be a client. I'd refused to cultivate the vet identity. But I was too green to carry my weight alone with that flying, entrepreneurial brand of leadership that so impressed me about my new comrades.

Besides, I was 26 and I'd never been to Europe. I now had the time and money, and a notebook filled with names and addresses of antiwar counterparts in a half dozen countries — all of whom I promised Tod and Jeremy I'd look up in the performance of what the Left termed solidarity work. My bags were stuffed with CCI brochures and reprints of news stories, which I would distribute with the appropriate zeal of a New Left Johnny Appleseed.

Vanessa

Vanessa Redgrave was then the thinking man's sex goddess of the silver screen, and I couldn't believe that the modest little house I stood before, the tiny front yard littered with children's toys and tricycles, and surrounded by a white picket fence, actually belonged to a great and famous movie star. From the side door Vanessa ushered me into the kitchen, and whipped up a delicious omelette as I laid out CCI's intentions and credentials. I was, frankly, numbed by this my first stumble through the Looking Glass into a world of celebrity I had only known, like most normal people, from refracted images à la cover photos on magazines that line the supermarket checkout counter. I'd seen *Blow Up*, of course, and *Morgan*, and had drooled over Redgrave's beauty like ten million other men.

Redgrave told me she wanted to do something to help the GI movement grow at the American military bases in Great Britain. She was going to throw a big party in London for American servicemen around the 4th of July. Did I have an interest in sticking around to help organize it, she wondered? Her suggestion was comradely, in no way overbearing. I hadn't known then just how political Redgrave was; the idea that a world class movie idol might be joined to a disciplined Trotskyist party (the British Socialist Workers Party) was too remote from my experience. I was only beginning my political education; the mysteries of Leninism, among many others, just starting to preoccupy my curiosity.

Begging off politely, citing my duties with CCI, I was simply dead set on blazing the traditional tourist trail. In my pocket was a first class rail pass, and, in the manner of the neophyte Yankee traveler I had no true purpose, only destinations — as many as I could squeeze into the shortest time possible. I was flattered when Redgrave asked me to return for the party to mix with the GIs and help make them feel comfortable. We agreed she'd write me in Amsterdam with the details.

Then she let me use the phone to call Jeremy collect back in New York with the news that Redgrave agreed to add her name to our list of sponsors. I went through an operator, told her it was Michael calling, and she informed me that the line was busy. About to hang up, and thanking her, she responded with words that even I sometimes wonder if I'm making up. But I'm not. She said, "Not at all, Sir Michael." Maybe the name Redgrave was needed somewhere in the course of this transmission, but what did she think, that it was Sir Michael Redgrave playing the Colonial?

Punching My Ticket

That line about no purpose in my travels is slightly exaggerated; I did chase the ghost of James Joyce for three days in Dublin, walking the route citywide that Bloom canvassed in *Ulysses*, taking a tram or bus to the Martello Tower, where "Stately, plump, Buck Mulligan" intones the "Introibo ad altare Dei" in the book's opening lines. But after that, it was a whirl of train stations and passport stamps, unremarkable but for a crossing to Helsinki with a beautiful Finn I picked up, then, stupidly, abandoned, and a day at the Prado in Madrid: is that really *Las Meninas* by Velasquez, I gasped, transfixed before the giant canvas in the grand and gilded stairwell?[46] Of all locations!

As for Paris, it's true the street life grabbed me the moment I emerged from St. Lazare, but I made no real connections there till returning late in August. Among the scattered tribes from home who milled about the American Express office in Amsterdam, I opened the airmailgram from London, and read the date, time, and directions for the party, signed, yes, "Vanessa."

London II

Some grand ballroom in a fancy hotel had been done up for the affair, and the groaning board was loaded with the best delights money and good taste could provide. A full complement swing band played pop tunes, and I stood next to Vanessa and her London-based pal, Mia Farrow, waiting for the bus load of American GIs to arrive. As they trickled through the door dressed in leisure polyester straight off the racks of the PX, faces shy as sheep, I began to feel ridiculous and out of place myself. When we of CCI talked with vets and soldiers, we tried to be in their element, not our own. You couldn't make these guys feel comfortable in such a ritzy atmosphere if you'd handed out lines of coke and c-notes to snort it as party favors.

The night was a bust. I avoided the GIs from a combination of inexperience and mixed emotions. One was out and out embarrassment over the ridiculous setting and insensitivity of bringing these guys to such a place, another, the desire to spend much of the evening jollying a very unpretentious Mia Farrow, who danced with me for a number of tunes and indulged my radical banter. When the airmen soon began to trickle out again, Vanessa stunned me with a crack, as if somehow I bore the blame for her *faux pas*. Later for that, I must have thought, while straining to keep my cool. If I'd been better seasoned to the sparring style of the Left I might have rejoined that the revolution is not a dinner party. I guess Chairman Mao said that.[47]

Portugal

On that sour note my grand tour was a wrap; reel two of this European adventure began, an intensive summer course at the University of Coimbra, financed by a small foundation grant. Portugal in 1970 was the great backwater of the continent; you could take a shave at the barber, hot towels and all, for the equivalent of a quarter — and I did, everyday. The escudo, under the Salazar regime — in power since c. 1926 — had remained at something like twenty-six to the dollar for decades in a country where every social and financial institution had been mothballed by the political fundamentalism of fascist repression.

The absence of a public political culture in Portugal gave the population a dour cast. The university, mired in some sterile brand of classicism, was a bore. But the country was spectacular, and the common folk one encountered, while sad of countenance, were generous and good-hearted. Our group at Coimbra was lively and multinational, and we made the beaches of Nazare' and Fiqueira da Foz our Lido that summer.

Then politics found us in a form reminiscent of the struggles over parietals throughout American colleges in the early sixties, when you could not go to your girlfriend's dorm room, nor she to yours. Two youths in our circle, an American lad and

At the University of Coimbra, summer 1970.

his Mexican sweetheart, were arrested, jailed, and charged with public immorality for having exchanged a kiss one evening in the Praça. The whole university went on strike, until someone reminded the guardians of national chastity that, whatever shackles they reserved for native youth could not be fastened so easily to the permissive offspring of corrupted democracies. The two innocents, truly mad for each other, were soon restored to their friends, and thenceforth spared the more surreal and antediluvian repressions of the host culture for the duration of their stay.[48]

My own love life remained a shambles. I'd briefly traveled for two weeks in Europe with my then current steady, a fellow NYU student named Barbara, then jettisoned that relationship, taking up with Caroline, a young Parisian girl at Coimbra. My French education had begun, though we could only speak to each other in Portuguese. We hung out at her parents' beach house in northern Portugal for a few days, then headed back to Paris by way of Barcelona, getting sloshed all through the Burgundy wine country between Dijon and Lyon, while comparing the *cassoulets* at several country inns. The romance should have ended there, but Caroline followed me to the States a few months later, or followed someone, because it's hard to imagine a person being less there for her than I was.

❖   ❖   ❖

My own contribution on the European front was meager, but competent enough for my comrades in New York to write, asking if I would take
on the role of CCI's national veteran coordinator. I'd managed to seed a few

National Committee for a
CITIZENS' COMMISSION of INQUIRY
on U.S. War Crimes in Vietnam

156 Fifth Avenue   •   Rm. 1005   •   New York, N. Y. 10010   •   (212) 533-2734

STAFF

Jeremy Rifkin, *Natl. Coordinator*
Tod Ensign, *Natl. Coordinator*
Mike Lihl, *Vet Coordinator, At-Large*
Peter Martinsen, *Vet Coordinator, West Coast*
Bob Johnson, *Vet Coordinator, East Coast*
Jerry Samuels, *Vet Coordinator, Canada*

SPONSORS

David Dellinger
Benjamin Spock
Jane Fonda
Richard Falk
Tony Randall
Richard Fernandez
Ossie Davis
Robert J. Lifton
Hon. Ernest Gruening
Stewart Meacham
Vanessa Redgrave
Balfour Brickner

NATIONAL COORDINATING COMMITTEE

Dennis Mora, Fort Hood Three, vet organizer **Howard Levy**, M.D., U.S. Servicemen's Fund (USSF) **Andy Stapp**, American Servicemen's Union **Donald Duncan**, USSF, Movement for a Democratic Military **Jan Crumb**, Vietnam Vets Against the War **Susan Schnall**, USSF **Ron Wolin**, Veterans for Peace in Vietnam (New York City) **Noam Chomsky**, Professor of Linguistics, M.I.T. **Fred Cohn**, Lawyer **Bill Davidon**, Professor of Physics, Haverford College, New National Mobilization Steering Committee **Douglas Dowd**, Professor of Economics, Cornell, New National Mobilization Committee **Don Freed**, Playwright **Eugene D. Genovese**, Chairman, Dept. of History, U. of Rochester **Dick Gregory** – **Phil Hutchings**, Writer **Mary Kaufman**, U. S. Nuremberg Tribunal Staff Member **Sylvia Kushner**, Chicago Peace Council **Helen Lamont**, Emergency Civil Liberties Committee **Paul Lauter**, Resist, New University Conference **Julius Lester**, Author **Conrad Lynn**, Civil Rights Attorney **Herbert Magidson**, Business Executives for Peace, Chairman, Individuals Against the Crime of Silence **Floyd McKissick** – **Joanna Misnik**, National Staff, Student Mobilization Committee **John Moran**, Professor of Philosophy, Manhattan College **J. B. Neilands**, Prof. of Biochemistry, University of California at Berkeley **Grace Paley**, Greenwich Village Center **Max Primack**, New National Mobilization Steering Committee **Mark Sacaroff**, Professor of English, Temple University **Ralph Schoenman**, Director, American Foundation for Social Justice, Secretary General, International War Crimes Tribunal **Jerry Schwinn**, Director, Committee of Returned Volunteers **T. G. G. Wilson**, M.D., Executive Director, Medical Committee for Human Rights **Melvin L. Wulf**, Director of Legal Department, American Civil Liberties Union **Eric Seitz**, Executive Secretary, National Lawyers Guild **Maxwell Geismar**, Author **Rabbi Abraham Feinberg**

Letterhead for Citizens' Commission of Inquiry.

potential fields of action in Stockholm, making contact with the organization of American deserters living there — a task I'd been specifically assigned to — and, in Paris, with luminaries of the antiwar faction of the American expat community, like Maria Jolas, and even with representatives of the PRG, Provisional Revolutionary Government of the South Vietnamese National Liberation Front, known to most as the Vietcong.[49]

Such were the times where an opposition in the midst of a national war could advocate for desertion by its own soldiers as a form of political resistance, and openly consorted with the enemy whose cause they actively supported. What was equally unprecedented was the scale on which veterans of that same war entered the lists of the antiwar opposition, even as the conflict raged on.

Corroboration ... Vindication

In July, CCI managed two major successes in the press. Late that month Jeremy had written me in Europe that things were escalating. He enclosed a news article on a torture piece, referring to an article by William Greider that had run prominently in the *Washington Post*. Added Rifkin, "P.S. Patton testified publicly and corroborated your testimony." My fellow lieutenant at Duc Pho and supervisor of our interrogation unit, who later wrote me that he found Tod and Jeremy's politics too radical, had spoken directly with the *Washington Post* reporter.

Greider's lead paragraph reads, "Seven Army veterans who served with military intelligence in the Vietnam war have offered public testimony that they witnessed or took part in brutal treatment of Vietnamese civilian prisoners, including interrogation by electrical torture."[50]

How, incidently, were such revelations playing inside the Pentagon? Concerning the veteran that William Greider, a highly respected journalist then working in the national press corps, had featured as the principal subject of his article and with whom he had spoken directly, a Pentagon report noted, "investigative efforts to locate Mr. Patton have been unsuccessful, and he is believed to be a fictitious person."[51]

Congress Versus CCI on the Meaning of My Lai

The Congressional report on the My Lai massacre had also just come out; it reads like a brief to shield U.S. policies in Vietnam from deep scrutiny, and, essentially, to ignore or cover up the widespread occurrences of atrocities by U.S. forces in Vietnam. In one despicable reference, the My Lai victims themselves become the accused: "it is reasonable to conclude that those 'civilians' [their quotations] present in the hamlet of My Lai 4, except those too young to do so, were there to aid the enemy in his cause." The report concludes: "What happened at My Lai was wrong ... so wrong and so foreign to the normal character and actions of our military forces as to immediately raise a question as to the legal sanity at the time of those men involved."[52]

The collective view at CCI was that what My Lai called into question was not the sanity of the men involved, but their relative guilt when compared with a much deeper complicity among the commanding generals and civilian architects of the war, whose tactical tools GIs employed to execute U.S. battlefield policies. CCI responded to the U.S. Army's indictments of the My Lai defendants by offering scores of Vietnam veterans to testify on behalf of those accused of the My Lai massacre. Jeremy Rifkin argued "that by pressing charges against only enlisted men and low-level officers, the Pentagon is scapegoating a handful of GI's for military strategies ... conceived at the highest levels of government."[53]

This question of guilt — or responsibility — for acts committed by individual GIs would become the most controversial position advocated by CCI during the entire campaign to publicize American war crimes, not least among fellow activists of the Left. Andy Stapp, former soldier and organizer of the American Serviceman's Union, and also a member of the Trotskyist Workers World Party, after listening to our argument about not scapegoating Lt. William Calley, the most notorious of the My Lai defendants, commented, "I agree. Stop the trial, and start the execution."

CCI didn't defend Calley's acts of butchery, but struggled to prevent the media and the public from becoming fixated on a single heinous crime in a genocidal war. We also hammered away at the principle that the U.S. itself had helped to establish in the conduct of warfare with the Nuremberg and Tokyo trials, to hold commanders responsible for the actions of their troops in the field. In the atmosphere of repulsion and horror that the revelation of My Lai helped create, it was not easy to maintain subtle and legalistic distinctions in the course of these discussions.

I am more surprised in looking back than I was at the time, that not one of the vets publicly denouncing American atrocities ever expressed any serious reservation about his personal vulnerability to prosecution. There were many heavy consciences among the vets, depending on the nature of the dude and the nature of the deed; but as a rule, we felt angry and abused, not guilty. And while it may be immodestly self-serving to suggest it, we made our experiences public to defend our humanity, not our skins.

Watching Our Backs

With its growing credibility in the media, CCI quickly acquired some additional big name sponsors.[54] But Tod Ensign's concern was clearly about credibility of a different, and equally important, sort. How was CCI going to prevent the Man from putting a ringer in our midst, a vet making outrageous accusations who could then be exposed as a liar? The media, in general, were never comfortable with CCI and the war crimes issues since we made no effort to hide the fact that our principal objective was to condemn the war, not some will o'the wisp juridical fantasy about restaging Nuremberg with our own leaders in the roles of the Nazis. If it wasn't for the confessions of the vets themselves, we would have been ignored. One provocateur, and the whole campaign could be dismissed.

On August 18, 1970, Tod had conducted a hearing at Richmond, Virginia, an absolute ten in terms of national press coverage.[55] It gratified Tod that the story had run in so many smaller towns and cities, like Winston-Salem, North Carolina, and Newark, New Jersey, or so he wrote to the CCI West Coast vet coordinator, Peter Martinsen. But the true purpose of Tod's letter was cautionary:

> It is essential that this coverage be continued and expanded. As you know, Pete, this credibility has been slowly built over seven months. We've made mistakes, to say the least, but each one has been corrected to the extent possible. Therefore it is imperative that anything exposed under the Commission's aegis be absolutely factual. One agent, and the Pentagon will discredit us and everything else we've done. Understandably then, we are insistent that effective controls (through you or us) be maintained over all witnesses and testimony.... In a word, only experienced persons should interview and prepare testimony for presentation.[56]

Experienced persons, increasingly in Tod's and Jeremy's eyes, meant someone like me. Both these guys were incredibly quick studies, and despite having never served in the armed forces, each had already acquired a detailed understanding of the American military culture in Vietnam. But there were gaps in their knowledge, and, sometimes, they lacked a feel for the subject. The mistakes Tod mentions are of a kind that a legal and logical mind like his could be embarrassed by. It was good politics, not false pride, that led the CCI twosome to lean more heavily on those whose personal experience with the war machine allowed for getting the facts of each vet's testimony straight.

Coming Home II

"By the time you receive this," Jeremy's urgent note began, "we hope to have spoken to you. If not, cable us home immediately." I was hiding out with my friend Caroline at her parent's very bourgeois apartment in one of Paris's more fashionable *arrondissements*. Jeremy had enclosed a draft, single spaced on two typed sheets, entitled *The Winter Soldier Investigation (An Inquiry into U.S. War Crimes in Vietnam)*. Hand lettered and circled in red ink was the word "confidential," and, next to that, my name and "for private use only." The proposal called for a national hearing spread over several days simultaneously in Detroit, Michigan, and Windsor, Canada, "beginning on or about December 8, 1970.... It is anticipated that up to 125 Vietnam veterans will attend to offer direct, eye witness accounts of war crimes committed by their respective units in the furtherance of U.S. military policies in Vietnam."[57]

Initially, Jeremy's cloak-and-dagger letter had struck me as a bit odd when it arrived in Paris. But the feeling had become acute between Tod and he that CCI was a potential object, if not of government infiltration, certainly of surveillance. "Don't mail anything c/o CCI," they warned repeatedly in their more recent communiques; Customs might flag the CCI name, and intercept whatever materials I was sending, which amounted to a bunch of typically incendiary left-wing lit from the movement's European sector.

Even from the low branch of intelligence gathering where I had briefly operated, one could easily grasp what vast funding and volume of manpower would be necessary, not just to tap pell-mell the phone lines of the Left, but to replay and process those miles of surreptitious recordings.[58] Government at all levels had to limit their targets of surveillance selectively, while exploiting the inflated belief among radicals that Left activism generally warranted serious attention from the listening posts of the national security apparatus. Low level paranoia, always debilitating, buzzed through the Left like static from a cheap radio, undermining, if not always destabilizing, appeals for unity.

But Jeremy's letter also invited me to become the group's national vet coordinator. Fully aware that I would now have a real role to play at CCI, I jumped at the chance. It meant admittance into a world of radical politics at a high powered level that should have awed me, but seldom did, probably because of my own intimate connection to the issue. This was a summons I could not ignore.

7. Antiwar Vets

The antiwar veterans' movement had shown moments of vitality since the late sixties, but had failed to create an identity apart from the larger movement in which, by early 1970, it functioned as a small but integral component. Publically expressed opposition to Vietnam among veterans who fought there underwent a quantum increase between the revelation of the My Lai massacre in November 1969, and the eruptions of student militance on hundreds of college campuses across the nation after the killings in early May at Kent and Jackson states, building upon massive mobilizations, on and off campus.[59]

Vietnam Veterans Against the War emerged as the singular voice of the vets' disgust for the war. VVAW's membership suddenly began to swell within an organizational structure that had been solidified over the preceding two years by a core of vet activists, notably the group's co-founder, poet Jan Barry Crumb. Over Labor Day weekend in 1970 VVAW would mount Operation Raw. A contingent of antiwar veterans spent three days marching and conducting mock battles through townships in New Jersey, deliberately chosen because they had been the sites of major battles during the Revolutionary War. The march terminated at Valley Forge, Pennsylvania, where two thousand demonstrators rallied in support of the vets, who ritualistically smashed their plastic M-16s, those eerily authentic models of our assault rifles that the Mattel Corporation now manufactured.[60]

What would become the vet style for the remainder of the war — the Kit Carson look — was firmly established during this amazing event. In their collective appearance, the shaggy, bearded vets recalled those tintype imitations of frontier scouts you costume for at souvenir photo shops in the far West — the absolute antithesis of the ramrod flag wavers in silly service caps who paraded behind honor guards and American Legion banners on Decoration Day when we were kids. The Vietnam vets, too, bedecked themselves in regalia, not the uniform of the parade ground, but their work clothes, so to speak, the garb of combat: government issue jungle hats, fatigues and boots. Behold America! The Winter Soldiers have returned from Nam to battle on the home ground with Sunshine Patriots who would prolong this war.

The vet style did not say hello to me personally. This aside is complicated, and I can't pretend to have sorted it through. I do know that whatever forces tugged at the identities of my ex-military antiwar contemporaries, transforming them, first and foremost, into vets, did not so direct my inner currents. I'd spent two reluctant years in the army; this did not entitle them to my identity. Anyway, I had another fantasy in mind, antiwar organizer. As for the fatigues, I packed them away, imagining they'd be useful someday when I had to change the oil on an automobile. One morning on East 9th Street, some bum or fellow urban scavenger found themselves a set of hand tailored officer's uniforms, including formal wear, draped over the garbage cans outside my tenement.[61]

Jane Fonda and the Origins of Winter Soldier

The natural allies in the Movement for the antiwar vets were those who'd been working with GIs. Enter Jane Fonda and company. Jane was indeed rare among the Hollywood types; she not only hated the war like many folk in the radical chic set, she truly longed to be a revolutionary activist.[62] And activist she had undoubtedly become, as organizer and headliner for an agit-prop theater group called FTA—"fuck the army" in soldier slang[63]—which played the GI coffee house circuit, and on an informal two month lecture and protest tour that took her by car cross country from California in the spring of 1970.[64] In the course of the rapidly moving events of that year, Jane Fonda became connected, through VVAW, to the work of CCI.

Since early in the year, CCI had been combing VVAW mailing lists for vets willing to testify publicly about their war experiences. The two organizations, separated by three floors in the same building, enjoyed a cordial, in some ways close, working relationship. Jeremy had written to me that he and Tod were introduced to Jane Fonda by VVAW's new president, a soft spoken but dynamic former air force captain named Al Hubbard, one of very few African Americans who joined the organization. It was at that meeting that Jane—who was then being closely advised by Mark Lane,[65] a crony of Ralph Schoenman's from the days of the Russell Tribunals—first proposed the Winter Soldier Investigation. We sat down with her, Tod recalled, Jeremy with his clipboard and foolscap and felt tip pen. He's impressive in that kind of setting. He really knows how to put it on. And he wowed 'em. He had Jane already realizing that she had to work with us.[66]

Jane asked for a draft of the whole concept, and, what follows is Tod's somewhat stand-up version of the subsequent episode with Fonda and crew[67]:

> So, I was dragooned into writing this fuckin' thing. And, of course, no air conditioning, we're sitting there in a New York August, sweat's dripping off as I'm typing.... We get it done, and Jeremy immediately wants to take it over to Maison Fonda. So, he calls her up—it's on a Saturday. And she says, I got some people here but—if you really want to, come on over. So we've got this docu-

ment, and we go over there. Well, who was *there* was Huey P. Newton, who'd
just gotten sprung from San Quentin. He was literally out the day before, and
he jumps on a jet — and where does he go? Jane Fonda's townhouse.

And so, I'll never forget in my life, I walk in there and here's this huge, hulk-
ing, bulked up guy with this really sweet face, you know. He was a very good
looking guy, with a really mild manner actually. And he's laying on her four
poster bed with a doll on the side of the pillow. And Jane says, show this to
Huey. And then, Afini Shakur was there, who was Zaid Shakur's sister — I think
she went off to Cuba. So Huey's saying, Right on, Right on. But not Afini. This
is objectively incorrect. This point here you make about the Pig, everyone
knows they're barbaric dogs.... Lecturing us. Right in our face. Jeremy and I
look at each other. What the fuck, this woman doesn't have a clue of what this
is all about. And Huey is on the bed. Jane's running around in the usual dithery
way. Mark Lane skulking over in the corner. And so, that's how the Winter Soldier concept was adopted.

The names of three CCI staffers, Jeremy, Tod and myself, were now
transferred to a new Winter Soldier Investigation letterhead, listing on its
"steering committee" Fonda, Lane, former Green Beret Don Duncan, VVAW's
Al Hubbard, Richard Fernandez of Clergy and Laity Concerned[68] — and in
their dual capacity, Ensign and Rifkin. My two comrades attempted to get
me on the board as well, citing a need for a greater vet presence, but, with
personality clashes and differences of temperament already evident among the
principals, both Jeremy and Tod believed in retrospect that Lane especially —
and probably Hubbard as well — had wished to lessen CCI's control.

It was agreed that the Winter Soldier steering committee would convene
weekly in CCI's offices. I attended my first meeting soon after returning from
Europe, walking in to see a pouty Jane Fonda typing the evening's agenda on
an old manual like a Katharine Gibbs virtuosa; along with Tod Ensign and
a former head of the USIA, she was the fastest typist I'd ever seen. Fonda and
I were oil and water the instant we met; subsequent events would prove we
were right to mistrust each other.[69]

As for the weekly meeting, it was — from the point of view of the CCI
senior cadres — superfluous to the organization's real division of labor. CCI's
modus operandi and work ethic drove the efforts that produced the results,
though quite a few VVAW members working elsewhere were quickly catch-
ing on to how to organize their brothers around the war crimes issue — a good
thing, from our perspective. But, for CCI, the Winter Soldier coalition was
always a Faustian pact prompted by two essential needs, to get Fonda to provide the funding and media profile for a national event, and to prevent Lane
from imposing his kooky stamp on any war crimes proceedings — especially
his idea of staging mock trials with veterans in the dock. Go out and try to
get vets to come forward with that strategy, we mockingly suggested.

Still, over the first two months the coalition went smoothly enough; differences were aired at meetings, and, in a least one instance, a consensus around disputed points was distributed to steering committee members in the form of a memo written by Tod.[70] It was agreed that the Winter Soldier Investigation would be held over three days, December 1st to 3rd. Jeremy had yielded on the venue, accepting "blue collar" Detroit over Washington, DC.

The "workerist" tendency in the movement overall was never dominant, but it was present along with a host of similar contradictions that bred friction among antiwar activists — between whites and nonwhites, men and women, pacifists and Bolsheviks, working class vets and middle class vets, who sometimes looked at each other across a divide similar to that separating officers and enlistees.[71]

CCI pursued a more limited goal: to organize working class vets to bring the antiwar message into their own communities. As an international border town, the selection of Detroit would also permit Vietnamese testimony to be beamed via closed circuit television from Windsor, Canada, across the bay to the Motor City. Neither Tod nor Jeremy objected to this; their main concern was that the event not be used as a platform for propaganda. In Tod Ensign's memo, referred to above, the first item read, "it is essential that the victims be limited to an elaboration of factual eyewitness accounts of war crimes. This should be made unmistakably clear to the appropriate parties involved." Furthermore expert testimony in all forms would be kept to a minimum, and the "focus primarily on testimony of Vietnam veterans."[72]

For CCI internally, one can now grasp how the Detroit/DC divide also played out in the long term political relationship of its two leaders. Jeremy leaned more and more toward engaging policy makers in their own back yard, not that he ever expected the government to try itself for war crimes. His hubris allowed him to fancy taking on the power structure directly. Tod was hardly disapproving of this strategy; he too enjoyed the occasional do-si-do down the corridors of power. But Tod had a more active penchant for grassroots work, and a soft spot for organized labor as an ideal that Jeremy didn't share. Tod also had strong ties to Detroit, where he'd gone to law school, and many contacts among radicals there, whom, as advance man for Winter Soldier, he hoped to rally to the cause. Jeremy's strategy remained media-driven, and he was skeptical about the prospects of turning out the national press corps and network television for a news event staged in what was then one of the most depressed and battered industrial cities in the nation.[73] His instinct proved disappointingly, but prophetically, accurate.

In the Meantime...

Since returning from Europe, I had been confronted with a dilemma of my own. When the semester began at NYU I was still enrolled in a doctoral program with a full course load. But my attention was leagues distant from the obscure rites of transformational grammar. I was doing what I'd been asked to do by CCI, chatting vets up by phone or in person, and gathering their testimonies.

In the deep background I attended to my disabilities, the one — TB — long under treatment, the other — what we would soon label post–Vietnam syndrome — only dimly acknowledged by the fact that I'd begun weekly visits to a shrink. For New York City dwellers of a certain class and formation, being in "therapy" was, to be sure, a contact sport for the emotions, and every bit as legitimate a topic for intermural culture-chat as a night at the theater or a hot new restaurant. Many of my closest non-vet friends, like Tod, sought the "talking cure" to lighten baggage from their own pasts; in my sessions, the war was not yet emphasized over other experiences. Whereas, any lingering effects of my one-time galloping consumption were subjected to a regimen of forty-plus pills a day, most of which were the size of a thumb joint and nauseating, and to periodic exams at the St. Albans VA in Queens.

My passion for the times grew daily. The pageantry of the downtown counterculture was exhilarating. Along St. Mark's Place, at the heart of the East Village, one witnessed an endless parade of fading *Bohemes* and fresh plumed flower children. Tie-dye, bell bottoms, Peter Max posters, psychedelic music clubs and concert halls — the Electric Circus and the Fillmore East — head shops and dope peddlers hawking loose joints. If you smoked reefer on the streets, you discreetly cupped the joint to your thigh whenever a cop passed on his sidewalk beat; black nationalists had taken out two young cops already in that neighborhood — in such an atmosphere, a collar for smoking a joint in public would be an act of self-ridicule.

A few blocks west, half of NYU's campus had been liberated. So papered with antiwar materials was the five story glass and steel student union across Washington Square, that it appeared wrapped like a work of monumental public art. Since Kent State and Cambodia, students themselves determined who could come and go within the building, now open round the clock. The argot of the ghetto, filtered through the rising profile and popularity of the Black Panthers, became the lingua franca of the movement: *right-on, power to the people, off the pig*.

A true opposition had arisen within the body politic, and the euphoria we felt within that milieu had an octane of reality high enough to fuel delusions of grandeur and fantasies of social revolution. Indeed if cultural and social practices throughout the United States are less racist, sexist, and provincial than what we knew before Vietnam, then our delusions were also less grandiose than many revisionist movement veterans have confessed in their recantations.

Added to the mix of movement types — students, peaceniks, old time commies and new age lefties — many of whom were weary after years of opposition to the war, were the fresh troops of antiwar veterans who'd come on the scene just in time to shoulder a significant load in the final years of the struggle. New York was a hub for that energy, some of which went toward exposing American genocidal policies, and considerably more toward building vet visibility at demos and street actions. The vets were on the march, and, on one late summer afternoon, I marched with them.

I won't swear to it, but I believe this was the only occasion in those years when I donned a pair of jungle fatigues, toted a plastic M-16, and joined a VVAW patrol for a round of street theater. Ed Koch, then our downtown Congressperson and putatively antiwar, was speaking at a small rally in midtown. The vets decided to run through the crowd "taking prisoners," so demonstrators might momentarily "feel" what it was like to "be" Vietnamese, in addition to supporting their cause. People were intimidated by our heathen cries; it was shock theater, a bit rough, but not violent. Koch was mouthing his cautious brand of opposition from a raised platform. He freaked out when he saw us rounding people up, and began frantically to look for an exit. Standing at the foot of the platform, I could see he was terrified. I tried to reassure him, and offered him a hand down. Seeing my vet get-up, he recoiled in horror, and screamed, "Don't you touch me."

If Koch's white collar was showing, well, in a sense mine was too. The street was not my style; it was many years since I'd been culled from the pack, and had come to see myself as caught between the classes. I'd never been a bloke's bloke, and besides, I was goal-, not process-oriented. The other vets got off on just being with each other; I got off on organizing the task, not the men. As September waned into October, I was focused on preparing a commission — the somewhat inflated idiom we still used for our efforts to publicize war crimes — for Philadelphia.

All CCI's efforts at gathering testimony were now geared toward maximizing participation at Winter Soldier. Three more commissions were planned before December, dress rehearsals for the latest recruits willing to step forward. In that same period we also learned of a parallel event being organized for late October in Stockholm, similar in composition to the Russell Tribunals, but, this time, within the exclusive political orbit of the Soviet Union. Mark Lane operated as a local contact for what was being called an International Commission of Enquiry on US War Crimes. In consultation with CCI,

Lane submitted names of several American veterans with summaries of their testimonies, two of whom would be flown via Moscow to testify in Sweden. The two men selected were myself and a vet from upstate New York named Danny A.

No one at CCI carried a brief for the Russians. For most New Leftists who'd been minted in the crucible of Vietnam, red diaper babies notwithstanding, the ideological squabbles of the Old Left had little impact — except when we clashed directly with party members, whether CP or Trotskyist, around immediate differences of tactics or strategy. We rejected the national obsession with anti-communism, believing that the imperial policies it shielded were the real danger to our national interest and security. While imagining sincerely that we served the Revolution, we functioned more like an outlaw band than a political cell; we took orders from no one.[74]

The Swedish-based Enquiry offered the chance for another grand adventure in Europe barely a month since my return. But my role would be ambiguous. In a small way I was becoming a leader in the movement; but I was going to Sweden as a vet. Psychologically I'd already begun to resist testifying to my own war experiences in any context devoid of a larger political analysis and message. Some part of me was wary about Stockholm; what shames me today is how the emerging animal trainer in me no longer wished to switch places with the performing bear.

Such inner conflicts were deeply unconscious in those days when one was driven by old ambitions to succeed in this urgent, entrepreneurial world of New Left politics. I may have been a piece of work in my own way, but I've never had a moment's doubt about the justice of our cause. In compiling the Philadelphia testimony, I worked like a daemon to ensure, above all, the veracity of each vet's account. I was particularly well suited to helping fellow vets distinguish between what they'd heard from what they'd seen or done. The emphasis on eye witness testimony was paramount, and my shit detector quick to pick up and challenge anything that sounded too bizarre, too outlandish; the truth was horrifying enough.

Philadelphia

The Philadelphia vets were already getting organized by the time we'd met them, and proved to be among the most compelling and powerful witnesses CCI would ever find. A former marine and forward observer, Ken Campbell, had directed artillery fire on two civilian villages without provocation, completely within the channels of his unit's command mission; he himself personally counted twenty dead civilians and twenty-five houses damaged or destroyed.[75] Another lad, with a name from central casting, Nathan Hale, described acts of electrical torture during the interrogation of prisoners; Hale possessed slides of such incidents.

Both these, and the other vets who participated, demonstrated enormous strength of character in facing the press, making clear the context of overall U.S. military practice in which they operated, but with deep regret for their individual failings. Among the war's architects, only the sleep of Robert McNamara[76] was, seemingly, disturbed by the shadows that his zeal for hegemony in Vietnam cast on the souls of boys like these who, innocently for the most part, tried to do his bidding.[77]

Moscow 1970: Ten Days That Shook My World

After Philadelphia, Dan A. and I met in New York and flew Air Canada from JFK to Montreal, where a scheduled Aeroflot flight would carry us to Stockholm via Moscow. Fate deposited us in Canada during the worst days of the Quebec Uprising. We were immediately detained and prevented from attending the press conference that Canadian comrades had scheduled for our arrival in the vicinity of the customs exit. Escorted through the airport, with riot troops visible everywhere cradling burp guns, we were interrogated over a period of five hours, then marched in handcuffs to an aircraft returning to New York and deported. Needless to say, we had protested in the strongest possible terms, but without avail; Quebec was under martial law, and Canadian equivalents of due process and individual rights à la Miranda had been suspended.[78]

Back at JFK two young agents of the FBI boarded our flight. Sternly, silently, they led us to some godforsaken underground corridors below the terminal building. In such a setting, one knows not what to expect. Undeniably nervous, I was strangely unintimidated. To their credit, the two Feds didn't try to strong-arm us. They took the tack that we were commie dupes. Appealing to our patriotism, they tried persuasion to pry us from subversive affiliations that must have struck them — quite sincerely — as an alliance with the evil one. They kept repeating, you guys answered the call, not like those goddamned cowards in Canada. How can you give aid and comfort to the enemy? We responded just as earnestly with our most heartfelt raps about the reality of the war. But they didn't get it. And, since we'd committed no crime, the dialogue ended in a standoff. Back at CCI there was a lot of huffing and puffing about this outrage, but reciprocal arrangements between the U.S. and the USSR allowed one Aeroflot flight a week from JFK, and, by the following night, we were again Moscow bound.

"Go to In-tourist. Young blond girl, Ludmilla. Soviet Peace Committee representative." These words stare elliptically from the back page of my 1970 calendar. Recollections of the actual flight are equally minimal. The plane was piloted in a manner that reminded me of combat patterns flown by troop transports in Vietnam, C-130s and Caribous. Straight up on take off, straight down on descent — exposing the barest profile to potential small arms fire. I've often wondered if I imagined this, but I don't think so. Every Soviet I met in that period seemed full throttle on the defensive.

The cabin of the *Ilyushin* was policed by female attendants who I'm convinced were trained at the Kremlin Academy for Prison Matrons. Collectively they prompted memories of Sister Caroline, my seventh grade teacher, the most feared enforcer at Our Lady of Perpetual Help, who had a swifter backhand than most tennis pros. There were no finishing school smiles, no "coffee, tea or me" patter on the lips of these bruisers, and one kept one's seat, and needed permission even to visit the john. In-flight perks, while limited, were elegant. Chilled vodka flowed on demand, and the grub was rich black bread with gobs of Beluga spread over beds of creamy butter.

Three days in Moscow are clearly insufficient for any serious judgments about the place or the people, even within the context of the times. But I can present a fair description of my few impressions. A Ludmilla did appear as scripted, and guided what turned out to be a small American delegation to our hotel downtown. Everything about this establishment was a cliche of what official Soviet culture had become since the short-lived promise of the October Revolution fifty years before. That the building itself was an architectural hoot, goes without saying. But only the perverted memory of an Eisenstein clone could have placed the babushka-clad char women on their hands and knees scrubbing the stairs that led to the lobby. In a dining room that made my high school cafeteria look like the Four Seasons, a very bad band played "Home on the Range," and similar pop favorites of the Eastern Bloc. Prickly waiters at Ratners back home would have found the service offensive, as thugs in soiled dinner jackets dispensed uneatable facsimiles of food; no wonder those people drink so much.

In 1970 Moscow was not a city the transient traveler could walk about at leisure. Once checked in, it was like the Roach Motel, you couldn't get out — or at least, not without an apparatchik at your elbow. After a day, a few of us rebelled and threatened to hit the streets, prohibitions notwithstanding. A quick and heated meeting was arranged between myself and the head commissar of the Peace Committee, who couldn't fathom my brand of communism any more than I could fathom his. Visually the encounter was a scene for the times.

Given my appearance, you could understand the man's hesitation in turning me loose among the natives. A psychiatric clinic, maybe. I had shoulder-length hair and a mop on my upper lip that Fuller Brush could have marketed. My clothes were vintage counterculture, a tie-dyed long john top and striped bellbottoms, blue and gold, that looked like they'd been cut from a beach cabana on the Riviera. He too was a cartoon version of himself, a stock character from the back lots of *A Watch on the Rhine*. We screamed at each other for about five minutes through an interpreter, which produced two tickets for *The Barber of Seville* that evening at the Bolshoi.

That was impressive. Half the house was papered, and one looked from the balcony over a sea of crimson-trimmed long coats sported by soldiers of the Red Army. This may not have been the taste of the average American serviceman, but Soviet troops thought it was great stuff; and so did Dan A. and I. Against the grain of my running put-down of the Soviet system, I have to acknowledge that the chap who accompanied us that night was the only non-Soviet-Soviet I ever met. You could tell Boris had a rakish side from the feather that adorned his fedora. Following the performance, and quite against orders I'm sure, he brought us by subway to the bar of the still swank St. George Hotel and treated us to a bourgeois round of cognac and — if memory serves — Cuban cigars.

Red Stockholm

Stockholm, by comparison with Moscow, was a somber place, devoid of comic mishaps that one can look back on with gallows humor. It was a dark time, standing before a self-appointed tribunal of careerists from the European Left — jurists for the most part, if I am not mistaken — pasty faced bureaucrats just as capable of managing a Vietnam of their own construction as their counterparts who managed the real war from Washington. Whether or not that sentiment is true or fair, I won't argue; but such was my feeling and lack of identity with those staging this affair.

I struggled to control the dimensions of my testimony, trading testy words with one chap in particular who was bent on making even more grotesque what in my eyes had been bad enough. The deep core of my horror about the war had never been the quality or number of atrocities I witnessed, but the utter degradation of the Vietnamese at the hands of all too many American men and boys who took pleasure in the day to day colonial rituals of domination and bullying.

But this view of our imperial arrogance, even when spiked by firsthand accounts of beatings and torture, was not sensational enough for Mark Lane, also present in Stockholm, who would later belittle my testimony. Lane was especially harsh with the other vet witness, Danny A., for telling the tribunal he'd witnessed the rape and murder of a Vietnamese woman by a black American GI that went unreported. For GIs to note distinctions of race was hardly unusual, and certainly not the overt act of racism that Lane sanctimoniously claimed.

A photo of me accompanied the article appearing on the front page of a Stockholm paper the next day.[79] The expression on my face confirms my depressed mood about the whole experience. First off, I was in over my head, still much too inexperienced to stand my ground in this company of the best and brightest. And secondly, perhaps because I remained so provincially American, I had no faith in the efficacy of the International Enquiry to accomplish any constructive end; more likely I believed the whole exercise was counterproductive — or would be if broadcast to the American masses back home.

One redemptive moment did occur for me in Stockholm, which, to explain, I must appropriate the spiritual vocabulary of healing and reconciliation. After the session where I gave my testimony, the three delegations from Indochina hosted a reception. For an hour or so, I circulated among a band of tiny diplomats, North Vietnamese, Pathet Lao, and Khmer Rouge. And still, even allowing for a lingering dose of youthful exuberance, I retain the most satisfying memories of those encounters. When backed to the wall the peoples of Indochina can be mean as snakes; but there's a capacity for sweetness in them that I've seldom experienced with peoples of other cultures. Alone among the international delegates, the Indochinese showed some delicacy of feeling toward my ambivalence. It was not just the common ground of politics we shared in conversation, but an exchange of human warmth; and that night I made peace with the enemy.

❖   ❖   ❖

In the mail when I returned from Stockholm were the bound galleys of Mark Lane's soon to be published *Conversations with Americans*. At CCI we had forecast a worst case scenario, that Lane's book would somehow undermine the credibility of our issue. Not that I will deny disliking Lane from day one, nor that I still nursed a slow burn from his treatment of Dan A. and myself in Stockholm. Jeremy and Tod too had their own reasons for distrusting Lane. We all wanted to contain his influence, but not yet at the expense of a fatal split in our fragile alliance. After all, we understood that Lane and Fonda were a boxed set, and it was Jane's connections that would finance what we all believed would be a major breakthrough for the issue in Detroit around the Winter Soldier Investigation.

In picking up Lane's book I was primed to be overcritical, not reckless.

But the shoddiness of his work was apparent from the start. In cadence and nuance the atrocities his vets recount are supercharged, like tales around a campfire. Lane seemed always focused on the most bestial accounts, and his interlocutors feed him the staged readings he solicits on cue. Generally absent, where not otherwise undercut by Lane's tabloid aesthetic, was any linking of individual GI actions to the logic of the military tools and tactics at their disposal on the field of battle. But a passage where a couple of vets on bar stools convinced the credulous Lane that they'd served in Vietnam with units which only existed on paper, invented for exercises in infantry training, was, for me, final proof that *Conversations with Americans* guaranteed our worst fears about its author.

I acted immediately on my pique over Lane's book. For a day or two in late October I steamed around the CCI offices, calling other vets who'd received the galleys, threatening to gather as many of their signatures as possible for a letter denouncing the book to its publisher, Simon and Schuster, a gesture made irrelevant by subsequent events.

Nationally, any mounting public concern about American atrocities was increasingly focused on the trials of the My Lai defendants. Additional revelations about war crimes were by degrees subordinated to the main event, the trial of William "Rusty" Calley in Columbus, Georgia, which would begin on November 17th.[80] CCI's own rhetoric surrounding the My Lai trials had likewise quickened. Tod Ensign publically demanded that all charges against those being prosecuted for war crimes be dropped because, he said, "The My Lai massacre is a logical outgrowth of policies set at the highest level — individual soldiers do not account for genocide."[81]

In reiterating the CCI political mantra Tod continued to argue, not only for the record, but for the immediate consumption of those in high places who might be taken by the seriousness of the charge — or simply the idea — that U.S. tactics in Vietnam systematically generated war crimes.[82] But it was in the arena of pubic opinion where we placed our major hope for relief, if not redress. We never believed the system would investigate itself, but we wanted some response — maybe a few more heads hung in shame among our leaders, like that evening at Tufts University where Jeremy had staged his private Nuremberg. Winter Soldier was our shot at competing, if only for a few days, with the Calley trial. Any schemes we plotted for getting close to that trial had, moreover, evaporated when it became clear that the defense as well as the prosecution were exploiting this forum to defend the war.

8. The CCI–VVAW Split

I myself can lay no special claim to powers of memory, especially after repression has sealed the vault where painful recollections lay. As for remembering exactly what "went down" during the melodrama later referred to by participants as "the VVAW/CCI split," my old buddies Rifkin and Ensign have each dredged up aspects of the conflict that my own memory has managed to misplace or bury; and I've been able, on occasion, to refresh their recollections as well both from what I recall and from the documented record. Thus what follows is an imperfect reconstruction of the circumstances surrounding the split, for which other sources, in particular Andrew Hunt's history of VVAW, *The Turning*, provide alternative, yet, for the most part, complementary interpretations.

Winter Soldier: How the Split Went Down

Tod describes my mood during those last days of October as "highly agitated."[83] I took a hard line against Lane, while Jeremy, for his own reasons, endorsed my view that Lane had become a liability the war crimes movement could no longer tolerate. In part I saw Lane as a threat to vet — and therefore my own — autonomy. Tod and Jeremy, whether from generational solidarity or political insight, had given vets in CCI's immediate circle the latitude in action one extends to comrades, not clients. Lane demanded the distance — and patronizing control — of a traditional lawyer-client relationship.

At the same time the Winter Soldier Steering Committee had been constituted without a Vietnam veteran presence that typified our constituency. The two vet members, Don Duncan and Al Hubbard,[84] had both at one time aspired to military careers; the men who populated the radical vet movement were not of this ilk. We were younger, lower ranking draftees and enlistees (or lowly junior officers) serving only to fulfill our minimal obligations. Behind my determined aim to oust Lane was the implied position that the Winter Soldier coalition represented a step backward in vets' — including my own — political development and empowerment as activists. Self-interest and principle were somewhat in alignment.

It was Jeremy who eventually forced an ultimatum on the steering committee, gaining that which I wanted, but lacked the power to achieve. Nor can I imagine for a moment, knowing Jeremy's strong willed personality as I do, that he acted to placate the ruffled feathers of his vet allies, even his then boon companion, yours truly. No, Jeremy wanted Lane out as much as — or more than — I did.

Tod has reflected often on this chain of occurrences, and speaks as freely about them as Jeremy remains guarded. He suggests that Jeremy and I rent an alliance that he was prepared to "muddle through." His loyalty to his comrades, and not his better judgement, Tod now believes, caused him to acquiesce to my and Jeremy's uncompromising decision. To which I respond that I have witnessed and admired many of Tod's talents and qualities over the years. Loyalty is prominent among them; "muddle through" is not. In the china shop of human affairs, Tod Ensign — who has indeed mellowed with age — could wreak havoc with the best of them. If there was inner conflict then, he kept his peace. Yet Tod protests with complete accuracy that he was not a prime mover in the breakup of the coalition, which shattered with blistering speed just three or four days after his return from the coast.

Tod rode the red-eye from Portland on October 28th, already with the sense of an impending showdown, after Jeremy called to warn him that the vets were spooked, and that I was insisting that Tod and Jeremy back us (the vets) up. Jeremy said he was seeking an immediate face-to-face parlay with Lane and Fonda to clear the air. The pair had traveled to the Boston area, where Jane was about to launch a month-long tour of college campuses to promote the Detroit investigation, and, not incidently, underwrite its costs with the hefty speaking fees a celebrity of her stature could command. The CCI contingent made its way to Boston and caught up with our coalition partners on Saturday the 30th at Lane's girlfriend's place in Cambridge.

Four of us stood before the building, when someone — most likely Lane — insisted that only members of the Steering Committee could attend. That left Bob Johnson and myself propped at the threshold, taking the news unkindly. Personally, I was fuming, suffering humiliation gladly not being among my strong suits. Although I'll bet Tod and Jeremy were just as happy to park my vet rage at the curb. Only Tod has provided an account of what transpired within, paraphrasing what he recalls Mark Lane to have said.

> So we begin talking, and Lane says, I've looked over some of these witnesses you've put together, and I certainly hope you're not planning to offer the kind of witnesses in Detroit that you sent to Stockholm. And I felt immediately attacked ... because I was being attacked. And I said, what do you mean? Well this one man talks about a black soldier raping a Vietnamese. How do you think that sounds. He's a racist. He hasn't got any testimony anyway. How many people did he kill? And Uhl..., I can't remember what he said about you, but he didn't like your testimony either.[85]

In Tod's account it is Lane who takes the offensive by turning the tables, challenging CCI's competence. Tod says Lane demanded an accounting.

"What are you doing down there in the city? What are you spending our money on?" Lane's threatening tone upset both Tod and Jeremy, and the meeting ended without a definitive move by either faction. Apparently, Tod and Jeremy felt the need to strengthen their veteran flank before going further. In any event, the four of us, joined by VVAW president Al Hubbard, retired to the Wursthaus on Harvard Square for a strategy session.

The only detail I remember clearly from that encounter is that Hubbard played us for suckers. During the meeting, his negativity about Lane and opposition to the man's continued involvement with Winter Soldier far outstripped even mine. As we dispersed for the evening, I had the distinct feeling that the plan for ousting Lane had been set in motion. With VVAW in our corner, CCI held all the cards, and, for his chances, Lane had — as they say in Brooklyn — *un gatz.*

Back in New York, the first thing Jeremy and I did early the next morning was visit the out-of-town newsstand on Times Square for a copy of the *Boston Sunday Globe.* We knew that Fonda had a scheduled interview the night before. The article was buried, page 51, but the contents, for Jeremy, signaled that the other shoe had finally dropped. The reporter quoted Lane on two points that CCI considered anathema. First, that "the group hopes to arouse the Pentagon to appoint an official War Crimes Commission," in effect, calling for the Pentagon to investigate itself. And second, "that the Detroit investigation ... is similar to the Nuremberg trials.... This time, however, American soldiers ... are putting themselves on trial ... and risking almost certain prosecution for their testimony."[86]

That evening Jeremy found Tod at his girlfriend Pam Booth's apartment in the Village. "We've gotta talk," Jeremy pleaded. "This is bad, really bad." Jeremy had tears rolling down his face, which greatly impressed Tod, who knew how emotionally undemonstrative his friend could be. He was just sobbing, and he said, "This guy is going to destroy everything we worked for. He's going to ruin it. We can't work with him."[87]

A quarter century later, Jeremy still recalled the confrontation with great passion.

> That's right, I said, we can't do this. We can't have vets on trial. Policy's on trial. Not the individual GIs. The whole point of this was to allow the GIs the opportunity to feel that they could talk about their experiences without being punished for them. Because, otherwise, it would end up just victimizing a handful of guys. And we'd never get to the policy itself that led to it. And so, we just couldn't have that. That was not acceptable.[88]

Acceptable or otherwise, Tod today regrets the decision. We could have taken a less extreme position, he says. But we didn't. Over the next few days we met with Al Hubbard, asking him to convey our decision to the Steering

Committee at a meeting scheduled probably that Thursday, November 4th.[89] Apparently Lane and Fonda had returned to New York for the occasion. "If Lane leaves, we'll work with the others," Tod recalls having told Hubbard. "And I'll always remember this," Tod continued. I said to Al, "We're not coming. We're boycotting. But I'll be in my apartment waiting for your call." Hubbard told Tod he would convey our views, and that we had his full support. About ten-thirty Tod's phone rang. It was Al who said, "We had our meeting, Tod." And Tod asked him, "Are you out or in, Al?" And he said, "You'll have to count me out," meaning he was staying with Fonda and Lane. We decided right away, as Tod puts it, "to go ahead on our own ... in Washington."[90]

Jane Fonda II

Several days after the split we were treated to the unannounced appearance of Jane Fonda at CCI's offices. When Jane discovered that her key no longer fit, since we had had the foresight to change the lock, she started pounding on the door and yelling, "Let me into my office, let me into my office." It must have been the weekend following the split. Jeremy and I were there alone, and the empty building reverberated like a tomb to the invasion of the slightest sound. Poor Jane. She had no audience but us. Speaking through the closed door, using his most annoyingly unflappable voice, Jeremy communicated a simple truth. "Jane, this is not your office," after which the actress, spouting threats and damning our eyes, stomped off.[91]

❖ ❖ ❖

In retrospect, the most serious consequence of the split was that, rather than cooperating, we were now competing with VVAW over turf in the war crimes movement. Since the Steering Committee had demanded summaries of all our testimonies — even though it was the height of hubris for Winter Soldier to lay claims to work indisputably accomplished by CCI — and since our relations with VVAW had so quickly soured — we fully expected a raid on our files.

Such imbroglios among like-minded groups on the Left were hardly unprecedented. The staff collective at the *Guardian*, the independent weekly of the Left for many years, had an internal fracas giving rise to an office break-in, and the sudden appearance of a rival dubbed the *Liberated Guardian*, while at *Liberation News*, a popular newspaper of New Left vintage, the New York offices were likewise ransacked, and the entire operation hauled off to

Vermont following a faction fight among the principals. For an earlier generation of New Leftists, it was the implosion of SDS in late 1969, creating splinters like the Weather faction, that forecast the youth movement's ultimate doom.

At CCI we were so paranoid about the VVAW unleashing its heavies to shanghai our work that we rounded up some muscle of our own. We called Andy Stapp of the American Servicemen's Union, asking him to dispatch his own bully boys for a security detail. With ASU watching our flanks in the corridors and outside the building, we loaded CCI's files into Jeremy's car and drove them downtown to my apartment for safekeeping. Stapp himself came by and commiserated with us about Al Hubbard's treachery. "He's either a fool or a pig, observed the colorful Stapp, ever the political heavy, but the upshot's still the same."

9. Organizing the National Veterans' Inquiry

November 1970

It took CCI exactly one month to organize — and finance — the National Veterans Inquiry (NVI), to be held over the first three days of December 1970 in a Washington hotel. In that short span, CCI produced its unfinished — and forgotten — political symphony. Never again would I work quite so hard, so willingly, so selflessly on any other political project; never again would my alienation be so integrated with my work, every ounce of potential harnessed to the moment and task at hand. I was now, as Tod has acknowledged, part of a triumvirate, adding talents to the mix that permitted Tod and Jeremy even more latitude to exercise their own.

Tod and I worked on shoring up and expanding our base of witnesses — without whose involvement there would be no inquiry. Jeremy concentrated on equally critical areas of media and fundraising, though, as with everything, we often operated in interchangeable roles. Admittedly my own versatility remained hampered by a lack of experience, but Tod and Jeremy proved themselves once more masters of the improvised spectacle; if chutzpah had been capital, these guys were on Easy Street.

We recruited dozens of supporters, all of whom contributed some vital element to the NVI's unspectacular success. Money came from a few special friends, not to mention members of the Ensign and Rifkin families, and from a modest shakedown of the Hearst Corporation that Jeremy pulled off at Avon Books. For the NVI was to have its own Boswell, one James Simon Kunen, a young writer of promise who had penned an offbeat chronicle of the 1968 student strike at Columbia University titled *The Strawberry Statement*. In Kunen's second book, *Standard Operating Procedure*, the author's running commentary — alternately comic or snotty, insightful or sophomoric, spurred or sapped by ennui — accompanies a transcript of the grotesqueries that one witness of American atrocities after another would testify to at CCI's public inquiry in Washington.[92]

CCI's proprietary right to the transcript was acknowledged with little resistance by Avon editor, Peter Mayer; indeed CCI's name appears on the book's cover. Mayer, as Kunen does report, agreed to pay for the transcript's production, to include the wages of a stenographer. We did indeed get the money — in the vicinity of twenty-five hundred bucks, as I recall — directly from Avon.

Dough came in from other quarters — not a lot — certainly not anywhere near as much as CCI lost in forfeiting Fonda's patronage. But enough to keep the phone lines humming over the next month, pay travel costs to Washington for ourselves on multiple occasions before the event, and for at least some of the forty vets who came to testify — who we also managed to shelter for several days thanks to volunteer housing. We rented the large banquet space and several smaller rooms at the obscure Dupont Plaza Hotel, most suitable in Jeremy's eyes for its proximity to virtually all the news bureaus of the Washington-based media. To each of these outlets we delivered — by hand — thick information packets with brief bios and summaries for all veterans expected to testify, and reprints of news clippings that covered CCI's earlier press exposure.

Jane Fonda III

Fonda fired one last shot in anger off CCI's bow in the form of a note spouting legalese and typed on VVAW letterhead.[93] She wrote that a check for her lecture at Rutgers on November 11 would come to CCI's address through prior arrangements. To avoid a criminal charge for conversion, she instructed us to present it to Al Hubbard who would accept the check for the Winter Soldier Investigation. We did just that. So it was that two of the three major events seeking to publicize U.S. war crimes in Indochina were launched in parallel with little contact among their feuding organizers.[94] Fonda added with a touch of acidity that CCI's efforts for a Washington, DC, hearing were not to be endorsed by WSI. Sour grapes. We, in return, publicly supported Winter Soldier, while hoping secretly among ourselves — may we rot in sectarian hell — that those assholes and class traitors on the seventh floor would fall on their tuchises. Politics then was always personal.

These hectic November weeks were crammed with memorable people and events. Of the many originals — as types or personalities go — among the vet witnesses, only a few stand out in memory after three decades. Take "Crazy" Joe Bangert, a nonstop monologist with an occasional turn at performance art. During one routine Joe dropped to the carpet in the lobby of the Dupont Plaza and mimed a piece of bacon being cooked in an electric fry pan. He reached over the imaginary edge and turned on the heat; after which he writhed and sizzled to a crisp. Jeremy loved it, but he kept repeating in a stage whisper, this guy's crazy.[95]

LBJ

My memory for that final month is mostly a blur. Only a truly improbable encounter with Lyndon Baines Johnson remains as clear in my mind as the day it happened. The weekend just before the NVI's inaugural session I was invited to attend a wedding reception for the younger of the sisters White, Victoria, whom I'd befriended during undergraduate days at Georgetown. Mrs. White graciously secured lodgings for me in the apartment left empty by her neighbors, then traveling, none other than retired Supreme Court Justice Tom Clark and his wife. Lyndon Johnson, fellow Texan and long time crony of William S. White, the *Washington Post* columnist, was at the reception surrounded by all the young Turks who were thrilled for this opportunity to debate the former president about his war policies. One very buttoned-down lad would comment later, oddly disheartened, that LBJ's geopolitical thinking was a pathetic anachronism, still linked to securing fueling stations in the Pacific.

But I formed another impression of Johnson that day, which is hard to square with my prior — and ongoing — judgments about a man who had so passionately waged aggressive war against the Vietnamese. Someone apparently told Johnson that I'd been in Vietnam, and suddenly I was stunned to see him standing by my side. Our eyes met. The gaze from that deeply troubled face was almost unbearably human, full of searching and empathy. Gently, he rested one of those lanky Texas arms on my shoulder, almost whispering, he drawled, "Ah understand." And then, with Lady Bird, he left. Till that moment, I'd only seen the war criminal; now I saw the man, and I've been soft on the guy ever since.

Over the next two days before the National Veterans Inquiry began on December 1, a Wednesday, I set up shop in Justice Clark's formal study and had a few vets up to help them organize their testimony. Could even a novelist conjure the large portrait in oil of Ramsey Clark, age five or so, dressed in a sailor suit, hair bobbed like Buster Brown, that overhung his father's desk?

The Inquiry

Wednesday arrived and the National Veterans Inquiry began with all due attention to the solemnity of the occasion. Dressed in their Sunday best, Tod, Jeremy, and Bob Johnson were the principal toastmasters providing interpretive comments and introducing individual speakers; I worked more behind the scenes helping folks make connections that needed to be made, acts of press agentry for the most part. Author James Reston Jr. would later record a brief account of my role at the inquiry in a book devoted to a campaign Tod and I were to launch the following year to demand amnesty for the war's draft and military resisters. Reston saw me in a light more flattering than I deserved; he wrote:

> I had first met Mike in Washington two years before at the National Veterans Inquiry, where he was the calm, professional contact for the Inquiry. He is of a new breed of anti-war organizer: replete with the radical analysis of the ills of American society, convinced that the Vietnam War is the epitome of those ills, and adept at stage-managing events that capture wide press coverage.[96]

How broad, incidentally, is the landscape of "wide press coverage?" Reston, two years after the fact, apparently retained an impression that the NVI was something of a media success. To others, including several members of the working press also in attendance, NVI's media impact was minimal; they, perhaps rightly, would contend that only those news stories with a claim to the national memory like My Lai can be judged to have been widely covered. Otherwise you're just yesterday's news and odds-on candidate for the sinkhole of history. It's certainly true that the media did not live up to the challenge Nat Hentoff posted in his column for the *Village Voice*, titled "Nuremberg III."

> Expect to see any of th[is] on the Cronkite, Brinkley or Howard K. Smith shows? Expect to see much of it in the *New York Times*? Let us watch ... Monitor the media starting December 1, and measure how much is reported of the National Veterans Inquiry into U.S. War Crimes.[97]

No, we didn't do quite *that* well; no print or TV reporter filed stories in succession for all three days. Some correspondents merely announced the inquiry, summarizing the testimonies along with CCI's stated intentions, which we'd provided them prior to December 1st[98]; others wrote only wrap-ups. And yet, however transient or impermanent the impact of this event, I side with Reston's view. The NVI garnered one helluva lot of media attention: network news, national wire service stories, the *Times*, the *Post*, and most of the nation's lesser rags as well. I don't mean to imply that the NVI came close in that brief three day span to becoming a household word. But if our efforts didn't ripple more visibly within the political arena, it wasn't for lack of media coverage.

The press can handle the broadly tragic and sensational, but the more subtle turns of history generally elude them. The significant presence of three former West Pointers at the NVI to introduce the various panels of testimony, one of whom, Louis Paul Font, was still on active duty, was all but completely lost on the media. Most reporters could find no easy peg for such an unprecedented breaking of ranks within this elite fraternity of professional officers, at least along this line of fracture, war vs. antiwar.[99]

LOU

After graduating from the military academy near the top of his class in 1968, Lou Font was seconded to Harvard for graduate work. Perhaps he breathed there the air of self-examination that once unsettled such earlier Harvard scholars as Emerson and Thoreau, prophets of a minority in the American kind prone to intoxication over ideas and principles. In every practical sense what Font did next was an affront to self-interest in proportion to the heights a boy of modest background achieves by meritorious advancement among elites. Font chose imaginative ground to protest the illegitimacy of the Vietnam War. He filed for a status he coined Selective Conscientious Objection. Thus, the former cadet made clear, he did not oppose all wars: only Vietnam. And in Vietnam he would not serve, even if so ordered.

The odyssey at Harvard ended with Font's swift return to active duty at Fort George G. Meade, Maryland, near Baltimore, where he and the army spent several months engaged in mutual harassment. Lieutenant Font was like a one-man CCI; with unflappable poise and straight arrow sincerity Font went before the press and threatened to bring war crimes charges against the high command under the UCMJ, the military's own Uniform Code of Military Justice. The army's threat to him was more viable, a court martial that could send him to prison.[100]

Font was among the best and the brightest that the army could have hoped to attract voluntarily in those days. The problem was that Font actually practiced the West Point ideals, duty, honor, country, that the body of his fellow officers found hazardous to ambitions for rapid advancement during a war like Vietnam. Had Font been alone, the army might have repressed his apostasy quietly and out of public view. But now it was too late. Other young officers still on active duty and opposed to Vietnam had organized themselves into a group called COM — the Concerned Officers Movement.

BOB

One of COM's active members participated in the NVI, a young doctor who'd been drafted into the service, if not unwillingly, with very little enthusiasm, directly after medical school. Robert Master appeared before the assembly — the press corps and a small public that the hearings attracted each day — in the uniform of a captain of the United States Army. In being there and speaking in opposition to the war, both Bob Master and Lou Font as active officers were claiming and exercising civil liberties which the military would have gladly denied them. But as the Pentagon knew better and more quickly than any other branch of government, the unbending military authority that had once so severely restricted the range of public actions among service members was being challenged and transformed from below. Master and Font, along with the two other former West Pointers present at the NVI, Bob Johnson and Gordon Livingston, gave elegant, if implicit, expression to the thousands of unobserved and under-articulated acts of resistance throughout the services, that culminated in the collapse of American ground forces in Vietnam over the next two years.

Like me, Bob Master had the fortunate misfortune of being assigned to a combat unit; he was a battalion surgeon, stationed on a fire base with the 101st Airborne. Bob opened the afternoon session that first day of the hearings speaking directly from his experience in Vietnam,

> where I witnessed the wholesale destruction of the entire fabric of Vietnamese rural life, the creation of a nation of refugees living in squalor, wracked by epidemics such as bubonic plague, without dignity, without independence. I speak to endorse wholeheartedly the efforts of those Vietnam veterans who ... courageously speak up at this time. I want them ... and everyone else to know that there are ... a growing number of concerned active-duty officers who are listening, who are supporting their testimony and the ends of this tribunal. It is our hope that the American people will come to realize that war crimes in Vietnam are not isolated, aberrant acts, but the inevitable result of a policy which in its direction of waging war against ... the Vietnamese civilians, is itself immoral and criminal.

Bob (Twenty Years Later)

I hadn't seen Bob Master for at least a decade, though my respect for him remained constant through the years. As might have been predicted, he'd become a physician of considerable social relevance, settling in the Boston area, where he'd helped pioneer clinics for the poor and the aging.

It must have been '94 or '95 when I called him after an overnight in Cambridge. We got together at his place, and I must have been talking about the NVI because he disappeared for a second upstairs, returning with a fist full of snapshots which he spread over the dining room table. They were photos of bodies, dead Vietcong, laid out in lines and rows, maybe forty of them.

Bob took the shots the day after his fire base with the 101st had been overrun by the enemy. He had stumbled around all that night treating the wounded and ducking bullets in the midst of a long and bloody firefight that claimed many Americans lives as well. Bob said he hadn't looked at the pictures for years, and that he'd never shown them to anyone else before that night.

Day Two

Bart

K. Barton Osborne pantomimed how he'd witnessed a Marine kill a VC suspect during interrogation by driving a dowel through the man's ear and into his brain; and the next day, newspapers all over the country featured a UPI photo of Osborne sticking a finger in his own ear.[101] Osborne's account of watching Marines hurl two VC suspects from an airborne helicopter during questioning also got the attention of many reporters present at the hearing that morning, print and TV alike. If the NVI produced a single superstar during its three days in the glare of prime time, it had to have been Bart Osborne, who enlisted in the army in 1966, then trained at the Intelligence School in Baltimore.

The army mints its spooks in two varieties, counterintelligence, as in my case, and "collection," as was the case with Bart Osborne. With considerable overlap in practice, the mission of the one is to deny and the other to gather intelligence. Both were elite services, but collection had the romance. To the degree such terms have meaning, Osborne was a true spy. Based in Da Nang, Osborne lived the life of a semiautonomous civilian under an assumed identity, or cover. He occupied himself with those sometimes messy intrigues that one might face who manages the dirty work of others, in this instance a network of South Vietnamese subagents whom he compensated on a cash and carry basis. The clients for whatever operational intelligence Osborne's private network managed to generate were local Army and Marine Corps units, and the resident spooks of the "Company," or CIA.

It was this mention of the Company in the mix of things that seemed to stir some momentary excitement in the media gallery. Almost to the point of agitation, Bob Schiefer sprang to action, demanding an immediate interview with Osborne in one of the private rooms CCI had reserved for such requests. Schiefer, then CBS correspondent at the Pentagon, was the only brahmin from network news to show at the NVI. Till Osborne began his testimony, Schiefer's sour expression radiated the contempt he apparently felt for the proceeding and its organizers. We in turn hadn't expected much sympathy from likes of Bob Schiefer, and considered him a flack for any boondoggle or rationale for aggression the military establishment wished to peddle before the gullible American taxpayers.

But Schiefer was also a reporter, and like his colleagues in the room that morning, he sniffed a story, maybe his only chance to get something from this agonizingly unpopular assignment past CBS anchorman Walter Cronkite that evening on the nightly news. Circumstantially, it appeared that Schiefer was to the political right of Cronkite; but the issue here would have been air time, a precious commodity in a show of only thirty minutes' duration. As for Walter Cronkite, who'd come of age as a correspondent during the euphoria of the U.S. victory in World War II, he was no friend to the antiwar veterans' movement.

Cronkite was typical of liberals who believe the responsible Left can't possibly extend farther on a given issue than they themselves do. The United States is probably the last place on the planet where an independent Left (excluding the loyal opposition within the Democratic Party) will ever contend for political power; but even as it plods along in its modest role of carping over injustices and attempting to raise the social and economic expectations of the masses, the Left always has the potential to upset the status quo. As evidence, I give you Vietnam.

As for K. Barton Osborne, I admit to having harbored the deepest ambivalence toward the man. Not a week before the NVI began, Bart seemed to materialize from nowhere. Of course, his explanation was plausible; he lived in DC as a grad student, and had read about the upcoming event in the *Washington Post*.[102] Osborne approached Jeremy first. Now, Jeremy's an upbeat guy, but not necessarily easy to impress. Osborne impressed him a lot, and Jeremy asked me to drop everything to talk with him. If this guy's for real, Jeremy bubbled...

If Osborne was for real, it would be my call to make that determination. Over the months the CCI regulars had refined what we called our verification procedure. In principle this meant following three basic guidelines. Each vet who'd agreed to testify had to provide a copy of his discharge papers, which, among other facts, established his Vietnam service record.[103] Then every potential witness would be closely questioned by one of CCI's vet coordinators — a role I played increasingly as the NVI approached — to gauge the general reliability of his account. And finally we would ask each vet for the names of others in his unit who could corroborate his testimony, though I don't recall any witness not participating for failure to satisfy this criterion; we had neither time nor resources to enforce this ambitious aspect of our policy.

I depended on my own feel for the subject to compensate for the unrealistic goal of matching witnesses from the same unit. If what a given vet was saying sounded and felt right, I trusted my instincts that he was kosher, not some government plant sent in to discredit us. Bart Osborne never felt quite right; I understand now that, paradoxically, he wasn't supposed to.

If this were a movie script, I could present my interview with Osborne as a take on "spy versus spy"; or "set a thief to catch a thief." But I didn't see the mutuality or irony of our pairing at the time. Nor did I possess the psychic agility, which has come with maturity, to engage a worthy adversary in some skillful mind game.

Osborne's personality was packaged far too tightly for me to move around in. With the other vets, an emotional transparency colored their accounts with an unimpeachable sincerity. But Osborne didn't wear his guilt or despair on his coat sleeves. He had the manner of a polished majordomo in a fine restaurant, self-effacing, but canny and self-assured. Bart delivered his testimony in the measured cadence of a talk show host, except sometimes he spoke in tongues, incoherent spook lingo, using terms like *cross cultural empathy facility.* He even paused smoothly once to ask the audience, can you all hear me? The egoless neutrality in Osborne's matter-of-fact but firmly spoken account of the most horrific murders of fellow humans, which, yes, he had witnessed but, no, had not himself committed, was, for me, a stunning performance.

Basically I had told Tod and Jeremy that I couldn't read the guy, and hadn't a clue where his motivations lay. But he was a specimen for the center ring, too fascinating to pass up. I think we all liked Bart from the start. He was easy going, unlike many of the vets, and pleasant company for a meal or conversation. So we ignored our doubts and agreed to let him testify. Sure, there's always a certain opportunism in political showmanship, but to this day, neither Tod, Jeremy, nor I have ever heard to the contrary that K. Barton Osborne wasn't everything he said he was.

GORDON

The other widely reported snip of testimony from day two of the NVI was an incident former West Pointer Dr. Gordon Livingston recycled from the letter he'd published a year earlier in *Saturday Review*.[104] Livingston's outfit in Vietnam had been commanded by Col. George S. Patton 3rd, whose chaplain prayed for a big body count at the colonel's nightly briefings. "Help us, oh Lord, to fulfill the standing order of this regiment: Give us the wisdom to find the bastards and pile on." It was like an item from *Ripley's Believe It or Not*, and you couldn't blame the reporters for tacking this bizarre note to the litany of bloody atrocities which otherwise pervaded their articles.[105]

Day Three and Beyond

Only a morning session had been scheduled for day three; it proved anticlimactic after the appearance of Bart Osborne. The "testimony was milder than the two previous days" was the opinion of the *New York Times*. Bob Johnson delivered a brief, but eloquent, summation quoted respectfully in the few press accounts to document that final day. In private Johnson had a spacy comic side; an image of Bill Lee, the zany former Red Sox pitcher, comes to mind. That morning Bob showed the bright, articulate side that must have gotten him into West Point. For content, he stuck closely to the CCI liturgy: he called on the Pentagon to stop scapegoating the My Lai defendants, and to halt the Calley trial. He then expressed the final appeal of the National Veterans Inquiry for an independent investigation into U.S. war crimes policies, the "prospect" for which "did not look overly promising," commented Jules Witcover in his article for the next morning's *Los Angeles Times*.[106]

A UPI wrap-up got scant coverage across the country, but the *Washington Post*, which had ignored the NVI once it opened, ran a thoughtful piece by columnist Nicholas von Hoffman under the ambiguous heading "Psychological Slavery." This was the condition from which Lou Font and Bob Johnson had freed themselves, according to von Hoffman, in contrast to a majority of their fellow West Pointers who put loyalty to the academy above any higher principles; in this case, a duty to acknowledge, as Von Hoffman put it, the "now warehouses full of evidence demonstrating that the United States, as a matter of policy, violates the Geneva Convention almost daily."[107]

For three days, forty-plus Vietnam veterans paraded troubled memories before the mostly skeptical members of the Washington press corps who'd come to hear them. One sensed the press had grown weary — and more wary — of the war crimes issue in the ten months since CCI had launched its crusade. There was no place left to go with these horrific tales. Most reporters knew damn well that no matter how hard CCI and the vets pushed, the war crimes issue would never reach a critical mass, a point beyond which the government could no longer avoid re-examining its war policies in the light of our charges. It just wasn't going to happen. By and large the reporters were pissed to be there, getting their stomachs turned — again — for nothing.

Still, they did what reporters do — they filed their stories, applying the most rote presentation of the facts that their craft permits. The six articles I have re-read from the coverage of the NVI on that first day are remarkably similar as individual compositions go; they vary in content in that each reporter assembles the litany of horrors that perhaps most startled or repelled him personally.

Gary Battles' account of grenades hurled into a well after a Vietnamese woman and child were thrown in, and the bits of flesh flying twenty feet in the air, made the cut in three of the six articles. It was precisely the shock effect of such nightmarish detail that CCI grimly trafficked in, while relentlessly associating each atrocity throughout the proceedings with a particular tactical practice or field policy.

A former grunt, Gary Battles could well have been cast by Martin Scorsese over Willem Dafoe as lead for *The Last Temptation of Christ*. Gary's burden of combat was so heavy, his remorse so profound, that he seemed near the brink of inconsolable despair. He was so emotionally unwrapped that we — the CCI organizers — actually debated whether to let him testify, only half-daring to fear that we had a potential suicide on our hands.[108]

In the end, it was Gary's call; as long as we believed he was telling the truth we had no more grounds to censor his account, nor thwart his willingness to make it public, than we had for any other credible vet witness. Ultimately Gary had no intention to remain quiet about his hellish experiences in Nam. Like me, like so many of the other guys, Gary Battles was a man possessed by newfound powers of conviction, and driven to proclaim the insanities of war.

Only two reporters even bothered to solicit some predictably absurd dissembling from the Pentagon. In an odd, unsigned piece for the *New York Times* where the name of each witness is annoyingly prefaced by the phrase "a veteran identified as," the reporter serves up this anemic homily from a Defense Department spokesperson: "Army regulations require personnel on active duty to report allegations of violations of the Uniform Code of Military Justice and/or the laws of ground warfare immediately upon their discovery." While Richard Dudman of the *St. Louis Post Dispatch*, seemingly tongue-in-cheek, inquired of the army's chief information officer who had served in Vietnam under William Westmoreland, whether the commanding general might once have said — as veteran Larry Rottmann claimed —"I want more emphasis on body count," the army flack objected, no doubt with fingers crossed, that "General Westmoreland never would have said anything like that."[109]

A Fantasy

My overall impression remains that the NVI was indeed widely covered. In general the press accounts were accurate and of a goodly length, starkly saturated with gruesome horror tales from the battlefield. Many reporters dutifully included fragments of CCI's politics and analysis in their coverage.

Despite the presence at the NVI of one or two distinguished journalists of Richard Dudman's stature, this was by no means the literary branch of the working press.[110] Can you imagine that, say, H.L. Mencken, the great cynic of American journalism, would have permitted his own bile, much less the unpopularity of the war crimes issue, to dull his wits or pen after witnessing the pageant of grotesques we laid before the press in Washington? Mencken's story would certainly have spared no feelings in official circles, and who knows what kind of drubbing the vets might have gotten; but a reader would retain a piece of Mencken's mind long after putting down the morning paper.

Or maybe the NVI required a more profound sensibility, say, a Hannah Arendt, whose reports on the Eichmann trial in Jerusalem for the *New Yorker* will perpetually froth with controversy owing to her association of Eichmann's monstrous deeds with "the banality of evil."[111] An active, daring mind like Arendt's might have stretched that insight to cover the utter ordinariness of the evil in our own Vietnam combat practices to which one veteran after another bore witness.

The NVI ought to have made more of an impression on the public consciousness at the time; it deserves to have been branded deeply into the historical record of the period. It didn't and it wasn't. CCI and the various constellations of vets, with the zeal of those who nurture and promote lost causes, carried on the "good fight" of the war crimes issue for another six months before transferring to other terrains the struggle in the belly of the beast against the imperialist dark side of the American Century.

Letting Down, but Not Letting Up

I remember a letdown when the curtain closed on the NVI, but I'm numb to the details. Tod stirs a vague recollection of the great party Bart

Osborne threw for all the vets at his DC apartment, which, for one reporter observing the same scene, was "an uncomfortably crowded place to drink wine." One man's treasure ... Tod talks about the enormous catharsis, "a sense of release ... completion." Maybe not so nice for Jeremy, whom Tod pictures for the second time in emotional collapse, "at the end of it having sat there ... sobbing." Tod's feeling permitted him a momentary disengagement. He and his old pal, Bob Holt, who'd worked with CCI briefly as Winter Soldier's administrator, left for Warsaw the next morning, and a month of pub hopping behind the Iron Curtain. Jeremy's and my feelings kept us stuck to the grindstone.[112]

10. Skirmishing in Washington: 1971

After the National Veterans Inquiry Jeremy and I kept up our runs to DC, working the national press around CCI's findings and probing Capitol Hill for an opening to set the war crimes issue on someone's congressional agenda. One afternoon in early January, returning home aboard the New York–bound Metroliner, we spotted reporter Neil Sheehan a few seats to our front. Just a week before, Sheehan had savaged Mark Lane and his book *Conversations with Americans* in a review for the Sunday *New York Times*.[113] Jeremy leapt at this chance encounter, and spent the remainder of the trip urging Sheehan to look on CCI's work as an antidote to Lane's reckless sensationalism. He must have been convincing because, before the month was out, Sheehan would cover CCI's ongoing campaign in two separate articles for the *Times*.[114]

As a personal attack on the author's credibility, Sheehan's review in the trendsetting *Sunday Times* doomed Lane's book to ignominy, canceling completely the ambivalent, yet by no means dismissive, reception the work had received from other critics a month earlier.[115]

Sheehan had approached his assignment more as reporter than reviewer. He quoted unidentified sources in the Pentagon who claimed that several of Lane's vets never set foot in Vietnam, much less participated in the brutalizations they describe. One vet told Lane the most outlandish fib: that his own father commanded a highly visible combat regiment in Vietnam, the 11th Armored Cavalry — even as the interview was being conducted. This, noted Sheehan, was "a simple and obvious fact," one the author might have easily verified. Such facts were "not relevant," parried Lane, arguing with Sheehan over the phone just before the review went to press. "The most unreliable source regarding the verification of atrocities," Lane lectured Sheehan, "is the Defense Department."[116]

Sheehan has the last word. The review's closing sentence strikes a pontificating note, and Sheehan does not fail to aim a parting dig at his charlatan foe. "Until the country does summon up the courage to convene a responsible inquiry"— until hell freezes over, Sheehan may as well have written if he'd chosen to be more direct — "we probably deserve the Mark Lanes." Arguably, Sheehan's engagement with the issue was an ambiguous one. While documenting the facts of aggression, he would never acknowledge or break with the hegemonic intentions that underlie American war policies; in a word, a classic fence sitter, neither hawk nor dove.[117]

As for the impact of Sheehan's review on the fate of the antiwar vets' movement, the record seems fairly unambiguous. "VVAW," concludes Andrew Hunt in *The Turning: A History of Vietnam Veterans Against the War*, "escaped from the imbroglio unharmed." Not even a disinformation campaign against VVAW hatched in the Nixon White House by high level staffers Haldemann, Erlichman and Colby — all later convicted and jailed for their roles in the Watergate cover-up — could tarnish the organization's sympathetic public image, nor stem its dramatic growth. VVAW continued to draw its primal energies throughout 1971 from the war crimes issue, and blossomed that year into a genuine mass movement — albeit of brief duration — within the larger national community of Vietnam veterans. Rising in prominence only during the late stages of the war's opposition, VVAW outlasted many other radical political formations of the sixties and early seventies.[118]

Sheehan would, nonetheless, briefly tread the dialectic between objective observer of the war crimes controversy and actual, if reluctant, player within its bounds. Quite early in his reporting Sheehan recognized the troubling "moral issue" attending certain facts about the Vietnam war, notably that "the majority of civilian casualties result from American and South Vietnamese air strikes."[119] In his review of Lane four years later, Sheehan reformulated this conviction with greater force: "the basic military tactics of the war, the air and artillery bombardments that have taken an untold number of civilian lives, is open to examination under the criteria established by the Nuremberg tribunal."[120]

By invoking Nuremberg, even if only for rhetorical effect, Sheehan fixed the seal of authority from our national newspaper of record to the movement's own line on the criminal nature of the American air war in Vietnam. By indicating, moreover, a broader trail of criminality traceable from the war's "basic military tactics," the former war correspondent had, unwittingly, made common cause with CCI.

11. Nuremberg, USA

Neither Jeremy nor I harbored the slightest illusion that Neil Sheehan had become a fellow traveler on the revolutionary trail; it was the legitimacy and readership of the *Times* we were after. As for motive, Sheehan could look to his own salvation like the rest of us. We'd brushed aside our own emotional fallout from the strenuous, year-long drive to organize the NVI. Now we pushed on doggedly, faithful to CCI's primary mission: to attract the maximum attention of the mainstream media to veterans' accounts of American atrocities in Vietnam.

If the public wanted to turn its face from the gore, like movie goers at a horror film,[121] then CCI remained committed to accommodate this ritual squeamishness with as many more pop up ghouls as we could reel before them in the months ahead. Whether, or in what form, our anguished cries reverberated in high places was of minimal concern, so long as we could help pump up the volume of national disgust toward the war by appropriating the very news outlets that official pro-war advocates had used for years to mute and befuddle the public.

We were guided only lightly by theory, and would never distill a strategic plan to press our call for an official war crimes inquiry, much less identify any true mechanism for putting such a plan into action. Consistent with the drift of politics within the late New Left, and despite our group's relentless single issue orientation, CCI's revolutionary rhetoric was increasingly strident and pretentious — even as our sights stayed ever focused on the immediate task of ending the war.

The Dick Cavett Show

Just days after buttonholing Neil Sheehan on the Metroliner, Jeremy and I sat in the audience for a taping session of ABC's late night talk show hosted by Dick Cavett. Through some prestidigious feat of New Left hucksterism, Jeremy had convinced the show's producer to include CCI's Bob Johnson in Cavett's interview with Telford Taylor. General Taylor had served as chief United States prosecutor at the Nuremberg trials after World War II, and was now a distinguished law professor at Columbia University, and a retired brigadier general in the Army Reserve.

Taylor had just published a scholarly work on war crimes titled *Nuremberg and Vietnam: An American Tragedy*.[122] In it, he wrote that if the standard used to judge General Tomayuki Yamashita — a Japanese commander in World War II held responsible for the conduct of his troops in the Philippines, and later hanged by the U.S. Army in occupied Tokyo — were applied to the American high command in Vietnam, men like General William C. Westmoreland might be vulnerable to trial for war crimes.

When Taylor reiterated this opinion even more explicitly in response to a question by Cavett, Jeremy rushed to a pay phone in the lobby and called Neil Sheehan in Washington. "You've got to get a transcript," he excitedly beseeched the reporter. "Telford Taylor just called Westmoreland a war criminal on national television."

Sheehan did just that. He secured and read the transcript, then he interviewed Taylor at home by phone. Sheehan's article ran in the next morning's *Times*, midway into the paper, but under a shocker of a headline — "Taylor Says by Nuremberg Rules Westmoreland May Be Guilty" — that must have singed the soul of at least one general officer when an aide whispered the news in his ear that morning.[123]

What a country, where such a thought can be expressed in open forum, a free press, not censored or suppressed as it most certainly would have been elsewhere on the planet, even in the most prosperous, stable and democratic places. What a gesture! What epiphany! A metaphor for the times, one might dare to suggest. All of which may or may not be true. But as a news story it went nowhere, a total bust. Like a shooting star, Sheehan's article rose from the pages of the *Times* and crested somewhere beyond the beyond, never to be seen or heard from again. What a country indeed! You could almost watch the contradictions being disappeared into its institutional pores before your very eyes; truly, this was the "one dimensional" Marcusian society supreme, just as Tod and Jeremy, and now I, believed.

Sheehan's story may have died instantly, but it was born living. It was, in fact, a true scoop because the Cavett Show wouldn't even air until Saturday evening of the same day the article appeared. Sheehan had assembled his story from a variety of sources: the show, the interview with Taylor, adding a few quotes from the general's new book, and, not unexpectedly, from the defense bureaucracy itself.

In Sheehan's lead paragraph we find the historical *j'accuse*, or what passes for such in the some-say, others-say brand of journalism practiced by members of today's fourth estate, much tamed since when, only two generations earlier, an Émile Zola, crusading to save Major Dreyfus, could address his readers as both guardian of fact and passionate participant in the drama he reported. Nor did Zola speak from the margins like radicals of the New Left, but from the very core of his nation's political life.

Still I find it amazing enough that, in the news the *Times* saw fit to print that day, the very first sentence of Sheehan's article contained the string of words, duly attributed to Telford Taylor, that "General William C. Westmoreland ... might be convicted as a war criminal." Sheehan went further. He associated other civilian leaders with the word Nuremberg, naming Dean Rusk, Robert S. McNamara, McGeorge Bundy and Walt W. Rostow — the greatest of the New Left's great Satans behind U.S. Vietnam policy — and thus, by implication, conjured the impossible imagery of an American Nuremberg. For one flashing instant these American war makers were lined up before readers of the almighty *New York Times*, and in the mind's eye of surely some, were pictured sitting on the benches where Nazis were condemned.

It would be absurd to suggest that CCI was the tail wagging the dog — our fling with Sheehan was just a two night stand — but with the power of the *New York Times* to yank a reaction to Taylor's comments from the Defense Department — not just some flack catcher on the night shift, but a couple of big fries — we couldn't help but feel we too had had our hands upon the halyard.

CCI's polemical batteries had been lobbing verbal charges at the Pentagon for a year, but this was the only time we learned immediately of a direct hit. If we inflicted a scratch on anyone, it was, at best, a wound of pride. One hopes, at least, that the then–secretary of the army, Stanley Resor had to stiffen his upper lip when revealing to Sheehan that the army had already "rejected a formal charge of war crimes under the Yamashita standard made against General Westmoreland by one of the Mylai defendants."[124]

Asked to comment on Taylor's legal opinions, the army's general counsel Robert E. Jordan 3rd argued in lawyerly fashion that "the Yamashita precedent did not apply to General Westmoreland in the Mylai case because the Army had determined that the general had taken 'reasonable precautions ... all that one would expect a major commander to take.'" The progeny of General Yamashita might be pardoned for seeing in Victor's Justice a mask for human sacrifice to the gods of revenge.

CCI's Bob Johnson has his cameo in the final paragraphs of Sheehan's piece when the reporter quoted his response to Cavett's question about our work, again giving the standard CCI recitation about widespread torture practices by Americans, about which allegations, Sheehan notes, General Taylor declined to comment. Nonetheless, adds Sheehan, the former Nuremberg prosecutor "shares with Mr. Johnson the belief that circumscribed official inquiries like the courts-martial of the Mylai defendants fell far short of what was needed."

The only other independently documented reference to Sheehan's January 9th article I know of occurs in a second article he himself wrote three days after the Cavett show. Covering CCI's latest tactical thrust, working with a group called the Concerned Officers Movement (COM), the reporter quotes himself.[125]

CCI's collaboration with COM,[126] a loosely organized antiwar network of junior officers still on active duty, dated from our initial contacts with Lieutenant Lou Font and Captain Bob Master in the weeks preceding the NVI. By mid–January 1971, CCI was helping other COM activists package their political opposition into public events like the press conference Sheehan himself attended at the Dupont Plaza Hotel on January 12.

The following morning the *New York Times* was again drafted as publicist for what was unmistakably by this point Sheehan's personal crusade, the call for an official government inquiry. Sheehan reinforced this advocacy through "five young officers" whom, he reported, "said today that they were asking the Secretaries of the Army and the Navy to convene formal courts of inquiry into the question of war crimes and atrocities in Vietnam."

There is an eerie foreshadowing in Sheehan's piece of an issue that would only fully explode within the U.S. body politic toward the end of the decade, the Agent Orange health controversy. In the young officers' letters to the service secretaries, Sheehan noted their reference to "a report published two weeks ago by the American Association for the Advancement of Science, which said the use of chemical herbicides in South Vietnam was causing catastrophic ecological effects."[127] Sheehan then abruptly reiterated the comments General Taylor made "on television," emphasizing once more the analogy to Nuremberg, before ending the article with an account of my own failed attempt, called into him that same afternoon before deadline, to hand deliver the COM activists' letters, along with a 300 page transcript of the NVI testimony, to Secretary John H. Chafee of the United States Navy.

Jeremy and I drove together to the Pentagon, and I went in alone with the documents. I'd gotten directions and walked rapidly through the long, sterile corridors, fury and loathing for the military molded to the furrows of my brow, before coming to the anteroom of the secretary's office. With a stare of contempt the equal of my own, a naval officer who served as Chafee's aide reached for the material, but I demanded a receipt. He refused, so I grabbed the package, vented a few unkind remarks, then fled the office in a rage.

On seeing me in this volcanic state, Jeremy's "What's going on?" had a tone of uncharacteristic spontaneity, which I promptly deflected with a torrent of political ranting to mask my ineffective performance. That business about a "receipt" had been pure improvisation. The point was to deliver the goods as advertised. Period. What the other side did with it — or didn't do with it — was not part of the script. But, in this reckless crossing to the enemy camp, I'd become entangled again in that old fear and loathing of military authority. My emotions ran amuck; I felt short of breath, my brain as swollen as my tongue. Politics aside, this was personal.

12. On Top Down Under

That Pentagon meltdown was not just about military authority. At 26 I was only beginning to construct a truly public self, one which — if I only knew what to say — could speak in a voice of its own. I was still very much in the throes of sorting through the trope-ways of an identity within the movement when from out of the blue came a letter inviting my participation at an antiwar conference in Australia. "We are endeavoring," it read in part, "to bring to this country a number of overseas personalities who could be key speakers."[128]

Imagine Cinderella's amazement at being summoned to the ball. That's how I felt. The invitation seemed that improbable. Certainly I hungered for anointment as an "overseas personality," someone standing in relief against the pageantry of social outrage engendered by the New Left; but the few lines I'd been given to date barely constituted a speaking part. No one at CCI had that national stature that the media and the movement conferred upon, say, the old guard of SDS, or the yippie royalty, and me, among our inner three-some, least of all.

The timing of the invitation's arrival lessened its immediate impact around the office. This was November, the marathon days for organizing the NVI, and the Australian conference wasn't scheduled till mid–February, three months down the road. Jeremy half-heartedly tried to guilt-trip me into declining, arguing that I was needed for the struggle on the home front, while Tod, impressed and perhaps a little jealous, countered that I'd be a fool to turn it down. Jeremy was probably right, but you can guess whose advice I followed.

The biggest battle surrounding this unexpected recognition was with my own self-confidence. In a second letter came a list of conference themes and topics, along with my assignment. "We would like you to present a major paper on 'the Development and state of the war in Indo-China.'" And could I plan to arrive the 15th of February, and remain at least three weeks for a tour of speaking dates throughout the country? In reply I demurred that my academic training was not in the area I was asked to address. Describing my practical activities within the antiwar effort as "organizing vets around the war crimes issue," I offered instead to speak on these experiences. "Let me reassure you," came the answer, "regarding the relevance of [your] contribution ... at the conference."[129]

I was reassured to the extent that this fantasy-laden junket was not about to be withdrawn. Common sense, if not consciousness, confirmed the logic and authenticity of my selection — certainly not as a "personality" — but as a credible eyewitness from the battlefield. There weren't exactly legions of young former officers — and none from the intelligence community — who'd crossed to the antiwar side with the intensity of my commitment. Besides, some political directorate — the Vietnamese themselves for all I knew — had undoubtedly endorsed my candidacy; my name wasn't just picked from a hat. Reading the list of international delegates, moreover, it was clear that the organizers of the conference were inclined toward substance over celebrity; except for one highly regarded French political scientist and academic, Phillipe Devillers, I didn't recognize a single name.

Winter Soldier Redux

Substance — circa late 1970 — did not yet mean the choice of a vet from the rank and file. Grunt power was on the rise, and it would not be long before former combatants — overwhelmingly from the enlisted ranks — would mount antiwar platforms at home and abroad under a strictly veteran sponsorship, typically VVAW's. An unexpected setback had momentarily stalled, then explosively hastened, these developments within the antiwar veterans' movement.

The historical impulse for this transformation was the Winter Soldier Investigation, which finally took place in Detroit exactly two months after the National Veterans Inquiry in DC. Despite its claim to three times as many veteran witnesses, WSI was virtually ignored by the mainstream media. Whether WSI's failure to light up the news can be laid to the lingering stench of scandal from Neil Sheehan's attack on Mark Lane — which many in the confraternity of the press may have failed to distinguish from an assault on the war crimes movement itself — has been the subject of an inconclusive debate within several specialized histories of the period. Some VVAW leaders eventually concluded that Washington was indeed a better bet for this undertaking than Detroit.[130]

Following the split with CCI, Lane had worked tirelessly behind the scenes in Detroit to bring about the WSI; after the *Times* review, his VVAW comrades reluctantly requested he refrain from further public association with the event.[131] In the end, Lane's energies — in partnership with those of Jane Fonda and a stalwart group of VVAW organizers — contributed to a much richer measure of success for the Winter Soldier Investigation than a fleeting moment of attention by the news media could provide. Winter Soldier cemented VVAW's organizational capacity for mobilizing antiwar vets on a scale previously unimagined, culminating in several actions over the next few months that no account of the antiwar movement's twilight days can ignore.

❖   ❖   ❖

All roads of opposition now led to Washington. Scent and instinct —
certainly not analysis or unity of action — notified virtually every pack and
gang within the New Left that the Beast was weakened and in retreat. Revolution was in the air. Not the revolution of the Declaration, or the Bastille,
or the Winter Palace. In the idiom of the hour this was a revolution of blown
minds. And it was spreading nationwide with the creeping inevitability of a
glacier.

In result, the world *before* Vietnam and the world *after* Vietnam, not
just in the United States but globally, would be two very different places.
Anyone formed in the culture of the fifties coming of age in the culture of
the sixties/seventies might reasonably argue the revolutionary nature of that
transformation, and mostly for the good. Even Power was reduced a notch
and Freedom gained in proportion; empowerment was not just individual,
but social and political; naturally, every advance has been — and continues to
be — challenged, sometimes rolled back, by reaction.

By 1971 a hundred tactics bloomed within the movement. Some were
self-deluding and dysfunctional. But every foot in opposition one way or
another joined to brake the imperial momentum that resisted an end to the
war.[132] If a given New Left group or activist nurtured the illusion that the balance of forces in the United States favored a transfer of power, even in the
glaring absence of any apparatus or program to make that dream reality, well,
that was too bad. Not all the casualties of war were on the battlefield; there
were Purple Hearts and Psycho Section 8's galore throughout the movement
too.

And now the masses — some in the streets — but most whose attitudes
only registered in polls as public opinion — were changing sides as well. While,
amazingly, in Vietnam itself, and on U.S. military installations everywhere,
rank and file troops lived in open rebellion and could no longer be counted
on as an effective implement of state violence.[133] We now know that, at this
stage of events, the strategy of the war managers and their allies among the
ruling elites was not to win in Vietnam, and, ultimately, not even to preserve
an independent Saigon, but to retire from the field behind a racist face-sav-
ing public relations campaign, the so called Vietnamization of the war that
Nixon characterized as Peace with Honor.[134]

❖   ❖   ❖

In our rounds to lobby a handful of progressive-thinking Congresspersons, only one door initially opened to us. It proved the ideal perch for CCI's

next major undertaking. Ronald Dellums had just taken office as the honorable representative from Oakland, California — home to the Black Panther Party and a constituency generally to the left of virtually every other American congressional district.

On a given day Dellums could spout anti-imperialist rhetoric as radical as any member of the Chicago 7 without damage to his standing among the home folk. Dellums's office was probably the smallest suite available on Capitol Hill. He was assigned an anteroom with inner office, and an annex down the corridor, cramped and unattached, in the old Longworth House Office Building. In that annex CCI set up a three-panel display of captioned photographs depicting American atrocities in Vietnam. And, on January 28th, we held a press conference there announcing "War Crimes Office Set Up in Congressman Dellums' Suite."

With Tod back from Europe to help organize the next wave of activity, CCI was now positioned to mount its latest New Left morality play within the very halls of Congress. Simultaneously, VVAW was working to bring thousands of vets to Washington for a movement "spring offensive" that would culminate in the historic May Day demonstrations. Hard feelings about Winter Soldier were submerged while CCI and VVAW collaborated, informally, on one final war crimes extravaganza.

❖ ❖ ❖

So little doubt did I have about my true calling as a radical activist, that I finally resigned from the doctoral program at NYU with enough credits for a master's I would never claim. The politicization of my private life was now complete, and I belonged body and soul to this new world within a world. Between them, the New Left and the counterculture had colonized enormous patches of American reality. Woodstock Nation wasn't just a fantasy if you changed that second word to Network. A movement activist roaming that "ribbon of highways" Woody Guthrie rhapsodized, conjuring the America of our ideals, could find a crash pad and communal meal in pretty much Anywhere, USA, during the early nineteen-seventies.

These transient encounters with fellow travelers, marked by political discussion and debate, were education in the truest sense, as one discovered that history speaks in tongues and community isn't always everything it's cracked up to be.[135] Sectarianism was rampant; still a pragmatic solidarity trumped most differences. One simply avoided the more robotic Leninists and the self-hating fringes, whether lumpenized banditos or their opposites — lost souls from the guilt-inducing perches of affluence — who grooved on pure adventurism.

13. A Personality Abroad

I'd been on the movement barricades for over a year, but didn't realize just how green I remained politically until reading the humiliating photo caption the day after arriving in Australia. A hastily prepared press conference had been arranged by the local organizers to welcome the delegation of three Americans, Peter Wiley, Patti Iiyama, and myself, all, unbeknownst to one another, on the same flight. The next morning, there's a group shot in the Sydney paper. I'm a total longhair now, shoulder length but kempt, still the trademark bushy moustache, but costumed in a subtle tweedy suit with club-style tie that makes me look both more together and straighter than I really am — a hip technocrat, or, maybe a young foundation executive. But I am not hip. I am, in fact, a political moron.

Responding to a reporter's question to define my politics, I managed some garbled nonsense that, reduced to three words, came out as "conservative revolutionary communist."[136] Now I knew well enough that such a formulation did not exist. No communist faction would tar itself with the modifier "conservative." This was a slander, a demeaning slur, an indictment, not a way any self-respecting communist would describe himself.

What the Australian antiwar conference needed for a bit of media attention just then was not, as things turned out, more seasoned movement heavies from overseas with airtight revolutionary raps, but a bonafide Vietnam vet. They didn't seem to have anyone yet down under for that particular role. The country had experienced several celebrated anti-draft cases, but no one who'd served with the Aussie unit in Vietnam had, I gathered, made much in public about their opposition. And, of course, there was nothing in Australia equivalent to a group like CCI, a self-appointed cadre who chose organizing antiwar vets as their primary political work. So, from a local media point of view, I was a ripe news peg for the goings-on in the Australian antiwar movement over the next couple of weeks.

My Australian handlers had clearly anticipated this possibility, and showed me a demanding tour schedule that would repay in kind their outlays for my airfare and upkeep. Not a half-hour from the airport I stood before a group of striking railways workers, and a bunch of tough looking gents they were. "What the fuck am I doing ranting at these guys," I was thinking, as I duly delivered my rap on war crimes. As it turned out, they weren't actually striking; they'd wildcatted for the day because, as one placard announced, "Railway commissioner refuses our right to hear M. Uhl American Ex-Serviceman." Originally the talk was to take place on company property. I

Addressing workers at the Chullora Locomotive Work Shops, Sydney, Australia, February 1971.

got a polite hearing from these trade unionists, probably considerably to the left of their U.S. counterparts, and, at least nominally, opposed to the war. But I knew these fellows were focused more on the loaves and fishes than the parable, and I was happy to serve as their excuse for a small skirmish with management over the terms of control in the workplace.[137]

I was then installed in the Sydney flat of an activist couple just long enough for a costume change. The agenda had me addressing the opening session of the conference that same afternoon for forty-five minutes, three times longer than the fifteen minutes allotted each of the other four speakers. Well, you wanted this, I kept saying to myself, but my doubts about pulling it off with any novelty or grace had me humbled, even in my own self-glorifying eyes. Really, my only true preparation for a spotlight anywhere near this intense had been on the high school stage, there abandoned after "going up" a half-dozen times, as actors say when they forget their lines, in the last of our three plays during senior year. Stage fright, in part, was a disability of the ill-prepared.

Fortunately I had learned that much and carried with me a twenty-five page paper I'd written in New York for the occasion, "Exposing U.S. War Crimes Through Veteran Organizing." Thirty years later it reads better than I remembered; I did stick pretty much to what I knew. A number of texts are cited, Taylor's *Nuremberg and Vietnam*, Chomsky's *At War with Asia* and "After Pinkville," and others, but I leaned most heavily on Edward Herman's *Atrocities in Vietnam: Myths and Realities* as a frame for my own polemic. The voices of veterans appear in the many fragments of testimony lifted from the NVI transcript and inserted strategically throughout my presentation.

When I stepped upon the stage that afternoon, I'd left the suit behind, and stood before the delegates in my tie-dyed hippie garb; I certainly wanted to appear self-assured in my radicalism. There was no problem if I kept to what I'd written; my line on the war and crimes of the American Imperium was in perfect harmony with the rhetoric prevailing throughout the revolutionary Left. Moreover, this was not mere posture, it had become my truth as well. What I dreaded was having to extemporize a revolutionary analysis on the hoof.

A fatal weakness afflicting our movement involved gut-checking one's comrades' politics, especially for any residual hints of liberal sentiment about the war. "The liberal is light as a feather, not heavy like Mount Tai," instructed Chairman Mao in his "little red book." At CCI we laughed at the lock-step Maoists in our midst who spouted such homilies, though we actually approved of this one. Maoists were one thing, Mao something else, widely considered among radicals of diverse affiliations as, with Fidel, the greatest revolutionaries of our times. If Mao's exhortations in the folk imagery of the Chinese peasantry seemed overly quaint to postindustrial ears, the Chairman's unambiguous political command to "Combat Liberalism" was adopted as a staple of rectification within the movement. To most activists it made perfect sense to aim the first blows of the Revolution toward advocates of bankrupt liberalism when you intoned a litany of names like McNamara, Rostow, the Bundy boys, and Kissinger.

Personally, I was unfazed by the threat of being labeled a liberal — that wasn't the ideology you were bred to defend — and therefore rebel from — where I grew up on the conservative shores of Republican Long Island. The person I was becoming was a lot closer to the person I felt at home with. But I still hadn't exposed my identity to a deeper introspection, and while I'd borrowed the shorthand rhetoric of the movement to represent my fury over Vietnam, this false voice of certainty would later yield to the writer's healthy skepticism that, however wedded to the ideals of humanism, took pride in the unpredictability of its own — sometimes cranky — originality.

In Australia my eyewitness account engaged an appreciative audience at the opening session of the antiwar conference, while my politics, sufficiently exhortatory and general, had that *nihil obstat* stamp of New Left orthodoxy. Later that evening, eighteen hundred people filled the Sydney Town Hall for a public rally against the war and now, with half the time to speak, I could only summarize my paper from hastily scribbled notes. Whatever I managed to say that night was cleaned up considerably for the *Tribune*, and the words reported were worthy of a Lenin. While a fair reflection of my angry views, they weren't mine:

Speaking at the National Anti-war Conference in Sydney, February 1971.

"Today it is the responsibility of every American to drive from power the renegades and criminals who govern the U.S. today, and the corrupt academics and the huge corporate interests that stand behind them," said Michael Uhl. "It's time to redistribute the power those small groups hold, both within America and internationally."[138]

❖   ❖   ❖

It's hardly news that politics and bad acting approach synonymity, nor that the public stage is a breeding ground for demagogues. The windy rhetoric and grandstanding antics of movement politicians were modeled on the very elites whose rule we opposed. Such power as the New Left gathered to itself, it wielded through all the familiar arrangements of hierarchy and inequality. But, perhaps because the movement played for limited — if momentous — stakes, never for all the marbles as some may have fantasized, spaces were set aside for pleasures that only occur when the spirit of competition is suspended.

Free of so many constraints of convention, free to think for ourselves and to associate with others on the basis of ideas and ideals, not just self-interest as dictated by market forces, I knew good times with strangers in the movement that I've seldom experienced before or since the years being chronicled here. However casual or transitory these encounters, there were genuine exchanges of affection that far outstripped that quick fix of good conscience that do-gooders thrive on when they bestow some act of kindness on a wayfarer in need. These good feelings were particularly concentrated in my brief contacts with the comrades who provided me with care and company while in Australia, and several sheaves of letters remind me still of how those friendships followed me home as correspondents and were sustained over several years.

The frailty of my constitution had not been evident in the year I'd combined graduate studies and work with CCI, despite the intense commitment and long hours. In the excitement and empowerment of those exertions, I'd managed to ignore the damage both the war and TB had wrecked on my stamina. But it didn't take my comrades in Australia long to witness how the strain of public speaking weakened me to the point where I began to lose my voice halfway though a given talk, and could continue only with difficulty by gulping water to lubricate every other sentence. To keep me in form for the weeks of touring they began to shave some lesser obligations from my schedule, and husband my energies especially for encounters with the media.[139]

A week before traveling to New Zealand for that country's antiwar conference, and the second leg of my speaking tour, Australian friends prescribed some R&R. A few Australian politicos and I rapped with American GIs on the streets of Sydney. These troopers, in for their own R&R from Nam, probably preferred "round eyed" over "slant eyed" women for their five days of freedom from the war, a hotly debated issue in bunker-bull sessions when I was there. We civilians preached the New Left gospel, and the GIs answered with Right Ons!—like Hosannas; what we thought we'd accomplish, I'll never know. Maybe words act like the wearing of amulets, if not proof against meeting that bullet with your name on it, they might inspire an extra measure of caution in the one who wears—or in this case—hears them.

There was a brief fling in Sydney, and my companion and I, and a few others—one a Catholic priest, which I—quite prudishly—thought very odd at the time—all went skinny-dipping at dawn in downtown Bondi Beach, the rough equivalent of the strand at Oak Street along the Gold Coast of Chicago; an exhausted penguin, who'd been involuntarily swept north by currents from its home on the continental icecap, emerged from the warm summer waters and stumbled about the sand. She looked like I felt, but recovery was no longer an option for her.

I then traveled to Melbourne and visited with friends in the CP who turned me on to the delights of the Australian wine country on the outskirts of the city. Unfairly, no doubt, I couldn't then imagine their counterparts in leadership positions of the party of Gus Hall, chairman of the CPUSA, and company being quite as laid back as these folk. Blame it on history. If humans are capable of making history, the opposite is also true: the Communist Party down under operated more openly than, and was not subjected to the same degree of repression and demonology as, its U.S. affiliate, whose most public members bore the markings of pariahs, and often behaved accordingly.

A comparison between the photos of me which appear in the Australian papers and those of New Zealand are the best evidence that I'd regained some strength and composure thanks to the regimen of leisure my Aussie comrades had enforced. Or maybe the Kiwi photographers just caught me at better angles, because, in their shots, I look five years younger and downright tranquil. But there's another facet to my transfiguration: I was on this kind of weird publicity high after departing Melbourne for Auckland.

A very peculiar thing took place when I checked in for that flight. As I approached the counter, the attendant, all perk and smiles, waving a folder at me, said loudly as I was still twenty paces off, "I have your ticket right here, Mr. Uhl." She even pronounced my name correctly, to rhyme with Yule. A few evenings earlier, I'd been interviewed for over twenty minutes on Australia's hour-long national news broadcast. Everyone who watched TV news in Australia in those days tuned into this nightly show on the country's only network.

In getting the celebrity treatment that comes with instant recognition, I experienced something of that immortal surge Andy Warhol signified with his quip about everyone being entitled to fifteen minutes of prime time. And still, I cringed at being seen but not known, becoming — however effervescently — a stationary target any stranger could sight in his scope. Was Big Brother watching? Indeed he was. Half my CIA file, modestly thin, contains the same set of overseas news clippings that I myself collected, plus a sheaf of dispatches — most of the contents blacked out in the copies the agency provided me — that the Company operatives in Australia forwarded to CIA headquarters in Langley, Virginia.

❖   ❖   ❖

In San Francisco before returning east I met with Tom Hayden, by then the non-leader of a Berkeley commune called the Red Family.[140] Hayden had contacted CCI a month or so earlier, a virtual summons to support a war crimes inquiry he was planning for the West Coast. The brochure from Hayden outlined the various types and categories of American war crimes, but gave equal emphasis to the Red Family's unstinting support for Vietnam's revolution and victory on the battlefield. This was the left-turn much of the movement had taken by now, us too, with, in my circle, considerable reservation toward the more exaggerated expressions of third world worship. There had been some resentment at the tone of Hayden's one-line note, hastily scribbled on the margin of his flyer. After the Mark Lane fiasco, neither Tod nor Jeremy wanted to risk a sketchy alliance with another prima donna who would only dance to his own tune. CCI would work with them, I would tell Hayden, but only on a one-shot basis with full cosponsorship.

Red Family indeed! Another ultra-leftist dream machine. I already knew about the group's extracurricular fixation with firearms; they trained and took target practice in the Berkeley Hills. Yet Hayden's track record in the movement was not so easily denigrated or dismissed. His media image of adventurism seemed to capture Hayden's less interesting talents for self-promotion, while obscuring his decade-long commitment to organizing in the civil rights movement, and later in marginalized neighborhoods of the inner city.

If a project stamped with Hayden's sponsorship, like the Red Family's agitation in Berkeley for community control of the police, seemed impossibly utopian, there was, belying the edgy polemic and pig-baiting, a commitment to the expansion of democratic possibilities. Rereading some of Hayden's writings from this period, I am struck by his grasp and elaboration of the historical, social, and political realities of the system we opposed.[141] He stands out as one of the most original minds among New Left theoreticians, even when his rhetoric of fury about the war obscured a visceral conviction that the true objective of revolution is democracy.

Like many of us, Hayden apparently practiced his democratic ideals less successfully than he preached them. His equally sharp-minded New Left contemporary, Todd Gitlin, chronicles how, "In 1971, Tom Hayden, trashed by his Berkeley lover and fellow Red Family communards for self-aggrandizing activities and 'male chauvinism,' left Berkeley altogether." Maybe Hayden's expulsion from the Red Family was really the highest compliment to his most cherished beliefs.[142]

My own contact with the Red Family was comically pathetic, like one of those pre-talkie Chaplin shorts, where the tramp commits some public *faux pas* and is instantly surrounded by a wall of disapproval from anyone and everyone in his vicinity. But the truth is, I don't really think that I'm the one who's always out of sync. No truly sane human being should be able to occupy most of the social spaces we create, where the ground seems to shimmer with a surreal glow, people are shadows, and voices crackle with mixed, more often incoherent, messages.

In that sense I remember my visit to the Red Family as walking through the movement version of a corny Coney Island funhouse, a sequence of distorted, mechanical — utterly predictable — interactions. The group occupied a compound of sorts. Behind the principal dwelling was a tiny bungalow, Hayden's private haunt, and across the street lived journalist Bob Sheer, a former editor of *Ramparts* magazine who seemed to enjoy a kind of emeritus status in the commune, free to live by a separate set of rules.

My reception was cool, almost unfriendly, as one communard led me around the place making introductions. I remember at least two exceptionally pretty women whose greetings were especially sour and intimidating. With just a look they let you know they'd had it with men and their sexist bullshit, so, back off, pig. I was taken over to meet Sheer, who wasn't in, but his mother was visiting, from the East I think, and we chatted in a familiar way. Sheer's worktable was covered with pamphlets and political tracts, and his mom told me he was reading everything he could get his hands on about the Chinese Revolution.

Finally I was taken into the presence of himself. Hayden was striking only in the utter ordinariness of his physical appearance. He was homely, his face lightly scarred by what was probably a bad case of adolescent acne. A schlumpy dresser with no flair to his costume, he anticipated the anti-style of the grunge look. His complexion wanted color, while his office body pudginess suggested a sensualist's inattention to exercise. In mind's eye, the archetype he resembled was the geek in high school who ran the audio visual equipment.

But always he was also a man of parts, and, as a movement elder, accustomed to being listened to. Unfortunately, brushed with my own light dusting of fame, I now imagined that I too could act, at least when cornered, as one entitled to a similar regard. Instead of conversation, we debated, somewhat heatedly, CCI's line emphasizing the nature of war crimes as policy over individual criminality and responsibility. Hayden punctuated his own arguments, barely a scintilla of which can I manage to reconstruct, by taking frequent swigs from a flask of Jack Daniels, not the fashionable Black Label of the poseurs and cognoscenti, but Green Label, a slightly cheaper sour mash distilled by the same company; there were always a few worldly eccentrics who made a point to order Green Label when I was a bartender years ago at Clyde's in Georgetown.

The meeting went nowhere. As Hayden waxed imperious defending the My Lai trials, I dug in to justify CCI's position. No understanding was reached, and soon thereafter I left for New York. CCI never heard from Hayden again (though he and Jeremy later became friends), and if the Red Family's war crimes inquiry ever took place, we never heard about that either.

14. In DC and Working Congress

Tod now says he had trouble getting his bearings as far back as late January after returning from Eastern Europe; he sensed the ground had shifted.[143] This uneasy vibe assayed Tod's general perception of a flux in the movement, but registered more intimately a change in dynamic within our own group. With Jeremy and I centering our efforts more and more in DC, Tod regarded with mixed admiration our successes in his absence, and fretted privately that perhaps no meaningful role remained for him at CCI.

By the time I returned from Australia, the situation had stabilized. En route east from San Francisco I had rendezvoused with Tod at the airport in Kansas City, where he awaited the arrival of Congressman Ronald Dellums. CCI was hearing more and more from future vets still on active duty who had run afoul of the command; by our lights this was a *de facto* resistance to the many tyrannies of military conscription and repression, sparked by the war, and spread widely and wildly throughout the rank and file of all the armed services.

Tod was accompanying Dellums to the military prison at nearby Fort Leavenworth where we had word of abuses toward prisoners who spoke out against the war and racism. This was to be an official inspection by a United States Congressman, Tod's latest brainstorm and weapon to harass the Pentagon; a U.S. Congressman, Tod had convinced Dellums, could not be turned from the gate of any military installation. Moreover, with our guys on the inside, we had a certain leverage to avoid the ceremonial fictions of the typical dog and pony show the brass orchestrates for such occasions. There would be a dose of reality to this visitation to confound the local guardians of military prerogative, maybe even make them squirm a bit at the discomforting challenge to their habit of acting unobserved and with impunity. Of course, Tod had his own legitimate access to such sanctuaries in the form of the attorney-client relationship.

I later got Tod's gleeful report on the morale boost to the brothers and the chagrin of their tormentors caused by Dellums' presence at Leavenworth that afternoon. Much as I would have enjoyed watching an Afro-topped Congressman and a long haired "commie" lawyer force civility, even deference, from the lantern-jawed bully-types who ran the prison, I'd had to decline Tod's encouragement to join them. As we sat at the airline gate waiting for Dellums's arrival, I could barely stay awake, my body no longer willing to support the denial of exhaustion.

I was road weary, but also curious about what Jeremy was up to. He had rented what Tod tagged a bachelor pad in the Calvert Street area of north-west Washington. It would turn out to be a throwback to undergraduate middle class tastes, one of those rehab flats transformed into an ersatz sheetrock palace with a sunken living room, cathedral ceiling, three bedrooms off the upstairs walkway, unfurnished, and so it remained but for the odd piece and a scattering of mattresses. Jeremy was camping there virtually full time, Tod said.

My curiosity was linked to a certain yearning for community that Jeremy and I began to imagine and improvise immediately after the NVI while Tod was away. There had been earnest consultations among friends and comrades in New York, going so far as to involve Tod's girlfriend Pam Booth, with Jeremy and me both pressing an oh-so-urgent appeal for our crowd to close ranks, form a political collective of our own. Jeremy leased the Washington digs, in part, with this goal in mind. Pam was somewhat charmed by our proposal, and Tod, simply incredulous; neither gave the suggestion serious consideration.

Tod thinks that he and Pam, roughly five years our senior, while finding leftist dreams of utopia no less appealing than Jeremy and I, were less ruffled by the New Left's preoccupation with the contradictions between private life and public politics. Something in their seniority — caution, sobriety, cunning — made Tod and Pam less susceptible to this new turn, this infusion of concerted opposition to the war with a charismatic vision of togetherness imported from the apolitical ranks of the counterculture: the two currents of the sixties had finally fused.

My own romance around domesticating political arrangements was, admittedly, somewhat dampened after exposure to the San Francisco collective, but I soon decamped for our little commune, more crash pad really, never housing more than four or five irregulars that spring. One was a cute blond — unarguably a dish — whom Jeremy fell for hard. Love, especially in its more lusty manifestations, transforms most of us. Jeremy did things for Terry that no one else short of holding a gun to his head might have expected. She was a smart, sassy kid and a product of the times: one part street waif, one part student politico, and one part — which dominated — disciple of a Buddhist sect that believed chanting a phrase over and over in pidgin Japanese could guarantee one's material dreams in the here and now. Jeremy's super-rational persona took on a strange, incongruous shading when, at Terry's persistent urging, he would drop to his knees before her makeshift altar, and chant ... for what? I'm guessin' it was just some kinky foreplay.

Okay, I didn't have a steady squeeze at the moment, so I was a little jealous. But I kept Terry at arm's length mainly because I judged the whole chanting–Buddhist shtick as bizarre, and, admittedly, I was boorishly intolerant of most any activity then not purely and radically political. Besides, sex was much less of a turn-on in our circles than politics; it was the movement that really got us off. So, except for a few hours at day's end when Jeremy attended love's labors, he was, as before, totally focused on CCI's agenda.

Whatever else transpired at CCI's Washington commune that spring was just a side show to the main event Tod and Jeremy had been hatching the whole month I was in Australia, and had presented to Ron Dellums and his staff at the end of February: a *Proposal for Congressional Hearings on U.S. War Crimes in Indo-China.*

❖   ❖   ❖

Hollywood attempts over these ensuing years to portray the movement culture coherently, or to represent its visual reality in the streets, never get close to the way I experienced those moments. There was always a quality of the fifties present throughout the sixties and early seventies; Hollywood's sixties is mostly foreground, dominated by close-ups of improbable protagonists working out the film's story line in a dialog typically overladen with individual psychodramas. Whited out is the background with its wide scope of social, economic and historical complexities, against which a given cultural happening that the film chooses for examination — hippie ritual, antiwar demo, college protest — derived its original source and meaning. Put simply, Hollywood produces bad anthropology, like B'wana's fantasies about the natives, who appear primitive only in relation to his own strengths, real and imagined. B'wana has no particular interest in seeing himself through native eyes.

The coexistence of the movement with its social opposite — what activists variously labeled the establishment, the system, the man, the ruling class — while never a pairing of equals, embodied a struggle over power that brought forth a new social contract based on important, if limited, gains, an indisputable advance in many ways over how we organized our lives in the fifties, sixties, seventies. As a culture we Americans are more inclusive and less provincial than before and during Vietnam.[144]

But even when some product of the Hollywood mill approximates the movement look or style — seldom enough — the gestalt or inner life of the participants is woefully off key. And not because the talent isn't capable of reaching those sensibilities and historical spaces, but because the work itself belongs to an entertainment medium first and foremost committed to its moment in the present; only rarely can we look to the movie industry to provide an insight into history, or even a fair representation of the past.

After all, Washington during that April of 1971 was not so different from the city I'd lived in four short years before when I'd last attended university here. The invasion of so many left wing activists in advance of events being organized for later that month only slightly altered the decor and intensity of the street life, and that only in the traditional white student neighborhoods on the fringes of Georgetown, in and around Dupont Circle and the Calvert Street area. Hollywood would model its movement type from a tiny minority among these folk, the wildest, most colorful freaks, and such bands of infantile leftists — to appropriate, slightly reconfigured, Lenin's term — who fancied themselves Americong guerrillas, but were more typically visual parodies of war painted native braves of a bygone era. Nonetheless, however the advanced teams of activists were packaged in coming to DC, and whatever their particular ideological persuasion, most of them, like our small group, occupied temporary digs and spent their time on logistics, and in earnest dialogue and debate to resolve the tactical issues at hand.[145]

Three major undertakings were in the staging phase: a one-day demonstration that would, it was hoped, attract a half-million opponents of the war to gather in the Mall and march between the Lincoln Memorial and the Capitol; the May Day action of civil disobedience on a massive scale, intending to disrupt business-as-usual throughout the government over a span of several days; and a sizable encampment — though no one predicted how large — of antiwar Vietnam vets, bound for Washington to demonstrate and lobby Congress. CCI's proposal, a repeat of the National Veterans Inquiry with fresh testimony before a rump congressional panel on Capitol Hill, chaired by Congressman Ron Dellums, while independently conceived, was coupled to a substantial veteran presence in the capital.

By the third week of April convoys of antiwar vets were pouring into Washington from the four corners, a massive incursion for peace dubbed Dewey Canyon III.[146] From sheer weight of numbers and with the overpowering aura of their moral force, the war veterans' illegal bivouac on the Mall, an encampment of several thousand, quickly became untouchable. There would be no repeat of the Bonus March of 1932 when the Hooverville shanties, constructed on a similar patch of government real estate, and from where World War I veterans laid siege to Congress to demand the war bonus that had been promised them, were stampeded and crushed by the regular cavalry.[147]

In April 1971, DC cops openly fraternized with the antiwar vets from perhaps some awareness of the common experience of military service. The usual channels of enforcement governing antiwar demonstrators were clogged in this instance, and it wasn't clear how the cops would respond to orders to forcibly dislodge the vets. Indeed many cops said publicly that they would refuse such orders. Their resolve was never tested. Conveniently, backroom contingencies were fashioned to simply neuter the court ruling that Attorney General, later convicted Watergate conspirator, John Mitchell, had won to sanction the vets' removal.[148] It is in such rare instances that one sees the face of Oz behind the screen manipulating, without benefit of rule of law, the true levers of power: "Gentlemen [sic], this extraordinary meeting of the executive body of the ruling class is now in session."

VVAW had suffered a minor embarrassment during Dewey Canyon when NBC *Nightly News* reported that Al Hubbard, the group's president, was not a former captain as he had claimed, but a staff sergeant, and moreover had not served in Vietnam — though, on this latter point, NBC may have, inadvertently or otherwise, trafficked in Pentagon disinformation. On the *Today Show* the morning following his exposure, Hubbard admitted lying about his rank; as a black man in America, someone whose credibility among the white majority was assumed to be low, he figured it wouldn't hurt to enhance his image by posing as an officer. But Hubbard still adamantly insisted that he's served in Vietnam — or at least had landed there repeatedly as a flight engineer.

VVAW's other leading cadres, including a recently recruited John Kerry, rallied to Hubbard's side. Al was well liked by his fellow vets, and credited with having guided the organization very ably since assuming its presidency. Despite this comradely support Hubbard's tenure had taken a fatal shot, and he would soon fade from prominence within the group, at the same time VVAW's public image, far from being damaged, shined on for some time as I have already noted.[149]

My memories of Dewey Canyon are mostly positive. I harbor a strong romantic emotion from one dark night of wandering throughout the encampment, the tents and groups of uniformed figures, some crouching around small fires — the fires being a detail I can't be entirely certain my imagination hasn't added to this classic military scene. There's only a single model for such a setting, old as war itself I guess. It resides prolifically within the literary inventory of martial campsites. No matter when or where such a camp appears, you're there with Caesar's legions, or among the English yeoman at Agincourt, exactly as Shakespeare pens it in *Henry V*.

It's a soldier's world, and the veterans these nights of Dewey Canyon were soldiers. Some even formed units, saluting and drilling among themselves, so totally had the military idiom seeped into their unconscious minds. I winced at such spectacles, judging them pitiful, but overall, experienced a calm of belonging so unexpected that my wistful memories of the night can only be explained by the staying power of this unwelcome self-discovery.

Not that I crashed Dewey Canyon just to commune with ghosts of soldiers past, or meditate on the eternal mysteries of camp life. I was there to drum up business for the Dellums Hearings, and one of the VVAW brothers put me on to a vet named Danny Notley, who some months earlier had been party to another massacre in Vietnam.

The night before our first session on the Hill, as Jeremy has reminded me,[150] we joined Danny as he told his wife some of the more unpleasant details about his time in Vietnam. They were a sweet couple, real good looking, both of them, and that's the only fragment from that difficult moment I shared in their lives that Morpheus has spared me. Danny became our star witness that April in the way Bart Osborne glowed for the media at the NVI the previous December.

My only regret about Dewey Canyon is that I was so busy preparing for the Dellums Hearings that I was unable to be there on the day my fellow Vietnam veterans stood at their tallest, and threw their medals in the face of their government on the steps of the U.S. Capitol.

The Dellums Hearings

I'm certain the decision to squeeze the hearings in between the big demo on the 24th and the actions around May Day was media driven. Given the newsworthiness of these events that were engaging tens of thousands within the movement, and mindful of Winter Soldier's minimal impact, this was a logical and responsible question about when in this action-packed calendar month one might expect maximum coverage for what would be CCI's final installment of shocking revelations from the front.

As subsequent developments reveal, the Dellums Hearings would also be CCI's supreme quixotic gesture at institutional chastisement where the war crimes issue was concerned. Over a four-day period, a mere score among the 500+ members of the House of Representatives would hear detailed, eyewitness testimony from combat veterans, many only recently home from Southeast Asia, on exactly how the American forces in Vietnam operated in flagrant violation of every convention of war. These hearing were unofficial, not sanctioned by the House leadership,[151] but the elected men and women who heard and questioned these veterans sat in an actual hearing room of the United States Congress.

CCI, working closely with Dellums's staff, assembled a credible coalition of Congresspersons to hear our testimony, beginning on a Monday morning, April 26, 1971. There was a diversity among the House members who participated that one did not yet intentionally construct in this still predawn of multicultural political correctness, a rainbow trio of women: New York's Jewish intellectual and outspoken feminist, Bela Abzug; the Jamaican born Shirley Chisholm from Brooklyn; and Patsy Mink, an Asian American from Hawaii. Parren Mitchell, John Conyers and Dellums himself spoke strongly for African American men, with Herman Badillo of the Bronx the lone *latino* voice (in a Congress embarrassingly under-represented by Hispanic members). James Abourezk, of Palestinian roots, was there and would, in subsequent years, become a strong advocate for Arab-Americans. Among the other white male liberals of various ethnic colorations, those appearing for at least one session were Ed Koch, Bill Ryan (who died at Jonestown in Guyana), John Seiberling, Henry Reuss, Phil Burton, Ben Rosenthal, John Bingham, Bob Kastenmeier, Don Edwards, Abner Mikva, a very young Don Riegle, and a token Republican, World War Two veteran and former Marine, Paul McCloskey of California, as radically invested in the rising stock of antiwar sentiment within the Congress as any of the hardcore progressive Democrats at this *ad hoc* gathering.

Heretofore, the limited effectiveness of antiwar liberals in Congress was mirrored by similar deficiencies within the antiwar movement; our collective powers to force a change in war policy were restrained by the slow pace of the larger public's rejection of the war. This gap now narrowed rapidly toward the direction of the Left. On a deeper level it remains unclear whether any individuals or groupings within governing circles ever seriously desired, much less sought to obtain, an official examination of charges linking American military policies to war crimes. There were certainly members of Congress, some in attendance at the Dellums Hearings, who flirted with the war crimes issue as a tactic toward ending the war — much like CCI — without any deep commitment to pushing for a full accounting.

One such maneuver, facilitated by CCI during the weeks we prepared for the Dellums Hearings, is revealing of how several Congressional liberals whipsawed key elements of the conservative House leadership into responding publicly to "war crimes allegations." Bob Eckhardt, a Texas democrat, and like LBJ a man imbued with the spirit of the New Deal, led the charge. The *New York Times* reported that Eckhardt was joined by three of his colleagues at a press conference in the Rayburn House Office Building to call upon the House Armed Services Committee, chaired by Dixiecrat F. Edward Hebert, "to conduct a public inquiry into alleged American war crimes in Vietnam."[152]

Hebert, quoted in the same article, was "seeking to prevent the liberal group from holding its own informal inquiry." And furthermore, Hebert had written to Eckhardt that if his group, associated, as the *Times* duly noted, with the "Citizen's Commission of Inquiry on U.S. War Crimes in Vietnam," had "any specific allegations of possible war crimes or related incidents and care to submit them to me, I will see that they receive the immediate attention of the Investigating Subcommittee staff." Which comment did not, Hebert later qualified to the reporter, constitute a commitment to "planned public hearings," as Eckhardt interpreted the chairman's words to the press. Rather, Hebert had only "promised that any allegations would be studied by the staff."

Such was the antiwar liberals' growing strength in the Congress that the normally all-powerful House leadership could not deliver on the threat to prevent Dellums from opening his informal hearings as scheduled. The first day's testimony, though virtually ignored by the media, was perhaps the most intriguing from the distance of history. CCI Vet Coordinator Bob Johnson managed to assemble a witness roster of six West Pointers who provided an eloquent overview of the military's mind-set, more "illustrative of policy, than shocking," as one army academy graduate expressed it.[153]

Press coverage would improve after Tuesday. Yet, the deliberative examination on the opening day of possible historical and institutional causes for American atrocities was, during this one brief moment, the stuff of a genuine inquiry, which no one in the press mistook the Dellums initiative to be; this momentarily spontaneous introspection by members of this powerful governing body around the conundrum of American war crimes might be the key artifact of CCI's lost opportunity for driving a more serious wedge into its call for an official probe.[154]

By the next morning the format shifted back to the issue's voyeuristic roots in daily journalism. Many lawmakers in attendance over each of the next three days, having warmed to the keen, if narrowly legalistic, aloofness of true inquisitors, were by no means mere transmitters of CCI's "war crimes as policy" formulation — an unpalatable line of reasoning even for this ultra-liberal crowd.

Only CCI's Bob Johnson had spoiled the somewhat clubby openended-ness of the discussion on the preceding day, doggedly debating Bela Abzug on the point of an individual's choice in the commission of atrocities. Here is a fragment of that dialogue which expresses the gist of their opposing views:[155]

> *Bela Abzug*: ... in the activity of men in the army are those who made a moral judgment to kill innocent victims, and those who made a moral judgment not to, and I don't quite understand whether you treat all acts the same, or whether you are suggesting that we do apparently. Is that your recommendation?
> *Robert Johnson*: I think given the framework of genocide in Indochina, where we have killed millions of Vietnamese, and there are five million refugees, it is somewhat absurd to focus on the guilt of any particular individual. With the atmosphere ... that exists in Vietnam ... there no longer is a moral frame of reference, there is no longer a moral judgment.

Abzug, like most of her colleagues on the Dellums panel, was a lawyer. Stimulated, perhaps, by the atmosphere of a pseudo tribunal, she framed her questions around assumptions of guilt versus innocence that are wired into American jurisprudence by way of English Common Law. First we determine innocence or guilt; if the latter, then we talk mitigation. But Bob Johnson and CCI were reversing this order for political, not legal, ends. Mitigation first, we demanded; then, hierarchy; if you want to prosecute the guilty, start at the top. Calley had blood on his hands, but he was the creature of policy, we argued, not the creator. If the moral absolutes seemed to fail Calley in the choices he made, what about the moral choices of those who put him in that village in the first place?

To drive this point home during Wednesday's session, the only veterans to appear were those who — over a span of several years — had served in the 11th Brigade of the Americal Division, the same unit as Rusty Calley, whose trial had ended two weeks earlier in his being sentenced to life (later commuted) for the premeditated murder of twenty-two victims at My Lai. CCI joined an unlikely chorus of voices in denouncing Calley's guilty verdict, though from motives diametrically opposite pro-war boosters like Barry Goldwater, the VFW, and the American Legion. Where Goldwater expressed dismay at the U.S. for "airing our dirty laundry before the world," CCI's desire was to expand ever higher up the chain of command, not suppress the public attention on the subject of responsibility for American atrocities. At the same time, the comments of some liberal politicians, like George McGovern, that "it's a mistake to make one man the scapegoat…, it's the policy that's wrong" were true echoes of the position CCI had been elaborating over the past year and a half.[156]

Wednesday's airing of more dirty laundry by the notorious Calley Brigade featured testimony from Danny Notley, the vet I'd interviewed at the Dewey Canyon encampment. Before two hundred stunned spectators who filled a mere fraction of the cavernous Cannon Caucus Room, Notley described a massacre at Truong Khanh, where, on April 18, 1969, at least 30 unarmed and unresisting villagers, mostly women and children, were gunned down in cold blood by members of his unit.[157]

As much as any of the heavily publicized antiwar events in those weeks, with Notley's account of the Truong Khanh massacre, the Dellums Hearings received gangbuster coverage in both the print and electronic media. The *Times* article, with a photo of Notley, ran to three full columns, and included, side by side, a hand drawing of the massacre site provided by Notley with a professional cartographer's rendition showing the provincial capital of Quang Ngai flanked by My Lai to the immediate north, and Truong Khanh just south of the city.[158]

The key word in the *Times* map was Quang Ngai, which any student of Vietnam's anti-colonial struggle will immediately flag as a traditional hotbed of national resistance over the many bloody decades that preceded the country's reunification in 1975. I point to this geo-historical fact again to suggest a possible context for the apparent disproportion in the barbarisms committed by the 11th Brigade during the unit's four years of fighting in this province. The logic being, in crude but simple language, that where you have more eggs, you will have more omelettes.

CCI did not consciously search for witnesses from the 11th Brigade, or from its parent division, the American. They seemed to come to us; I, myself, after all, had served with the 11th. Jeremy and Tod had been quick to concentrate these assets, and use them to underwrite the obvious argument that Lieutenant Calley and his heinous acts were not such great exceptions within the operational sphere of the American Division. But we recognized that it was valid to ask, were the depredations attributed to this division, and to the 11th Brigade in particular, greatly out of proportion with how the land war was being fought by other leg units elsewhere in South Vietnam?

It's doubtful. In our introduction to the published transcripts of the Dellums Hearings, we wrote that CCI "had amassed hundreds of testimonies from vets, covering virtually every major unit and military operation from late 1965 to early 1970."[159] Added to these testimonies were VVAW's Winter Soldier Investigation, and subsequent hearings that the vets continued to hold, CCI–style, throughout the hinterland over the next year.

Calley may have been quantitatively more monstrous than other GIs whose actions we know about, and the 11th Brigade — owing perhaps to added pressures placed on the unit by the intensely politicized population it was called upon to "police"— quantitatively more barbarous than the other American fighting forces, but the pattern of war crimes and the policies they sprang from existed in the Delta, in the Central Highlands, along the DMZ, at Hue, throughout the Parrot's Beak along the Cambodian border, around Cu Chi, Bien Hoa, and Saigon — everywhere — throughout the entirety of South Vietnam, and parts of Cambodia and Laos as well.

Anything that happened at the Dellums Hearings after Notley was anticlimax. Thursday's testimony focused on the air war and pacification, and featured Fred Branfman, a former educational adviser with the International Voluntary Service stationed nearly four years in Laos. Branfman told the panel of an atrocity on a magnitude far greater than Truong Khanh. The Plain of Jars, a fertile valley in Laos roughly the size of New York State, was, he testified, "the most heavily bombed region in the history of warfare," reduced to "a lake of blood and destruction."

Fred Branfman also lived in DC, and Jeremy and I saw something of him socially — or what passed for social contact in the all-business political culture of the movement. Everyone at CCI was very impressed by the research Branfman had assembled on the secret bombing of Laos, not least a phenomenal collection of eyewitness drawings depicting the living hell of life under perpetual bombardment.[160] But even for a group so primed to expose U.S.

battlefield and strategic excesses — what with the all consuming nature of Vietnam's struggle — we could never give more than lip service to what was happening throughout the rest of Indochina.

With Dellums a wrap, we devoted what meager resources that remained from our depleted finances to publicizing Truong Khanh. Tod, as Danny's lawyer, guided the official follow-up through a channel briefly opened with Pentagon investigators. At the same time, and completely unbeknownst to CCI, an enterprising reporter for the Associated Press in Saigon took it upon himself to investigate Notley's charges. His scoop, datelined May 9th in Nghia Hanh, Vietnam, broke in the *Chicago Tribune* on May 8th; anxious to file, the reporter must have bolted to the nearest phone, and outdistanced the international dateline!

The *Trib* headline ran "5 S. Viets Back Ex-GI on Atrocity." According to the *New York Post*, which only carried the story two days later, five women were interviewed by the reporter in what was euphemistically labeled a resettlement camp "not far from now deserted Truong Khanh." *Deserted*, mind you! Both papers carried direct quotes from former residents of the village whose collective recollection "agrees in some respects, and disagrees in others, with the account by former ... sergeant Notley." One woman, identified as Mrs. Nguyen Thi Mai, told the reporter she

> was in the fields, but could see American soldiers in the hamlet. In the afternoon they took thirty people from several houses where they were hiding and shot them. Then they went to several other houses and took about thirty other people, old people and children, and shot them. Then they burned the bodies.[161]

The main point where the survivors' accounts seemed to vary from Notley's was in doubling the number of victims. The AP reporter also obtained an army after-action-report which substantiates that Notley's unit lost a man to a booby trap on April 17, 1969, and then called in a bombing strike on Truong Khanh the following day. These were the very points Notley had emphasized in his testimony. Then the army's version deviates from what Notley told the Dellums panel, and from what the survivors at Truong Khanh told the AP, inventing for the official record the fiction that Notley's "reconnaissance patrol found 18 bodies of Vietnamese men of military age."[162]

The literature of Vietnam is resplendent with tales of how the U.S. military in Vietnam calculated its body counts, listing any dead gook as a legitimate enemy kill, an illusion no less mythic than the Grimms' fantasy of Rumpelstiltskin spinning gold from flax. In Nam it was the easiest trick in the world to spin 18 male guerillas of "military age" from 60 dead women and children. Not until just six months before the Paris Peace Accords between the U.S. and North Vietnam were signed in 1973 did someone finally wonder in print — it was *Newsweek*'s Saigon Bureau Chief, Kevin Buckley — "say, where are the weapons?"[163]

Tod charged that "the Army is not anxious to attack the matter. They are trying to put it [Truong Khanh] to rest." A statement from the U.S. command in Saigon that the army "had no reason to investigate" because "all those who were involved, if there was such an incident, are gone now" seemed to confirm Tod's opinion. While from across the Potomac came the Pentagon countercharge that "Notley and the Citizens Commission of Inquiry had refused to cooperate." To which Notley rejoined, they just "want me to make another scapegoat like Lt. Calley," and Tod clarified that "they want him to reveal names of low ranking soldiers." This was CCI's political no-no, a viewpoint with which most Vietnam vets in our circles, including Danny Notley, readily acquiesced to as in their own self-interest.[164]

CCI's documented link to Danny Notley's account ends with an interview in the *Washington Post* conducted after the New York press conference. Here it is Notley who voices CCI's somewhat revised, and perhaps final, demand for an official inquiry. The veteran called on "President Nixon to set up a special citizens' commission to investigate the fighting tactics which he says make such atrocities inevitable." "Will Notley cooperate with the army in investigating these charges," Tod was asked? "When, and only when, such a panel is convened," Tod insists, "will Notley provide 'full details' of the events at Truong Khanh."[165]

And there the incident rested, truly a *denouement* without an ending. In revisiting these movement experiences I am sometimes tempted to find a flaw in our actions when some other explanation might be more suitable. If, after riding Truong Khanh for several weeks, CCI, as the record clearly suggests, simply walked away from one of its most damning war crimes charges, then that was probably the only possibility we perceived. Professional investigators may have found other means for prolonging the half-life of this dramatic exposé in the news, the legislature, perhaps even the courts. But CCI could never sustain such a campaign given the hand-to-mouth nature of our funding, and the intensity of our disgust and distrust toward the establishment. We never claimed to undertake this effort in a spirit of cooperation with the war makers — already judged war criminals in our eyes.

Years later Tod told me, reflecting somewhat guiltily, that, when Nixon's White House counsel, Fred Buzhard, sought him out as Danny Notley's attorney just after Truong Khanh was made public, he ought to have made more of an effort to contact him. We'll probably never know exactly what it was that the late Buzhard wanted, because, basically, Tod blew him off. He did this, Tod now thinks, from intimidation: "who was I to consult with this high powered Harvard lawyer-type in the White House?" But I maintain that, if in April 1971 you were a true radical and full-time activist in the antiwar movement, like Tod, it was impossible, even obscene, to imagine a real dialogue with the enemy; so why bother?

15. Mopping Up

Faint Echoes

The accumulated outrage from non-movement quarters concerning America's conduct of the war remained fluid. But here or there in these last months of CCI's existence a reverberation of our pleadings would echo back. The New York *Newsday* would, for example, distinguish itself as the only American newspaper in the mainstream to editorialize for "a full-scale congressional inquiry into war crimes and war crimes responsibility," urging support for a bill Ron Dellums and 21 cosponsors had submitted to Congress and which Tod and Jeremy had a strong hand in drafting.

The *Newsday* editorial was everything CCI might have hoped for as a response from a free and independent press. "Daily," it reads, "we are being exposed to more revelations, more new horrors. The instinct is to ... dismiss them as the fevered concoction of the anti-war zealots or publicity seekers.... We seek comfort from, of all places, the Pentagon, which assures us that they are being investigated.... But the atrocities are being reported more rapidly that they can be disposed of.... The goal [of such an inquiry] would not be vengeance, but truth — and ... some measure of expiation.... The alternative ... is clear. We will pass on, not grandeur, but guilt to our children ... and will have lost the 'decent respect to the opinions of mankind.'"[166]

The most significant commentary on the nature of the American war that spring, however, once again came from Neil Sheehan. He wrote another lengthy article, this time an omnibus review of the Mark Sacharoff bibliography, thirty-three recent titles touching on some aspect of the war crimes controversy.[167] Sacharoff, a professor of English at Temple University, and a long time CCI board member, had been compiling his list over the preceding year and giving it wide circulation.

This was "perhaps the most important issue of the *New York Times Book Review* ever published," or so editorialized the *Washington Post* according to John Leonard, the *Times* editor who had commissioned the piece from Sheehan.[168] In my view, having given the record on these matters a fair scouring, this March 1971 work of Sheehan's was the single most important document on American war crimes ever to appear in print, period. Not only for where it ran — the *New York Times* — but for being written by a confirmed insider who proclaimed objectivity for muse and method, and whose attitude toward the New Left and the antiwar movement — by no means atypical among Sheehan's colleagues in journalism during the Vietnam era — bordered, at times, on contempt.

One may logically extract such a judgment from Sheehan's choice of language, like "childishly indiscriminate" where reference to "much of the intellectual community and students" of the New Left appears in his copy. Perhaps the very idea of a party or movement of true — as opposed to loyal — opposition, the existence of which most societies outside the United States take for granted within their own bodies politic, is as foreign — and therefore repugnant — to Sheehan as to most Americans of a similarly unexamined conditioning.

Yet, not unlike the transformations undergone by innumerable New Leftists, certainly those like myself not bred to liberal or leftist political views, Sheehan had seemed to discover that only the accounts of the war presented by texts like those in the Sacharoff bibliography, virtually all authored by confirmed critics and opponents of U.S.–South East Asia policy, provided a framework for integrating and interpreting his own first hand experiences in Vietnam, "what he'd seen, and then repressed," as John Leonard puts it.[169]

As badly as the review was taken by the *Times* brass, John Leonard recalls, it was the threat of Sheehan's conversion that really upset the paper's editorial chieftain, Abe Rosenthal. Rosenthal, according to Leonard, feared "that Sheehan would blow his objectivity before he would deliver his coverage of the Pentagon Papers." But wouldn't that event not take place for another two months, I reminded Leonard? And didn't Daniel Ellsberg, a former Marine and Pentagon official, and colleague Tony Russo, then his fellow analyst at the Rand Corporation, deliver the Pentagon Papers to Sheehan after having been so favorably impressed by this review? "Ah no," Leonard replied, "Sheehan had the papers before the [review] appeared.... I know for a fact ... because he told me."[170]

It is certainly clear that Sheehan, in the preparation of this essay, was digesting more than the Sacharoff texts; not so much what one might learn from the Pentagon Papers, but from a credible reading of the laws and conventions of warfare. Throughout what is essentially a tautly transcribed interrogatory with himself, Sheehan lattices references to the army's Law of Land Warfare, the Geneva and Hague conventions, the broad principles of the Nuremberg and Tokyo tribunals, seeming to indict, in turn, each of the military means upon which American conduct of the Vietnam war depended: unrestricted and indiscriminate bombardment of civilian populations, forced relocation of civilians, routine destruction of hospitals and other noncombatant targets, reprisals, massacres and battlefield atrocities, and torture of prisoners.

In subjecting the war against civilian society in Vietnam to close examination over many paragraphs, Sheehan juxtaposes two damning facts: his own observation that "devastation had become a fundamental element in their [U.S.] strategy to win the war," and a quote from the Army Field Manual. "Devastation as an end in itself or as a separate measure of war is not sanctioned by the law of war." At its most fevered point Sheehan's argument contemplates "whether the United States intervention in Vietnam was itself a violation of the Nuremberg Principles forbidding wars of aggression," a crime against humanity, and therefore the gravest of charges to be levied on a modern warring nation.

From the brink of such an apostasy that may indeed foreshadow conversion, it is interesting to see by what rhetorical logic Sheehan now retreats. He asks, quite reasonably, "how is this country to determine whether war crimes were really committed in Vietnam and who is responsible for them?" In surveying the institutional options, Sheehan concludes that "the army ... will not enforce military law and judge itself"; nor can "one expect the Nixon Administration, of its own accord, to institute any meaningful inquiry into war crimes." The one "sole hope," too, is doubtful, for "there does not seem to be the stomach for such an inquiry in Congress now."

In fact there will never be an inquiry. Sheehan knows it; CCI knows. And, since "not even the wildest of anticommunist politicians has predicted the conquest of the United States by the Vietcong," there will certainly be no Nuremberg, no Tokyo, no victor's justice. If there were, toys Sheehan with mock absurdity, even cabinet members like "Orville Freeman, the Secretary of Agriculture under President Johnson, could acquire responsibility."

And while all available evidence may "demand a national inquiry into the war crimes question," Sheehan consoles the reader that "nothing the United States has perpetrated approaches the satanic evil of Hitler and his followers." In failing to take action, however, "the nation's conscience" must bear the shame of "hypocrisy," and the loss of an "opportunity for humanity" that such an inquiry would signify. The do-gooder nation will simply fail to do what it thinks it always does anyway — good — toward those whom Sheehan describes as "the weaker peoples of the globe."

With the agility of a fakir hopping over hot coals, Sheehan leaps us from the treacherous surface of the ideal to the solid underlayment of the real. We discover that it is not — Sheehan's learned disputations notwithstanding — the rule of law that orders the dynamic circumstances so ably catalogued by the *Times* critic, but — *toujours* — the rule of might. It's the System. It's Chinatown, Jake. It's the way things are, the way they've *always* been. It's human nature. Nature versus nurture. The curse of the bambino. Individuals change, not societies.

Like the rich young man in the New Testament parable, Sheehan turns away from the choice that tempts him from self-interest. He does not "blow his objectivity," and goes on to bring the Pentagon Papers to public light in a series of articles for the *Times*. Like the rest of the world we at CCI did not learn of this impending triumph until it happened. And so our many attempts to contact Sheehan during this interval were unsuccessful, because the reporter's attentions were clearly elsewhere. Sheehan did good work on Vietnam, maybe even good works. But, let's face it, rich young men always seem to be a tad more practical than Jesus was.[171]

❖ ❖ ❖

Writing almost exactly one year later — March 13, 1972 — in the preface of an obscure scholarly work about the air war in Indochina, Neil Sheehan notes that the authors of this study began "from antiwar motives," but could "not come to a firm judgment on the question of war crimes." For Sheehan, however, "the evidence speaks for those who wish to hear it," and he seems in little doubt that the air war constitutes "a massive war crime by the American government and its leaders." The preface closes with a forecast that American forces will likely be "driven from the Indochinese peninsula by the Vietnamese communists," an outcome Sheehan openly cheers as "an unparalleled example of the triumph of the spirit of man over the machine." There is no further call here for an official inquiry, and, as far as I can determine, this would be Neil Sheehan's final public sermon on the topic of American war crimes in Vietnam.[172]

End Game

As President Nixon moved to diminish public attentiveness to the war by substantially reducing the American presence in Vietnam, thereby shifting the burden of fighting — and the military casualties — to the Saigon army, committed activists within the antiwar movement imagined possibilities for consolidating the many organizational and intellectual assets of the opposition in anticipation of the postwar years. This collective struggle we had forged to slow our nation's imperial aggressions was, who could deny it, a dynamo of such considerable dimension that one quite naturally assumed its perpetuation as a network of entities, however loosely affiliated, to continue the advance of diverse and radical agendas.

As individuals, and ensemble, our little squad at CCI looked toward such a future, while continuing to seek and appropriate in the short run every opportunity to use the war against itself. But the lull of steamy summer days now seemed to put the movement on half-shift, and we too — the core three-some at CCI — while not inclined to slow the pace, did scale down our routine preoccupation with war crimes in an effort to broaden our involvements.

Ever since Tod escorted Ron Dellums to the Leavenworth stockade CCI had become something of a backstop for GI complaints — resistance, in our terms — that now flooded the Congressman's office. By mid–May we were already coordinating with local GI organizers for a summer of surprise congressional visitations at military brigs and stockades throughout the country.

I myself enjoy the priceless memory of having witnessed at Fort Dix several months later a version of what I'd missed at Fort Leavenworth when, without warning, Ron Dellums entered the headquarters building of this northern New Jersey army base. The chief of staff, a colonel, cuppa joe in one hand, lighted butt in the other, wore a flat out *what-do-you-want-Boy* look all over his face as he eyed the tall, good looking, and smartly dressed black man who stood smiling pleasantly before him. You could sense his brainwave was stalled on some trite image like, *token Negro at Pepsi Cola*, as it slowly decoded that the man was holding the ID card of a bona fide United States Congressman. "Ah-ba-ba," the colonel sputtered, then took a pratfall, coffee and cigarette colliding as he burnt his own finger in the process of submitting to a handshake. After which our smug little party, including a couple of Washington based journalists,[173] went off to inspect a training unit for dissident GIs, confined, illegally we believed, under stockade conditions.

These congressional raids on military turf were, for CCI, frail gestures of counter-harassment toward an all-powerful Pentagon, while providing some civilian cover and protection for pockets of rebellion in the armed forces that were so vital to the antiwar cause. In the big picture, as we fully grasped, it was the war that spread dysfunction through the ranks of the American military. We at CCI merely exploited that condition to stage our politicized performance art in the midst of the enemy's camp; for each of us — Tod, Jeremy and myself — got off on watching these commanders and their retinues mouth unwanted lines in our agitprop productions.

Without meaning to, we pissed off a few organizers who worked with GIs at the grassroots, and resented our cavalier ways, swooping in from the big city for a dose of instant glory while they slugged it out day to day with the brass. They had a point; but what was the alternative? There wasn't any career track in the movement, no set distribution of labor. It's not like anyone was in it for the money. Just a handful of activists made a living wage with decent benefits in staff positions backed by some institution, usually religious or academic. The rest of us worked freelance, content, if not over-joyed, with subsistence life-styles, sowing some radical oats and generally feeling good about our lives and ourselves, if not our world. Romantic lip service aside, none of us at CCI was fit for duty at the grassroots. Given our aggressive and restless imaginations, we created work that suited our talents, telescoping our engagement over a national field of action, while following no one's lead but our own.

This leadership phobia, so characteristic of New Left political culture, had a paradoxical composition, a healthy respect for decentralization mixed with the suspicion that most expressions of authority in our ranks were either media-driven or attention-seeking by ego trippers. We'd all witnessed how many leaders in our movement became overwhelmed by their status as celebri-ties, obscuring, in the process, that many had come to prominence precisely because of their talents to lead — if not, alas, to organize.

Problem was, by mid–1971 we all wanted to be famous. I know I did. Tod did. Bob Johnson already had some sense of his own celebrity.[174] He left the group around this time to try his luck on the lecture circuit, while con-tracting with a New York publisher to coauthor a work critical of West Point. And, of course, Jeremy, who has gained some measure of fame over the years in the rare job description of "futurist" had already, on many occasions, shown his aptitude for commanding an audience. At strategy sessions with the May Day Collective back in April even movement honchos like Rennie Davis and Mike Learner,[175] both afflicted with disabling wounds of self-importance, had begun to lend an ear to Jeremy's earnest, articulate, and good natured polemics.

Oslo

By the end of June Tod was off to Oslo accompanying a delegation of vet witnesses for another round of the international commission, the inau-gural session of which I had attended eight months before in Stockholm. It's perverse, but I still get a small buzz from one particular letter in the CCI files, a proof of sorts that CCI retained the American war crimes franchise in the eyes of many activists, including interested Europeans working the same issue. Hans Goren Frank, the Commission of Enquiry's secretary general, wrote, "As you have a good contact with U.S. soldiers and officers that have testified to war crimes committed by U.S. troops in Indochina we now kindly ask for your cooperation in finding and arranging for a number of veterans that are willing to testify before the Commission in Oslo."[176]

At CCI we looked upon the organizers of the Oslo inquiry as moldy old

lefties who, under the best of circumstances, seemed uncomfortable with anyone not subject to vertical political discipline. They especially didn't have a
clue how to handle these high spirited U.S. proletarians who had only recently
acted with such barbarity on the battlefield, and now dressed like hippies and
spouted the hard line rhetoric of social revolution. The delegation Tod helped
assemble, however, was creamed from our larger cohort of vet contacts. Not
only could each of these witnesses relay shocking tales of American atrocities
from firsthand experience, but they were individually better informed and
more talented politically than the crusty apparatchiks could have known.

Ken Campbell, cut in the mold of the worker intellectual, was fiercely
opinionated and had the natural gift for shop floor leadership; he later took
his doctorate and went on to teach political science at university. Bart
Osborne, though shadowy in personality, gained credibility in his willing and
exceptionally articulate testimony about the campaign of covert terrorism in
Vietnam that supplemented more standard American combat policies. Larry
Rottmann, a former information officer, was something of a sullen man, but,
among the soldier poets created by Vietnam, his stark, sardonic miniatures
belong to the best, most authentic writing the war produced. I hardly knew
Randy Floyd, a well-spoken ex–Marine fighter pilot who'd testified at the
Dellums Hearings, and like Notley, had come to the war crimes issue in its
later stages directly through VVAW. He was the rare pilot in that conflict
who, painfully aware of the air war's indiscriminate wasting of Indochina and
its peoples, was willing to denounce the policy publicly. The two other vet
delegates were Danny Notley and Nathan Hale. I never really got to know
either man, but they both struck me as innocents, Hale, the former interrogator with a Huck Finn sort of sweetness, and Danny, a young super-sol-
dier now tortured by his battlefield memories, almost overpowering in his
forthrightness and sincerity as a witness.

But the Oslo conveners apparently saw these men through other lenses,
a pack of wolf children, modern Casper Hausers.[177] Ruled thus incompetent,
and prone perhaps to run amuck, the vet delegation was sequestered on a
island an hour from the Norwegian capital where a kind of bacchanalia awaited
to appease their tormented souls. Ken Campbell captures the action in published excerpts from his diary. "About fifty guys and girls were waiting for us,
and they had an entire pig roasting over a pit, named Nixon II. Much beer,
vodka, food, song and dance." Plus — wink, wink — a little skinny dipping in
the bracing waters of the fjord, confides the diarist.

Well and good. Sounds like a great party. Only, by noon the following
day it began to dawn on Campbell that "our guides acted more like guards."
Finding they were not permitted to attend the conference, and by 3 p.m.
beginning "to get a feeling of confinement," the vet delegation decided "to go

ashore one way or another. We got our bags, went down to the dock and demanded the boat. We were prepared to take it," which proved unnecessary. The vets booked hotel rooms in Oslo, then called a meeting with the commission organizers who had by now gotten precisely what they'd feared from these veterans — trouble, not due to inappropriate deportment on the latter's part, but the effect of their own clumsy misconceptions. During this heated get-acquainted session it soon became clear to those voices governing the commission that the vets were no more mad or rabid than the average political radical, and therefore no suitable reason remained for their being marginalized from the proceedings.[178]

Tod returned bearing anecdotes about these and other miscues from the Oslo adventure. He said that when news of the vets' rebellion reached the conference, he was confronted by an American delegate with deep roots in the CPUSA. "This will go bad for you," she openly threatened, as if Stalin's minions yet roamed the globe with rock picks to smite their opponents on the Left. Tod just laughed in her face. Another story was more disturbing and concerned the vets, who, after Oslo, did some touring within European leftist circles. At an antiwar rally organized by Lotta Continua in Bologna — the great industrial bastion of Italian communism — they were introduced from the stage. It seems Bart Osborne missed his cue to salute the crowd with a clenched fist and had his arm rudely hoisted aloft by two of his vet companions, as one of them would later sheepishly confess to Tod. The halls of heresy, too, are filled with many orthodoxies.

CCI fueled its tank partially on true belief of a similar octane. But our addictions to revolutionary zeal and its antithesis, demon hunting, were tempered by a strange conjuncture of native traits that Tod, Jeremy and I all shared: a pragmatism geared toward achieving some measurable result for our actions, like ink in the morning press; a shrewd capacity for the dismissal of appearances, which each of us expressed in attitudes, moods and voices that ranged from high toned convictions worthy of Thoreau, to the deviltry of the pitchman at a medicine show; and we were each developing a genuine taste for civic intervention in the public arena, especially for those entrepreneurial variants of the political game one could, to whatever limited extent, play according to rules of one's own invention.

We were empowered as much under unique circumstances of the American experience as by our own concerted efforts. This privilege to act out radical political fantasies was indeed wrested from a power structure tinged with oligarchy by the counterpull of mass opposition. Yet, in the absence of repressive measures that our actions might have automatically brought forth in most contemporary societies, there echoed a deep sounding of the freedoms our ancestors had forged in democratic struggles of their own. But the state's tolerance had its calculated limits. As long as the nation's large, self-disciplined blue collar element remained inert, and the poor and the colored races distracted by the immediate cares of survival, a benign state could indulge the shenanigans of its most alienated sons and daughters among the white middle and affluent classes, drawing the line only at violence. Is it any wonder that an activist could imagine that when Bob Dylan sang, "Pump don't work cause the vandals took the handle"— one could so readily identify with the vandals.

A New Movement

Armed with the cocky confidence of those who see themselves as players, the CCI three piled into Jeremy's car and made our second trip to Chicago that summer to attend a preliminary meeting among fellow activists, some of whom were hoping to form a "new American movement" for the postwar years.

We were all three, moreover, of a similar headset politically as we approached the meeting in Chicago. The initiative was Mike Lerner's, the May Day tribalist who had befriended Jeremy during the Washington spring offensive.[179] Neither Tod, Jeremy, nor I had participated in the May Day demonstrations on principled grounds. I suppose we shared the Trotskyist view that, as a mass tactic, civil disobedience was counterproductive, even, perhaps, elitist. It's not that we doubted that acts of civil disobedience could be individually courageous and effective, but they could never serve the average citizen as a model for political action. Most people couldn't afford the luxury of getting themselves arrested, even if their anger and commitment might have justified such an act of conscience. And we feared the underlying message of May Day was that one's political purity could only be affirmed in such acts of individual bravado, and that this would deepen the alienation from the movement of the paradoxically conformist and communal-minded Middle Americans we viewed as our own constituency.

A related problem was the growing trend in the movement toward Third World worship, manifest openly among elements of the May Day Tribe, and most ostentatiously—and destructively—among members of the Weather underground. It seemed that many in the movement were down for everyone else's revolution but their own. CCI endorsed all the "antis," like most of our New Left co-thinkers—anti-militarist, anti-imperialist, anti-racist, anti-capitalist—but we never became anti–American. Jeremy in particular had been developing a program to supersede the war crimes issue that was aimed at reconnecting movement energy and forces with the radical heroes and heroines and traditions found everywhere throughout American history. He would audition this line of thinking in political circles for the first time in Chicago.

The first organizing meeting for the New American Movement was held in the stark surroundings that typically house such events on the Left.[180] It's always linoleum and metal folding chairs, and nothing of the cushy, corporate-sponsored amenities one finds — and expects — across the ideological divide. Theory, ideas, analysis — smoothly articulated — these are the comfort foods of the materially undernourished Left. The moral pageantry afoot often suggests a petty reenactment of the Diet of Worms without the gentry, princes of the Church, or the emperor. And every man — and now woman — his and her own Luther with a list of thesis to expound. My recollections of a fleshy, sensual Mike Lerner, presiding over — virtually dominating — this gathering remain crossed in mind's eye with the elemental willfulness and self-love one has come to associate with aspects of the Great Reformer's personality. Lerner, while not in Luther's league of course, was even then a pretty smart cookie as can be seen in the prominence he would later achieve as counsel to Hillary Clinton, and creator of the magazine *Tikkum*.

I don't really think this meeting in Chicago can be cast in a historical light. But, for me, it was a deeply impressive moment, the first time I ever sat in council with so many leading American leftists of my own generation. The roster was a modest sampling, but entirely representative. From the *old* New Left came three founding members and past national officers of Students for a Democratic Society, Heather and Paul Booth, and Steve Max. Lerner was accompanied by at least one of his mates from the Seattle Eight. And, among those with radical pedigrees of a slightly older lineage, were Alice Lynd and husband, Staughton, the activist-historian who was fired by Yale for traveling to North Vietnam in violation of a State Department ban; James Weinstein, long associated with leftist journals like *Studies on the Left*, *Socialist Revolution*, and later founder and publisher of *In These Times*, made an appearance; and, if memory serves, Dorothy Healey, once a very big name in the California branch of the Communist Party, was also there.

I remember sitting quietly for the most part in the ranks along with at least half the attendees who lent their ears to the other half who did most of the speaking. I may have been the only veteran present, though I doubt I would have identified myself as such. Certainly the whole vet/GI dimension of CCI's political work had no airing here except by refraction in a point Staughton Lynd kept hammering away at: the New Left was totally isolated from the American working class, even from its most organized and progressive voices throughout trade unionism. Lerner argued forcefully that NAM should openly designate itself a socialist organization, while Lynd took the opposite view that socialism — with its associations to European Marxism — was an instant turn-off for most Americans.

Many of the modern Left's canonical themes were being rehashed here. Always juxtaposed at the deepest strata in such exchanges is the résumé of totalitarian Stalinism, and its mirror opposite, the red-baiting of a legitimate and democratic opposition, which in a free society might include, or even be led by, communists and socialists of many stripes. In the more dynamic foreground of the discussions in Chicago much attention was paid to certain innovations of New Left political culture. There was, for one, a stout tendency among those present to struggle in the name of socialist feminism around entrenched customs of male precedence. And there was as well the usual preponderance of distressing incivilities, gut checking, and rank pulling in the manner people addressed one another; the old SDS crowd was particularly snotty, hovering on the edges of each session with the disdainful aloofness of conspirators.

Any striving toward reciprocal exchanges in these intellectual trials always loses ground, it seems, to the peculiar vulnerabilities and psychodramas that afflict the participants. Yet the tensions that sharpen people's tongues do no less for their ideas, and the old SDSers, when they spoke, did so still with considerable panache and sometimes wisdom. The one true teacher in Chicago was Staughton Lynd, a philosopher of that native strain evolved first from the Puritan scolds, later mellowed through eclectic, indulgent filters of the Emersonian skeptics and reformers. But while Lynd's orientation toward homegrown radicalism gave scope to CCI's ideological drift,[181] we were not in his camp around the bugaboo of socialism; Jeremy, perhaps, but not me, and certainly not Tod.

It was still only 1971, but Jeremy had begun to ruminate on how radicals might engage the nation's upcoming bicentennial year of 1976. His focus as an organizer remained on Middle America, and he now contemplated a strategy for involving the grassroots around an agenda for change that made no direct reference to the military or the Vietnam War. Jeremy received a polite, if critical, hearing for his proposals at the NAM meeting. I don't recall Tod playing much more of a role at the meeting than I did, but, if he and I were less enthusiastic about the counter-bicentennial theme than Jeremy, we most definitely shared our comrade's general class analysis and orientation toward this mysterious realm of Middle America.[182]

In the end, NAM proved more left-wing intellectual club and debating society than embryo of organizational agency for direct political engagement.[183] The radical American Left tends to exist in incubators such as this which perpetuate its life force and sustain its incursions into reality, quite powerfully under certain circumstances, as Vietnam is but the most recent example. Whereas the cadres birthed in these intellectual hothouses go on to retell the Left's story from one generation to the next.

Certainly no other classroom I'd ever been in delivered education to match what I'd learned over a year and a half of antiwar activism. The NAM meeting was, for me, a kind of final exam, self-graded according to one's capacity to follow, not merely the arcane historical and textual references, but the more subtle turns of mind and phrase that sought to sway the outcome of the motions the assembly would be voting on. I left Chicago no more certain of my immediate future, but more unshakably committed than ever to the activist life, sustained in my happy bubble of alienation by monthly checks from the very system at which I hurled my lances.

16. A Farewell to War Crimes

It was a liberal Republican, Representative Ogden Reid of Westchester, New York, whose individual initiatives neatly bracketed whatever limited show of interest the U.S. Congress demonstrated — exclusive of the Dellums *ad hoc* hearings — around the outcry over American atrocities in Vietnam. Reid had helped to sponsor an open forum on the Hill back in early 1970, the subject of a paperback co-edited by CCI mentor Erwin Knoll.[184] And in August 1971 the House Government Operations subcommittee Reid sat on heard "what was believed to be the first Vietnam veterans to publicly testify under oath before an open congressional subcommittee on specific allegations of torture and murder by U.S. government personnel."[185] The two vet witnesses were Bart Osborne and myself.

The subcommittee was investigating the CIA–sponsored Phoenix Program, designed to target and assassinate Vietcong civilian leaders. Reid and his staff had shoehorned Bart's and my testimony into the proceedings in "rebuttal"[186] of prior testimony by the program's creator and field marshal, William E. Colby.[187] Colby, who had testified a fortnight earlier, "cautiously conceded" the occurrences of "unjustified abuses" in many Phoenix operations. But the man who would later head the CIA and who, some years after retirement, would be mysteriously found dead in the waters near his weekend home on the Chesapeake Bay, was "categorical" in his contention that "Americans play only a supporting role in the bloody business."[188]

Osborne's sworn evidence blew holes in Colby's calculated mendacities about U.S. noninvolvement in these "abuses." "They all died," he said about the VC suspects brought into the U.S. interrogation centers during his own

15 month tour in Vietnam. Asked to estimate the number of those killed, Osborne replied, "several hundred." Most of the victims, he emphasized, were tortured and murdered, not by Vietnamese operatives of the Saigon regime, but "by personnel of the U.S. interrogation group at the Da Nang Marine base."[189]

Shocking as this charge was, it would not penetrate the dense, arrogant exterior of plausible denial that Colby and all agents of covert action are schooled to assume the instant any untoward discovery or accusation arises from their activities. That's our line, shrugged Spy Master Colby, take it or leave it. The U.S. Congress, itself so thoroughly complicit in responsibility for the Phoenix assassinations, quite naturally took it. Reid and his colleagues on the subcommittee — most vocal of whom was another antiwar Republican, Paul McCloskey — had been audacious in publicly questioning a government brahmin of Bill Colby's stature. But their efforts, beyond the principled expressions of personal disapproval and outrage and the paper trail for history they managed to place on the record, accomplished little. The subcommittee was already poaching on turf sacred to the House and Senate Armed Services Committees, the only bodies in Congress with direct jurisdiction over the military, and thus the power to cause such policies as Phoenix to be seriously probed, abandoned, and — ideally — repudiated.

What it probably came down to in the public mind was Colby versus Osborne: Spy versus Spy. My plausible denial over yours. Naturally, Bart's dramatic account dominated all the press coverage of his and my joint appearance. I thought it interesting that the two or three corpses Bart had produced for the National Veterans Inquiry had increased to the population of a small village. So, either Bart was exaggerating before the subcommittee to a degree impossible to determine, or, after the NVI, Winter Soldier, and Oslo, he now felt more secure in his role as star witness of grotesqueries practiced by the American intelligence community in Vietnam. He was also under oath; then again, so was Colby.

I had labored to prepare my own statement, a "perspective gained from the field," in which I do not describe a single atrocity.[190] Instead, my testimony constructs the argument that Phoenix, as a program targeting high ranking Vietcong Infrastructure (VCI), was a hoax. Neither American nor South Vietnamese Intelligence, I contended, had the capacity for high level rub outs in the thousands being claimed for Phoenix by Colby.

Citing my own operational experience, I suggested that such numbers more likely resulted from the daily contacts between Vietnamese civilians and American infantry forces, made volatile within the vulnerable reality of soldiers operating in a countryside populated by a peasantry generally loyal, not to Saigon, and certainly not to us, but to the Vietcong. Phoenix really was,

I claimed, a concentrated campaign of terror "derivative of overall policies that have led to the indiscriminate killing of thousands of Indochinese people," and was created precisely to cover up and justify such policies. The infamous "mere gook rule" put any peasant in the cross hairs, and death confirmed his or her status as a VCI. The essence of my testimony was a reflection of my experiences, and of the interpretation I believed them to deserve. I assume the same was true for Bart Osborne. Not so Bill Colby, who, called upon to defend a criminal policy, had either come to believe his own propaganda, or, more likely, simply lied.

I readily acknowledge my animus toward Colby, another of those figures on a par with Kissinger, the Bundys, McNamara, Rostow, and the like, still viewed by many diehards from New Left circles as war criminals never brought to justice. This animus toward Colby would one day fuel the story line for a screenplay outline I'll probably never get around to writing. When Colby disappeared in the spring of 1996 he was missing for nine days before his body was recovered. Following the autopsy the cause of death was ruled as hypothermia and drowning. My fantasy suggests an alternative scenario, loosely based on the few reported facts of the case.

It was disclosed that Colby had gone alone to his weekend retreat, a house secluded at the far end of a road on a point that juts into the bay. But in my story Colby doesn't go off boating by himself, then collapse from exposure and drown. Rather, on the evening of his arrival, overcast and misty, a team of Vietnam-era radicals approaches the house from the water just after dark. Colby can be seen through the kitchen window preparing and eating what will be his last meal. He is overpowered and, throughout the night, subjected to a People's Trial. When the defense of his Vietnam policies falls short, Colby is condemned and injected with a solution that cannot be traced, his body and canoe taken to the tributary where it will later be discovered. Such is the *deus ex machina* of one radical who's not really out for blood but for justice in the courts of history, for which this account of CCI and the war crime movement may serve as one among many guiding briefs.

❖ ❖ ❖

CCI's agitations around U.S. atrocity-producing combat policies in Vietnam ended with these hearings. VVAW would adhere to this tactic for the better part of the upcoming year, conducting CCI–style hearings throughout the country. The war crimes issue provided vets an obvious nexus to whatever public antiwar opposition remained.[191] But attention to revelations of war crimes committed by American soldiers would never again rise to public prominence, and the issue evaporated many months before the war would end.

Standing before the dust jacket display of *G.I. Guinea Pigs* at the War Crimes Museum in Ho Chi Minh City, summer 1994.

The public either did not — or did not want to — believe that the veterans' accounts of battlefield atrocities were the logical outcome of American war policy. This ambivalence toward the vets and their message was not so hard to understand, given the "my country right or wrong" attitude that as yet pervades our culture. Without a genuine public outcry there would be no real pressure for an official war crimes inquiry. And, as I have noted previously, the unalloyed endorsement by the masses of the veterans' self-revelations was never an objective in which CCI activists had invested a great deal of optimism or expectation. We had quite soberly defined our efforts as contributing to a larger and powerfully diverse movement organized to discredit and stop the war.

It was clear to any close observer of the war, well before Nixon's presidential landslide election of November '72, that U.S. and allied ground troops would soon be withdrawn, if not from all of Indochina, then at least from Vietnam. Not having dared to imagine that Saigon could fall to the North just two short years after the Peace Accords were finally signed in January 1973 — on roughly the same terms first suggested by North Vietnam in 1965[192] — we reckoned we'd be fighting official U.S. efforts to prop up the Saigon regime with military aid and air power for years to come. Our commitment as individuals to oppose our nation's unseemly imperial reach had not slackened one iota; indeed our dedication to the larger historical canvas of social struggle was never greater. The war crimes issue had simply run its course, and it was now time to move on.

Wasn't It a Time

I would never again work closely with Jeremy Rifkin, but our affection for one another through the years has, I believe, remained mutual. Jeremy's turn to the work of the People's Bicentennial Commission in late 1971 reflected his strong personal frustration with the style and isolation of working on the Left. He wanted a larger pond for his activities, which his talents, personality, and dynamic work ethic have helped him achieve. As a public figure and commentator on a host of environmental, social and economic issues, Jeremy's name has not quite attained the status of a household word, but he enjoys a degree of recognition that is only just shy of that charmed circle of true celebrity. This is not for lack of effort, but because Jeremy's political instincts remain, at core, uncompromisingly radical and controversial.

As the preeminent watchdog over the corporate commercializing of breakthrough research in genetics, Jeremy's relentless staying power stems from a youthful preoccupation with the fascist ideology of eugenics and its drive to engineer a master race, the subject he chose for his graduate thesis at Tufts in 1969. Woven through the high moral tone of Jeremy's environmental campaigns around the greenhouse effect, the destructive economics of producing a human diet of protein based on cattle raising, and the genetically engineered adulteration of animals, vegetables or grains, is a modern vision of low tech self-sustainability. And Jeremy's ideas for democratizing the global economy, despite getting a polite hearing in the more enlightened managerial boardrooms, are not generally sympathetic to capitalism's predatory requirements.

Tod Ensign, on the other hand, had cast his lot unambiguously with the activist Left, with all the appetite for intellectual gymnastics, internecine conflict, urban culture, and revolutionary zeal such a choice embraced in the New York City radical milieu of this era. In the ensuing years his programmatic opposition to American militarism has remained steadfast. The organization he and I would later found and direct together, Citizen Soldier, remains doggedly in existence, under Tod's sole stewardship since 1981, involving him in scores of invaluable crusades since Vietnam on behalf of human rights within the armed forces.

Tod, like Jeremy, in my judgment, has done much good over the past thirty years. I'm the one who dropped from intense activist politics, at least until the days preceding the invasion of Iraq. When I left Citizen Soldier in 1981, it was to start a family long delayed and launch a fragile career in writing, first from Brooklyn, then from Maine.[193]

In late 1971 when I returned from Washington to live in New York, Tod and I formed a strong personal bond, and a working partnership that endured a decade. Our first organizational collaboration was Safe Return, a committee that permitted an ongoing focus on the war, while simultaneously addressing what would evolve into a major postwar issue, the campaign for a universal amnesty.[194]

Safe Return demanded total amnesty for all war resisters, but selected for its particular backing American military deserters, whom we styled "self-retired veterans." Those prior travels to Europe had connected us to exile com-

With Tod Ensign circa 1971.

munities of American deserters and draft resisters living in Paris and Sweden; along with these folks and diverse resister groups exiled in Canada, we helped to forge a lively international pro-amnesty coalition. For Safe Return, this drive, which extended over the next several years, was organized around the dramatic public tactic of surfacing and repatriating individual deserters who volunteered with great courage for trial as test cases for amnesty.[195] Despite falling considerably short of its objectives, the amnesty effort did gain, in the form of presidential pardons and discharge reviews, a few modest successes that otherwise may have never been achieved.

In a Paris café, fall 1971.

Those ten years in the East Village working with Tod, hanging at our office in the Flatiron Building, traveling the planet on one radical political junket after another, are the subject of a sequel to this work, a memoir of New York's left-wing political and cultural life in the seventies. During those years Tod and I could put in long hours when the task demanded. But we also displayed compatible temperaments for the many unhurried pleasures New York laid before its *corps de flâneurs*.

Frequently after work we'd meet at Tod's place around midnight, chat over wine and maybe smoke a joint, then wander east from First Avenue into the demimonde of the downtown jazz scene. We might stop for a little "leg" along the way, a platter of ghetto starch, fried chicken, mashed potatoes and slices of Wonder Bread smeared with margarine. Above naugahyde booths in the storefront eatery hung hand-painted signs that read, "No Nodding." At the entrance to Slugs, we'd pay the one-drink minimum, find a table near the stage, and later pour some red from the bottle Tod had tucked beneath his coat, eyes and ears riveted on the big league band, group, or ensemble whose music blasted over us, wave upon wave, with the hippest jazz you could hear anywhere.

My love life had also improved by then, though I can't credit New York for that. After a romantic drought of some years, I'd finally connected with the first girl I felt good waking up next to since Katie. Only 19, Ann was still a coed. I'd met her at the Watergate complex, where she interned that summer of '71 for Larry O'Brien, head of the Democratic National Committee. After May Day, Jeremy and I would mosey over there on occasion to evangelize the younger, antiwar elements of the Democratic Party.

Just before beginning her senior year at Wellesley, Ann joined me, along with Tod, his sister Deb, and Pam Booth on a trip to Haiti. Tod and I had picked up some cheap nine-day package tours from an African-American travel entrepreneur at Sweet Basil, a jazz bar we frequented in the West Village. We only saw a small segment of sad, exotic Haiti under Baby Doc, unpaved Port au Prince, Petionville, the Ton Ton Macute, Joe Le Cue, Olafson's, the ashen-faced poor, avocados the size of volley balls, drumming like you'd only hear in the *candomblé* of Brazil, and the Bonano family reputedly running the local joke-of-a-casino along the wharf on the one concrete strip of road in town, called Harry Truman Boulevard. I hate to admit it, but we had a pretty fair time.

That winter I drove up to Wellesley, and, at one of those Sunday Teas, sat watching Ann play clarinet in the well-known string quintet by Mozart; that's the moment I discovered how the erotic can differ from the sexual. The next year Ann moved in with me in the East Village. I don't know what I was thinking. The two of us were actually talking marriage. Feeling somewhat desperate, even possessive, I hadn't begun to fathom yet, not even intellectually, that a person couldn't love and possess the same object. I was with this desirable, talented, and dynamic young woman who wasn't remotely ready for commitment; that I might never be was a fear yet to be imagined. Fortunately Ann had more sense than I. When we started grating on each other's nerves, she moved out. And I mourned briefly another lost infatuation.

I'd known the slough of despond when Katie dumped me, so far down I volunteered for Vietnam. But when Ann split my life was on the upswing. In my fashion I now engaged the world I used to hide from. There was a bounce in my step when I hit the pavement each morning, and a purpose. I was the righteous Michael, the avenging angel possessed of a new faith, and wild to battle on against the wickedness and snares of the (imperial) devil. I was the goyishe Yeshiva boy, sitting at the feet of rabbinical New York Marxists, chewing *Kapital*, word by word, line by line, grooving on the labor theory of value and the fetishism of the marketplace as if I'd been given the keys to the vault of knowledge. The street was a spectacle I never tired of. Life in the neighborhood bars and cafes was charged with human vibrancy and urban cool. One devoured the high or avant-garde arts as much or little as inclination demanded. Where else could you see Andre Gregory's *End Game*, Meredith Monk's *Quarry*, and the Royal Khmer Ballet in the same season? Wasn't it a time? And it was mine. *Amour propre* would out. And I was glad of it.

Postscript on War Crimes

In November 1971, the Americal Division was quietly disbanded. In one news report there's an extraordinary quote from a senior officer who remained in-country when his "196th Infantry Brigade was quietly detached" from its departing division. "Nobody in the brigade gives a damn about this war anymore, including me. We will all be happy to go home, and when we do the enemy will march down out of the hills and take over."[196]

By then, no one could remain a happy camper with the Americal. The final blow to the division's much soiled reputation had occurred the previous June. The army accused General John W. Donaldson, formerly a colonel and commander of the Americal's 11th Brigade, "of murdering six Vietnamese civilians ... in the winter of 1968–69," exactly overlapping the period I served under his command in Vietnam. As noted earlier, Donaldson's notoriety as a "gook hunter" circulated openly through the brigade's rumor mill. And although he was fingered by the man who piloted his own chopper, Donaldson never stood trial. Charges against him were eventually dropped for "lack of evidence," but his once promising career as a professional officer was over. He was, after all, the first general officer accused of war crimes since a General Jacob H. Smith, who had commanded a brigade in the Philippines in 1901.[197]

❖   ❖   ❖

Readers might conclude that the U.S. government was, and has remained, remarkably successful in ignoring its criminal responsibility for the war of aggression against Vietnam, and for the atrocity-producing tactical and strategic policies that defined U.S. prosecution of that war. With equal adroitness, one might argue, did a succession of administrations in Washington squash or sidetrack every call and effort to convene a full blown investigation into these war crimes accusations. A postwar consensus would subsequently emerge, with the apparent acquiescence of the nation's principal news and media outlets, and — though with slightly less unanimity — throughout academe, to prevent a full accounting of the war crimes controversy from appearing in official and mainstream histories of the war. It remains official U.S. doctrine that the My Lai massacre was an aberrant action, and that the "war crimes industry" was manufactured by the antiwar movement in coordination with its friends in Moscow and Hanoi to embarrass our government and undermine its war effort.

The phrase *war crimes industry* had been introduced into the postwar literature by Guenter Lewy in his semi-official history of the war, *America in*

Vietnam.[198] Among American historians, three broad lines of historical argument on the meaning of the Vietnam War have emerged over the years: the hawkish, or conservative line; the dovish, or liberal line, and the radical, or antiwar line. Lewy's work is very much an apology for the prowar line of thought, based substantially on records provided to the historian by the Pentagon, whose quoted sources and official rationales generously decorate Lewy's text.

Of all the historical summing-up that follow in the immediate wake of the war, only two authors, Guenter Lewy and Norman Podhoretz, seemed to perceive the work of the Citizen's Commission of Inquiry as sufficiently threatening to warrant engagement directly and by name. Podhoretz makes no attempt at objectivity; his bitter prose simply dismisses CCI in the vein of the obsessed neocon whose gods of youthful idealism failed him long ago.[199] Whereas Lewy, in an entire chapter devoted to the war crimes industry, "Atrocities: Fiction or Fact," lines up a few hastily constructed straw men and mows them down with the sharp edge of sophistry befitting the prestidigitation of a state propagandist.

The tenor of Lewy's position is that "In an unsuccessful and unpopular war like Vietnam..., atrocities are blamed on one's own nation's army," for which wild assertion Lewy offers not a single proof or argument. As for those issues bearing directly on the work of CCI and VVAW, two veterans, Lee Meyrowitz and Ken Campbell, have responded ably to Lewy's principal objection that our motives were "political."

> The veterans who testified at these war crimes hearings had ending the Vietnam War as their ultimate objective. But does this mean, therefore, that the atrocities described did not happen, or if they did happen, that they were not war crimes? These former infantrymen, pilots, artillery observers, and interrogators did not testify to witnessing or participating in atrocities in Vietnam because they opposed the war; rather they opposed the war *because* they had witnessed or participated in atrocities. Lewy did not appreciate this crucial distinction.[200]

❖   ❖   ❖

I close this account with a wild speculation of my own, and point a trail that someone else may wish to follow. Is it just possible that the contemporary world's heightened, if selective, interest in the prosecution of war criminals derives some portion of its historical legitimacy and momentum from the widespread exposure once given to American atrocities in Vietnam? And will the existence of what we are told is a permanent world body to investigate and try future violations of the laws of war one day lead back to a reexamination of American conduct of the war in Vietnam? Or will our crimes in Vietnam join with, say, slavery and the genocide of Native Americans, ever lurking as one more "hideous scandal in the background of American history?"[201]

Chapter Notes

I. Days of Slumber

1. I tracked down the following note from music licensing consultant Ralph Berliner of New York City: "Ernie Kovacs loved music and its possibilities as accompaniment for humor. His musical choices were certainly eclectic. His main theme song was called 'Oriental Blues,' by Jack Newlon, which borrows heavily from 'Rialto Ripples Rag,' a quirky piano number by George Gershwin. Robert Maxwell's 'Solfeggio' became so associated with Kovacs' derby-hatted apes, that it became better known simply as 'The Song of the Nairobi Trio.'"

2. Beginning and ending for most kids then with *Mad Magazine*, published each month by "the usual gang of idiots"; there was the *Monocle* for the older, more literary sophisticates.

3. Family trips to the City, other than to relatives in Queens, were to the annual Easter show at Radio City Music Hall, to Madison Square Garden for the circus, or, on occasion, to one of the three major league ballparks.

4. Only in the mid-nineties would I learn that George, now called Jorge — and identified as a native of Costa Rica — had become something of a recording star. He had joined forces with an Iranian guitarist and carved out a comfortable following among fans of world music under the rubric *Strunz & Farah*.

5. This being today a university that is widely known for its all–African American basketball team!

6. Sugar Loaf Mountain, one of Rio's signature tourist attractions.

7. Leonel Brizola died in 2004.

II. Days of Wakening

1. Two classic contemporary works on the Vietnam era GI movement are David Cortright, *Soldiers in Revolt: The American Military Today* (Garden City, New York: Doubleday, 1975; reprinted by Haymarket, 2005), and Matthew Rinaldi, "The Olive-Drab Rebels: Military Organizing During the Vietnam War," *Radial America* 8, no. 3 (1974).

III. Days of War (1)

1. My own account appears twice in the Vietnam literature, in Christian G. Appy, *Working Class War: American Combat Soldiers and Vietnam* (Chapel Hill: University of North Carolina Press, 1993), p. 130; and in Mark Baker, *NAM: The Vietnam War in the Words of the Men and Women Who Fought There* (William Morrow and Company, 1981) pp. 51–52, which was Appy's source for this material. My best memory of what actually took place is that which appears above.

2. Abbreviation for "combat assault," a military operation involving no set number of troops, usually *inserted* in the target area by helicopter.

3. MACV — Military Assistance Command Vietnam, and below MIT — Military Intelligence Team.

4. The account of Donaldson's downfall was widely covered. The case later resurfaced in an article about Colin Powell, "A Soldier's Story," that Charles Lane wrote for the *New Republic*, October 16, 1995. He writes: "On June 2, 1971, the Army's criminal division

lodged murder charges against General John W. Donaldson, the former American Division chief of staff with whom Powell worked closely for eight months. The case was based on sworn complaints from Donaldson's own helicopter pilots to the effect that Donaldson, without provocation, had shot and killed six unarmed Vietnamese civilians from the air in late 1968 and early 1969." This is the time frame during which Donaldson commanded the American's 11th Brigade.

5. In his *America's Longest War: The United States and Vietnam 1950–1975* (New York: Knopf, 1986; p.155) historian George C. Herring concluded, quoting Army Chief of Staff General Howard Johnson, that "as much as 85 percent of the ammunition used [by American forces] was unobserved fire."

6. Charley-Charley — Command and Control Helicopter; the Huey or "slick" used for the commander's personal conveyance; "zero, zero one zero" equals ten minutes.

7. Each "click" on the dial of the standard army issue compass represented one kilometer.

8. KIA, killed in action; WIA, wounded in action.

9. When General John Donaldson was later charged with "gook hunting," Powell provided an affidavit in support of his former boss in Vietnam, claiming that the pursuit of Vietnamese males of "military age" by helicopter was an "effective means of separating hostiles from the general population." It was such reasoning, wrote Charles Lane in the *New Republic* article cited above (note 4), that led to the dismissal of charges against Donaldson.

IV. Days of War (2)

1. The beer was actually Carling Black Label, and the advertising jingle ran, "Mable ... Black Label."

2. The incurably sardonic American GI had a recipe for ending the war: Separate the good Vietnamese from the bad. Put the good Vietnamese on boats. Nuke the country. Sink the boats.

3. Three years later this became my introductory piece of published writing in *Winning Hearts and Minds* (McGraw Hill, 1972), the first anthology of Vietnam Veteran poetry from the war, appearing several months before the signing of the peace accord.

4. Bobby Seale of the Black Panther Party, in *Seize the Time* (Random House, 1970), p. 408, provides the following gloss for this "revolutionary term": "Motherfucker actually comes from the old slave system and was a reference to the slave master who raped our mothers which society today doesn't want to face as a fact." And, quoting Eldridge Cleaver, "I've seen and heard brothers use the word four or five times in one sentence and each time the word has a *different* meaning and expression" (italics in original).

5. Pretty girls.

6. The *ao dai* is the traditional outfit of Vietnamese women, a flowing jumper, often white, cut high at both sides, over loose fitting pants, often black.

7. The view from those routinely targeted by B-52s is graphically described in *A Viet Cong Memoir: An Inside Account of the Vietnam War and Its Aftermath*, by Trung Nhu Tang, a former minister of justice with the South Vietnamese National Liberation Front (Viet Cong), with David Chanoff and Doan Van Toai (New York: Vintage, 1985), p. 167. Tang writes: "nothing the guerrillas had to endure compared with the stark terrorization of the B-52 bombardments ... the high altitude ... invisible predators ... an experience of undiluted psychological terror, into which we were plunged, day in, day out, for years on end." When operating over North Vietnam rather than in the South, sophisticated anti-aircraft weaponry leveled the playing field to a greater extent, and many B-52s were shot down.

8. Our fallen comrade's name appears on line 31W17 on *The Wall*, the Vietnam Memorial in Washington.

9. Gide (Vintage, 1958) has Michel recall his illness with the following words, "My fatigue in the meantime was growing greater every day; but I should have thought it was shameful to give into it. I had a bad cough and a curious feeling of discomfort in the upper part of my chest" (p. 13).

10. The politics of jockeying for command time is a key stratagem for advancement in rank within the armed forces.

V. Days of Reckoning

1. The quote is from "Human Nature: Justice versus Power," in *Foucault And His Interlocutors*, ed. Arnold I. Davidson (University of Chicago Press, 1997).

2. The full name of the organization was the National Committee for a Citizens' Commission of Inquiry on U.S. War Crimes in Vietnam, whose founding by Ralph Schoenman, a former personal secretary to Bertrand Russell, had been reported in the *New York Times* on Sunday, November 30, 1969. CCI was a direct descendant of the International Tribunal on War Crimes that Lord Russell had sponsored — and Schoenman helped to organize — in Stockholm, Sweden (May 2–10, 1967) and Roskilde, Denmark (Nov. 20–Dec. 1, 1967) two years earlier, with the participation of Jean Paul Sartre, Simone de Beauvoir, Khrishna Mennan, and Dave Dellinger, among other intellectuals and jurists of world renown. The Times article ("Peace Group to Set Up Panels on Atrocity Charges"), without byline, quotes Schoenman on what would become the guiding themes of CCI's work over the course of its brief existence during the next year-and-a-half, the gist of which I summarize here: that First Lieutenant William L. Calley Jr., a principal participant in the March 16, 1968, My Lai massacre, whose court martial was about to begin at Fort Benning, Georgia, should not "be used as a scapegoat" for atrocities in Vietnam which were a matter of American policy, formulated, not by lowly lieutenants in the field, however deranged, but at the highest levels of government and military command. More than twenty boxes holding records of the Citizens' Commission of Inquiry, and those of its successor organizations, the Safe Return Amnesty Committee, FORA (Friends of Resisters for Amnesty), PIC (the Portugal Information Center), and Citizen Soldier, are housed in the Department of Rare and Manuscript Collections of the Cornell University Library.

3. The two were Arthur Felberbaum, a Trotskyist activist of long standing who later founded the New York School for Marxist Education, but was at that moment affiliated with CCI, and poet Jan (Barry) Crumb, a founder of Vietnam Veterans Against the War (VVAW) who had served in Vietnam in 1963; each cut a figure in New York radical circles for a time, and both their lives intersected with the events this chapter remembers and chronicles, though their parts may not appear much in the writing of this particular account.

4. The real pariahs at Valley Forge inhabited the amputee ward, which TB patients wearing surgical masks would pass through on the one morning a week the PX was emptied and we were permitted to shop there. It's impossible to describe — or forget — the expressions on the faces of young men, propped up on their pillows, whose limbs were pruned to stubs by mines or booby traps in Vietnam.

5. Months earlier when my commander in Vietnam had dressed me down about my unmilitary moustaches, I'd folded like an old book; now, in the spirit of my former comrade Lt. Patton, I was ready to take a stand against command intimidation. The colonel would look foolish seeking approval from a general officer at a regional command to slap an incapacitated junior officer fresh from the war zone with an Article 15, the standard non-judicial punishment, over such a trivial matter and I knew it. Exploiting this advantage, I dared the colonel to do his worst, then turned on my heels and left him standing with the veins in his head about to burst, an event even more delectable in memory, no doubt, than it was in fact.

6. The My Lai massacre took place on March 16, 1968, but would only come to light publicly in November 1969, several months after I left the hospital; the invasions and carpet bombings of Cambodia and Laos, the Christmas bombing of Hanoi and Haiphong, had all yet to occur.

7. Chomsky's other writings were also exerting an influence on my political development by this time. His "After Pinkville," in *The New York Review of Books* that January, provided the first important conceptual framework I would appropriate for understanding my own experiences in Vietnam.

8. That Christmas, John, whose roots were Boston Italian, presented me with a bottle of "dago red," and this poetic parody of his literary idols: *Lo this vintage is no prize, it might in fact burn out your eyes, and give you pains, eat out your brain, but it will make you wise. This gift is not in retaliation, but merely a seasonal salutation, a thought not worth a penny, one thought amongst so many. Forget ole Chomsky and Levine, and with this fire, drown your spleen, until you see but red and green, until your humors turn to cherry, and make unsaintly Xmas merry.*

9. By late 1969, as CCI principal Tod Ensign puts it, "the veterans were not particularly present. The G.I. movement, we were aware of that ... the coffee houses..." (interview with Tod Ensign, April 16, 1995). For the only really extensive accounts or analyses

of the GI movement, see David Cortright, *Soldiers in Revolt: The American Military Today*, and Matthew Rinaldi, "The Olive-Drab Rebels: Military Organizing During the Vietnam War," cited above. The subsequent history of the antiwar veterans, and of the essentially working and underclass character of those who did the fighting, is well covered in such postwar sources as Andrew Hunt, *The Turning: A History of the Vietnam Veterans Against the War* (New York University Press, 1999); and Christian Appy, *Working Class War: American Combat Soldiers and Vietnam* (The University of North Carolina Press, 1993).

10. Cointelpro was an FBI managed program engineered by the Nixon administration to undermine the organized Left, and, in particular, destroy the Black Liberation Movement.

11. I met these folk only once or twice. An anecdote of Tod's about one of their meetings provides more detail on a political culture which most in those years did not experience, many do not wish to remember, or, if born to subsequent times, find hard to even imagine. Seems the psychiatrist had some distant family connection to Lev Davidovich Bronstein, alias Leon Trotsky; but he was no "Trotskyite!" One night Tod watched the shrink play the heavy as he opened a meeting by putting his loaded *piece* on the table before him, right next to the text by Joe Stalin that was the subject of the evening's study. You couldn't write a better scene. Such theatrics — taken quite seriously by the participants at the time — are amusing to look back on, at least in those cases where fantasy did not leak into some misadventure.

12. Ensign interview.

13. See footnote 2 at the beginning of this chapter. Much of the account of CCI's early months, before I joined the effort, comes from CCI's internal records housed at the Cornell University Library, and from interviews conducted by me with Ensign and Rifkin. Attempts to interview Schoenman for this account were unsuccessful, whereas, by the time of this writing, Arthur Felberbaum had already passed away. One of the best accounts of Ralph Schoenman's colorful adventures on the Left, before his founding of the CCI, can be found in the delectable memoir of the anti–Vietnam War Movement in England, *Street Fighting Years* (Collins, 1987), by Tariq Ali.

14. Ensign interview.

15. Rifkin interview.

16. The *Guardian* Extra Edition, December 1969. There is a considerable literature on the topic of the My Lai massacre; one of the most detailed and readable accounts is Michael Bilton and Kevin Sim, *Four Hours in My Lai* (Penguin Books, 1993).

17. Ensign interview. It is unlikely that this criticism of polemical excess can be laid at the feet of journalist Jonathan Schell, who also spoke at the Diplomat that night. The Harvard educated Schell was a patrician by birth, but positively Orwellian in his skepticism of U.S. aims and policy in Vietnam. He authored the definitive expose of the American air war, initially in the pages of the *New Yorker* magazine, now assembled in Jonathan Schell, *The Real War: The Classic Reporting on the Vietnam War with a New Essay* (New York: Da Capo Press, 2000), collecting Schell's original two reports, *The Military Half* and *The Village of Ben Suc,* while adding his subsequent retrospective on the war.

18. Fred Halsted, *Out Now: A Participant's Account of the American Movement Against the Vietnam War* (New York: Monad Press, 1978).

19. Halsted, *Out Now,* and Todd Gitlin, *The Sixties: Year of Hope, Days of Rage*, (Bantam Books, 1993).

20. I don't mean to ignore here those three or four Vietnam veterans who, on several prior occasions, had already publicly denounced American atrocities in Vietnam; I simply wish to emphasize that their "testimony" was lost on the general public in the U.S., owing to the media's reluctance to legitimize the settings — the Russell Tribunals, for example — in which they were presented. Coverage in the *New York Times* throughout 1967, for example, was particularly hostile to Lord Russell personally, as well as to his stance and activities against the U.S. war effort.

21. For those initiated into the jargon of the Left, the abbreviation "CP" automatically translates as "Communist Party," in this instance, the Canadian branch of that essentially pro–USSR, which is to say Russian, political apparatus.

22. Dr. Gordon S. Livingston was an important early sponsor of the CCI. Livingston, a 1960 graduate of West Point, had served as regimental surgeon on the staff of Col. George S. Patton, commander of the 11th Armored Calvary. Livingston's "Letter from Vietnam," published in the *Saturday Review*, September 20, 1969, is one of the most

thoughtful and convincing recitations from an American participant of what was wrong with the Vietnam War.

23. Personal communication, September 19, 1997.

24. This phenomenon was observed by Robert J. Lifton, MD, who uses this phrasing in *Home from the War*, Simon and Schuster, 1973.

25. "Anti-War Group Plans Meetings in Annapolis," *The Evening Star* (Washington, D.C.), March 6, 1970; dateline Baltimore.

26. Erwin Knoll, then Washington correspondent for *The Progressive,* and co-editor Judith Nies McFadden assembled a transcript of the proceedings in an instant paperback, *War Crimes and the American Conscience: Congressional Conference on War and National Responsibility* (Holt, Rinehart and Winston, 1970). Knoll would become a tireless supporter of CCI's efforts over the next two years.

27. Don Frese, "War crimes unit stages Vietnam horror showing," *Evening Star* (Annapolis, Md.), Mar. 12, 1970.

28. "Eyewitnesses report on U.S.-Viet horrors," *The Baltimore Afro-American*, Mar. 17, 1970.

29. Ensign interview.

30. Adding insult to injury, the *Times* ran another notice on Dec. 20, 1969, stating that the "U.S. Court of Appeals Rejects Schoenman Bid for Passport." The blurb reads in part, "Mr. Schoenman's passport was lifted after his return from Sweden, where a so-called war crimes tribunal had convicted the United States and President Johnson of military atrocities in Vietnam." One monument to this work that Ralph Schoenman has left behind is the 1968 book, initially self-published, *Against the Crime of Silence: Proceedings of the International War Crimes Tribunal*, and reprinted in 1970 by Simon and Schuster as a Clarion Book, edited by John Duffett, with a preface by Noam Chomsky.

31. See Chapter I.

32. Tod Ensign provided this brief memorial for Pamela Booth: "I would describe Pamela as a 'first wave' feminist, back when women's liberation meant more than just the question of WHO was on top. She was an early advocate for women's health in the broadest sense of the word. She worked to raise the important issue of women's CONTROL over their bodies — not just when they were pregnant, either. She had returned to Columbia where she earned a Masters of Public Health

degree — of which she was very proud. It makes me sad to think of her and her premature end. RIP."

33. Adam Fisher, "Group Tells 'True Nature' of War," *Springfield Daily News* (Springfield, Mass.), Monday Evening, April 6, 1970.

34. Douglas Robinson, "Ex-Pilot Alleges Civilian Slayings: Tells Citizens Inquiry 33 Were Killed by a Major," *The New York Times*, Tuesday, April 7, 1970.

35. "New massacre claim probed," *The Boston Globe* (UPI), April 8, 1970.

36. In addition to Chomsky, CCI board members regularly consulted in these early stages were Mel Wulf of the ACLU, Herb Magidson of Business Executives for Peace, Mark Sacaroff of Temple University, and Andy Stapp of the American Serviceman's Union; this group was soon extended to include Richard Falk of Princeton, Robert J. Lifton of Yale, Chaim Shatan, a New York psychiatrist, Marcus Raskin and Richard Barnett of the Institute for Policy Studies, and Peter Weiss of the Center for Constitutional Rights, among several others.

37. "3 Viet Vets Charge 'Routine Use of Torture by U.S. Troops,'" *The New York Post*, April 13, 1970; Timothy Ferris, "2 Vets Say GI's Tortured Captives," *The New York Post*, April 14, 1970; Jim Stingley, "Ex-GI's Charge Viet Prisoners Were Tortured," *The Los Angeles Times*, Weds., Apr. 15, 1970. For the first time, the principal weeklies of the Left also ran stories: "GI's reveal new atrocities," *The Guardian*, April 18, 1970; "Torture Techniques Reported," *The Militant*, Friday, May 8, 1970.

38. The self-quotation comes from the draft, in my possession, of the talk I delivered at Clarkson College of Technology, April 11, 1970; the term *standard operating procedure*, as applied by CCI to atrocity-producing U.S. field policies, appears in print first in Ferris, "2 Vets Say GI's Tortured Captives"; the term *aberrant* had become common usage in government circles since the My Lai revelation, whenever official reference was made to allegations of U.S. atrocities throughout Indochina.

39. In some early accounts, there is an almost partisan tone to the sympathy expressed on behalf of the vets, as if the chair long left empty for them at the national table of debate on the war had been finally and gratefully filled. *The Springfield Union*, April 7, 1970, had commented, "The three men were dressed conservatively in sports jackets and

ties, and their presentation, made in a question and answer format, was articulate, dignified and moving"; a far cry from the wild-man TV and movies images of Vietnam veterans that were later enshrined within the popular culture.

40. Larry Rottmann has written some of the most interesting, and — to the degree such a word can be applied to this literary form in the United States — lasting Vietnam War poetry by an American. His early work appears in the volume he helped to edit and get published, *Winning Hearts and Minds, War Poems by Vietnam Veterans*, edited by Larry Rottmann, Jan Barry and Basil T. Paquet (1st Casualty Press, 1972; reprinted that same year by McGraw Hill).

41. Douglas Crocket, "Two ex–GIs say troops torture prisoners in Vietnam," *The Boston Globe*, Friday Morning, May 8, 1970; Dave O'Brian, "Ex-Intelligence Officers List War Crimes Witnessed," *Boston Record American*, Friday, May 8, 1970; "Lethal Nerve Gas in Vietnam Charged," *The New York Times*, May 8, 1970; "'67 Yank forays in Cambodia told," United Press International wire story, *Chicago Sun-Times*, Friday May 8, 1970; Richard W. McManus, "'Unofficial' atrocities attributed to Pentagon," *The Christian Science Monitor*, Friday, May 8, 1970.

42. Based on my long exposure to Noam Chomsky's political writing over the years, I can see that, as was and is often the case, his comments placed him ahead of the curve. The *Globe* printed only Chomsky's bitter remark that the American government was made up of "desperados and lawbreakers," and that "it's senseless to talk about the law in these times." The *Christian Science Monitor*, on the other hand, reported Chomsky's revelation about the secret war in Laos, where the U.S. was at that time conducting in excess of 500 bombing sorties per day. This was yet another "premature truth" possessed by the antiwar Left which mainstream media, in general, was not ready to touch.

43. Gitlin, *The Sixties*. The "teach-in," rendered passé by the rapid radicalization of student bodies everywhere, was suddenly attractive to college administrations looking for ways and means to contain what was beginning to look like outright rebellion on campuses all around the country.

44. I think of myself as in the vanguard of upward mobility of the working class.

45. I later confirmed this account in an interview with Noam Chomsky, February 15, 1995.

46. I also spent an hour in fascination before *Los Desastres de la Guerra*, Goya's stark drawings and engravings of scenes of atrocities committed in Spain during the Napoleonic Wars, in a gallery that most of those present in the Prado that morning, owing no doubt to the discomforting nature of the subject matter depicted, avoided like the plague itself.

47. Culture note: Children of the millennium, Generation X, my own son, Simon, for example, of the more vaguely designated Gen Y, have no frame of reference in their social experience for understanding the phenomenon of Mao's *Little Red Book*, with its place on every lefty's bookshelf, even if one quoted the Great Helmsman's pithy sayings only with considerable irony.

48. By early 1976, some months after the Revolution of Carnations in Portugal finally swept the fascists from the stage, Tod Ensign and I were back in Lisbon, playing occasional correspondent for *The Progressive* magazine, and attempting to broadcast the good news of Workers and Soldiers Control to an audience of American radicals through an organ of our own, the Portugal Information Bulletin. See also Carl Feingold, Tod Ensign and Michael Uhl, "Portugal: The Meaning of November 25," *Radical America* 10, no. 2 (March–April 1976).

49. The paper trail on which my account of these events from June through August 1970 is based includes copies of personal correspondence between Ensign, Rifkin and myself, and a sheaf of reports and internal documents generated by CCI, all of which are stored in the group's Cornell University Library collection, and on the interviews conducted with the principals, already cited.

Jeremy Rifkin's letter to Maria Jolas, a native of Kentucky whose husband had been a close associate and literary executor of James Joyce, is the clearest expression of the group's actions and intentions to that date: "The Commission believes that the only way to convince the American public that a policy of genocide is being pursued is by encouraging active duty soldiers and veterans to testify publicly about their personal involvement in war crimes in Vietnam ... we had held nine hearings in U.S. cities at which some twenty-five former soldiers have testified on the use of systematic torture, mass murder, etc."

(letter dated June 19, 1970; Cornell University Library #7033, Box 1).

50. William Greider, "Ex-GIS Tell of Torturing Prisoners," *The Washington Post*, July 19, 1970. Greider's article had gone out on the *Post* wire service, and was carried widely, in such papers as *The Des Moines Register*, *The Providence Journal*, and the *San Francisco Chronicle.*

CCI scored a second coup the following day, when Steve Noetzel, a former Green Beret living on Long Island, "called today for an immediate congressional investigation of the military's policy of systematic torture of Vietnamese by U.S. military intelligence personnel in South Vietnam." The veteran gave a grisly account of atrocities he had witnessed, and the article concludes with a quote from me as a fellow Long Islander, lifted from a CCI press release: "Michael J. Uhl, another lieutenant who served in intelligence, said, "I have personally witnessed the use of field telephone wires that were attached to the fingers and elbows of the suspects. Most of the time the suspect danced with pain and fell to the floor. Obviously, this technique did get people to talk" ("LI'r Charges U.S. Tortured Vietnamese," *Long Island Press*, July 20, 1970).

51. The Army Criminal Investigation Division (CID) report quoted here is reproduced from the National Archives depository in College Park, Md., located in Case File 52 and titled "Murphy-Patton Allegations" (CCI).

52. *Investigation of the My Lai Incident*, Report of the Armed Services Investigating Subcommittee of the Committee on Armed Services House of Representatives, Ninety-First Congress, Second Session, July 15, 1970.

53. Timothy Ferris, "Pacifists Offer My Lai Defense," *The New York Post*, July 7, 1970; on what basis the headline writer at the *Post* invented the notion that CCI activists were "pacifists," is a mystery; it was never a way in which we saw or presented ourselves.

54. Jeremy Rifkin listed these in a letter he sent to me in Portugal, dated July 20, 1970. He wrote, "We've got some new sponsors for the Commission. Dave Dellinger, Sen. Gruening, Jane Fonda, Toni Randall, Ossie Davis, Ben Spock, Stewart Meecham, Richard Falk, Bob Lifton et al." Ernest Gruening of Alaska, with Sen. Wayne Morse of Oregon, were the only two members of the United States Congress to vote against the 1964 Gulf of Tonkin Resolution, the unofficial declaration of war against Vietnam. Meecham was a leader in the American Friends Service Committee, Falk and Lifton, highly regarded academics, the former at Princeton, the latter at Yale.

55. Carl Shires, "Atrocities in Vietnam Said 'a Way of Life," *The Richmond News Leader*, Aug. 18, 1970. The story, featuring the testimony of four new vets, also ran in the *Washington Post*, the *International Herald Tribune*, the *Detroit News*, the *St. Louis Post Dispatch*, the *Minneapolis Star*, the *San Francisco Examiner*, and the *Wheeling News-Register*, in addition to the *Winston-Salem Journal*, and the *Evening News* in Newark, to give only a sampling of the coverage.

56. Letter dated Aug. 20, 1970; Cornell Collection. For Martinsen, see page 132.

57. Letters and document in author's personal collection.

58. As of August 2000, the FBI apparently possesses the computer technology with software called Carnivore to do just that.

59. See, for example, Halsted, *Out Now.*

60. The event was preserved in the film *Different Sons* (Brooklyn, N.Y.: Bowling Green Films, 1970).

61. In an interview by the author, already cited, Noam Chomsky quite rightly referred to Vietnam veterans as "an authentic group," authenticity in this case expressing Chomsky's understanding of the working and underclass origins of those Americans who did the fighting during the war. The point is ably defended by historian Christian Appy throughout his *Working-Class War.*

62. Jane confessed this ambition to Jeremy one evening at CCI's offices. Rifkin interview; Ensign interview.

63. *Fun, travel and adventure* was how army recruiters interpreted FTA.

64. See Hunt, *The Turning.*

65. For better or worse, Mark Lane was not highly regarded in the New Left circles of New York that I frequented. An attorney, he was best known as author of *Rush to Judgment*, a book on the Kennedy assassination advancing the conspiracy thesis. Many criticized this work, and Lane's subsequent book about war crimes, *Conversations with Americans* (Simon and Schuster, 1970) as shoddy and sensationalistic. Mark Lane's own views on the Winter Soldier experience can be found in Hunt, *The Turning.*

66. Ensign interview.

67. Ensign interview. The CCI–VVAW relationship is discussed in some detail in Hunt, *The Turning.*

68. An East Coast–based committee made up primarily of antiwar clergy, the most prominent of whom was the pastor of New York's Riverside Church, Rev. William Sloan Coffin.

69. It is perhaps unfair to describe Jane Fonda as "pouty"; she had an arduous shooting schedule most days filming *Klute*. The expression and mood she brought to those meetings at CCI was remarkably close to the character she'd created for the film, choices for which she was awarded an Academy Award.

70. Memorandum dated August 31, 1970, and titled "Items Agreed To" (Cornell University Collection).

71. At a VVAW national convention some time later, Larry Rottmann — with whom I had "testified" in Boston in May 1970 — was reputed to have agitated from the seats with a sign reading, "Free John Kerry's Maid." Senator John Kerry of Massachusetts, a junior naval officer who had served in Vietnam, had been actively, but briefly, associated with VVAW. The anecdote was told to me by an eyewitness at the conference, Vietnam veteran and poet/memoirist, W.D. Ehrhart, and also appears in Hunt, *The Turning*.

72. Tod Ensign had elaborated on this point to Mark Lane directly in a letter dated August 29, 1970, two days before the memo. He wrote, "One of the people we approached for sponsorship, Dr. Robt. J. Lifton, expressed real concern about the nature of the Vietnamese testimony.... We really need to get a commitment and clear understanding as to the precise nature of this testimony (from the PRG) or, I'm afraid we're going to have more problems with this aspect of the WSI" (Cornell Collection). The PRG — Provisional Revolutionary Government — was the governing entity of the National Liberation Front (Vietcong), the South Vietnamese communists and their allies. One criticism Ensign did not confide in this letter, he told me privately, was Lifton's strong opposition to Lane's involvement with CCI and the war crimes issue, period.

73. One of the classic texts on Detroit in hard times is Dan Georgakas and Marvin Surkin, *Detroit I Do Mind Dying: A Study in Urban Revolution* (St. Martin's Press, 1975; revised ed. 1999).

74. Richard Rorty makes the strange case for the Cold War and the anticommunist social democracy on the American Left in *Achieving Our Country* (Harvard University Press, 1997); practically anything by Daniel Singer

argues the opposite, neo–Marxian position; for example, "Exploiting a Tragedy, or Le Rouge en Noir," a book review in *The Nation*, December 13, 1999.

75. Ken Campbell has provided his own accounts of these activities in "Vietnam Veterans and War Crimes Hearings," in *An American Ordeal: The Antiwar Movement of the Vietnam Era*, by Elliott L. Meyrowitz and Kenneth J. Campbell (Syracuse University Press, 1990); and Kenneth J. Campbell, "The International War Crimes Conference, Oslo, June 1971: Excerpts from the Diary of One of the Witnesses," in *Nobody Gets Off The Bus: The Vietnam Generation Big Book* (1994).

76. For one take on the repentance of the former secretary of defense, see "Bombing for the Hell of It," a review of Robert McNamara's *In Retrospect: The Tragedy and Lessons of Vietnam*, by Carol Brightman and Michael Uhl, *The Nation*, June 12, 1995.

77. Joseph H. Trachtman, "Common Procedure in Vietnam: 5 Vets Charge Murders," *The Philadelphia Inquirer*, October 20, 1970.

78. *The New York Times* ran stories on three successive days about the uprising, October 23–25, 1970. The front page story on October 23 noted that the "Canadian government invoked emergency powers against French Canadian separatists...." My own deportation order, dated October 20, 1970, states as the reason for expulsion my membership "in a prohibited class," unspecified other than as not being "a bona-fide non-immigrant." The line for my signature reads, "refused to sign."

79. "*USA-officeren som vittade om krigsförbrytelserna.*" Aftonbladet, Söndagen den 25 oktober, 1970.

80. Certainly the premier eyewitness account of these proceedings is Mary McCarthy's series of articles for the *New York Review of Books*, centered on the trial of Calley's commander, Captain Ernest Medina. Much of McCarthy's writing on the Vietnam War is collected in *The Seventeenth Degree: How It Went, Vietnam, Hanoi, Medina, Son of the Morning* (Harcourt, Brace and Jovanovitch, 1974).

81. James Long, "War Atrocities Termed Commonplace," *Oregon Journal*, October 28, 1970.

82. After the war, two staunch apologists for U.S. Vietnam policy, Guenter Lewy and Norman Podhoretz, addressed and attempted to dismiss, this and other CCI formulations

about American atrocities in works that will be discussed below.

83. Personal communication with the author, August 5, 1999.

84. It would come out later that Hubbard himself may never have actually served a tour in Vietnam. This matter is taken up in context below.

85. Ensign interview.

86. Evelyn Keene, "Jane Fonda's newest cause: probing US 'war crimes,'" *The Boston Sunday Globe*, November 1, 1970.

87. Ensign interview.

88. Rifkin interview.

89. I base this date placement on two letters written by Tod Ensign, copies of which are in the CCI Cornell collection. On Nov. 4th, Tod wrote inviting a Canadian comrade's participation at Winter Soldier in Detroit, while a letter to Dan Amigone in Buffalo on the following day, dated Nov. 5th, is the first documented reference to the split. It reads in part, "We have broken politically with Mark Lane."

90. Ensign interview.

91. Jeremy confirmed this escapade when I reminded him about it years later. "We were all kids," he said. "We were with Jane Fonda" (Rifkin interview). What, I have often wondered, was on Jane Fonda's mind when she found the door locked that day, and the CCI premises, presumably empty? Had she intended to walk off with CCI's files of the veterans' testimony?

92. *The Strawberry Statement: Notes of a College Revolutionary* (Avon, 1969); *Standard Operating Procedure: Notes of a Draft-age American* (with the cooperation of the Citizens' Commission of Inquiry on U.S. War crimes in Indochina) (Avon, 1971). Both works by James Simon Kunen.

93. Cornell collection.

94. The *third* event referred to here was an ad hoc Congressional hearing CCI would organize on Capitol Hill four months later, in April 1971.

95. Joe has remained a lifelong activist in veterans' causes, and was for some time during the nineties in Hanoi where one friend reports he'd opened a gin mill modeled after Rick's Café from the movie *Casablanca*. Joe appears at his articulate best in the documentary film *Sir! No Sir!*, released in 2006.

96. James Reston Jr., *The Amnesty of John David Herndon* (McGraw Hill, 1973).

97. *The Village Voice*, November 26, 1970.

98. *The Chicago Daily News*, for one, ran a long piece on the weekend preceding the NVI. William McGaffin, "Slaughter not unusual: ex–GI," Nov. 28–29, 1970.

99. The American Civil War, of course, had caused a split among West Point grads, and active duty army officers and men, of a grave but different sort.

100. Robert C. Maynard, "War Foes Blame U.S., Commanders for Viet Atrocities," *Washington Post*, November 25, 1970. The press conference was also used by CCI to officially announce the upcoming National Veterans Inquiry. Soon after the NVI, Louis Font was allowed to resign from the U.S. Army under honorable conditions.

101. For example, "Yanks tortured Red prisoners, two GIs testify," *Chicago Daily News* (UPI), December 3, 1970.

102. See note 101.

103. Every ex–GI is given a form DD 214 which summarizes his service history and describes the nature of his discharge. For practical, not political, reasons, CCI had insisted that only veterans honorably discharged be allowed to testify.

104. See note 24.

105. A sample of the press from Day Two, all dated December 3, 1970, includes the *Chicago Daily News* article cited in note 112; Jerry Oppenheimer, "'We could hear them screaming,'" *Washington Daily News;* "Red POWs Pushed Off Copters Witness Says," *Los Angeles Times;* "Ex-CIA man speaks of Vietnam killings," *The Times* (London); "Ex-GI Says He Saw Americans Commit Executions, Atrocities," *The Florida Times-Union;* "Viet Veterans Recall War Crimes," *Charlotte Observer;* "A Tale of Torture and Murder," *Daily Freeman* (Kingston, N.Y.); "GI's threw 2 Viets to death, agent says," *Detroit News;* "Torture was policy, Viet war vets say," *The Cleveland Press;* "Billings Veteran to Testify at 'War Crimes Inquiry,'" *Billings Gazette* (Montana).

106. "War Veterans at Inquiry Feel 'Atrocities' Are Result of Policy," *The New York Times*, Dec. 4, 1970; Jules Witcover, "Veterans Ask Inquiry Into Alleged Atrocities: Meeting Charging U.S. with War Crimes Ends with Ex-GIs' Accounts of Torture," *Los Angeles Times*, Dec. 4, 1970.

107. "'War Crime' Inquiry Hears of Bombing," *San Francisco Chronicle* (UPI), Dec. 4, 1970; Nicholas von Hoffman, "Psychological Slavery," *Washington Post*, Dec. 4, 1970.

108. "Vietnam veterans assert that twice as many of their brethren have died by suicide since the war than died at the hands of the enemy. I, for one, have no inclination to dispute this number, though accurately estimating suicides in this population is even more difficult than counting the homeless." Jonathan Shay, "The Betrayal of 'What's Right': Vietnam Combat Veterans and Post-Traumatic Stress Disorder," in *The Legacies of Vietnam, The Long Term View: A Journal of Informed Opinion* (Massachusetts School of Law, 2000).

109. The case for General William Westmoreland's obsession with "body counts" is convincingly made by Lewis Sorley in *A Better War* (Harcourt Brace, 1999). My review of this book, "The jaws of victory," appeared in the *Sunday Boston Globe Book Review*, August 1, 1999.

110. Richard Dudman was bureau chief in Washington of the *Saint Louis Post Dispatch*. His was also a Vietnam war correspondent, and author of the book *40 Days with the Enemy: The Story of a Journalist Held Captive By Guerrillas in Cambodia* (Liveright, 1971). For the record I note that several vets, including myself, were interviewed by I.F. Stone for his newsletter, a brief reference to which appeared in I.F. Stone's Bi-Weekly, December 14, 1970.

111. *Eichmann in Jerusalem: A Report on the Banality of Evil* (Viking, 1963).

112. Kunen op. cit.; Ensign interview.

113. A review of *Conversations with Americans* by Mark Lane, *The New York Times Book Review*, Sunday, December 27, 1970. "This book," begins Neil Sheehan, "is so irresponsible that it may help to provoke a responsible inquiry into the question of war crimes and atrocities in Vietnam."

114. These articles are cited in context below. See notes 175 and 176.

115. David Schoenbrun's review "American Atrocities in Vietnam," which appeared in the *Washington Post* the same day John Leonard's critique of *Conversations with Americans* ran in the *New York Times,* Wednesday, November 18, 1970.

116. In late October, Mark Lane had publicly called on "the Pentagon to appoint an official War Crimes Commission," the very position he now claimed to oppose in his dispute with Sheehan. See page 166.

117. In two essays, written twenty-five years apart, Neil Sheehan's views on the Vietnam War, while complex and engagingly readable, remain essentially unchanged: the war, a well meaning mistake, not an act of aggression. "Not a Dove, but No Longer a Hawk," *The New York Times Magazine,* October 9, 1966, in Reporting Vietnam Part One: American Journalism 1959–1969 (The Library of America, 1998); *After the War Was Over: Hanoi and Saigon* (Vintage, 1991).

118. VVAW's organizational history is the subject of Andrew Hunt's *The Turning: A History of Vietnam Veterans Against the War* (New York University Press, 1999); a related work is Richard Moser's *The New Winter Soldiers: GI and Veteran Dissent During the Vietnam Era* (Rutgers University Press, 1996).

119. Sheehan, "Not a Dove."

120. Sheehan, review of *Conversations with Americans.*

121. "Two weeks later, the New Years Eve edition of the *Voice* carried Nat Hentoff's parting eulogy for the NVI, "Why doesn't somebody do something?" In his column, Hentoff concurs with Jules Witcover's opinion (*Los Angeles Times,* December 8, 1970) that the event was "little noticed," while providing a lengthy summation of testimony "that was left out of the [New York] Times."

122. Taylor's book (A New York Times Quadrangle Book, 1970), had been favorably reviewed by John Leonard in the same "Books of the Times" column where Leonard examined Mark Lane's *Conversations with Americans.* There Leonard noted that the "logic" of Taylor's argument about war crimes in Vietnam "leads upward — to the policy makers."

123. *The New York Times*, Saturday, January 9, 1971.

124. Ibid.

125. Neil Sheehan, "Five Officers Say They Seek Formal War Crimes Inquires," *The New York Times,* January 13, 1971.

126. A COM spokesperson told Sheehan that the organization has "about 600 adherents, including about 20 officers in South Vietnam." Sheehan, ibid.

127. Activists in the antiwar movement had been publicizing this point for years. See for example Carol Brightman, "The Weed Killers," *Viet-Report,* June–July, 1966; the health aspect of the Agent Orange controversy was, in part, the subject of a book written by Tod Ensign and myself which appeared in early 1980: *G.I. Guinea Pigs: How the Military Exposed Our Troops to Dangers More Deadly Than War* (Playboy Books). There is a tragic

irony associated with this press conference. One of the young officers, LTJG Peter Dunkelberger, was subsequently invited to discuss his grievances with the then Chief of Naval Operations Admiral Elmo Zumwalt at a formal naval dinner party; Zumwalt would later become an advocate for veterans in the Agent Orange controversy when his own son succumbed to cancer, possibly resulting from herbicide exposure in Vietnam.

128. Letter from John Lloyd, secretary, Vietnam Moratorium Campaign, Melbourne, Australia, November 18, 1970. Cornell Collection.

129. Exchange of letters between John Lloyd and myself: Dec. 10, 16, 17, 30, 1970. Cornell Collection.

130. The most extensive retrospective of this debate among participants, with a detailed account of the Winter Soldier experience, can be found in Hunt, *The Turning.* See also Tod Ensign, "American War Crimes and Vietnam Veterans," in *Against the Vietnam War: Writings by Activists,* ed. Mary Susannah Robbins (Syracuse University Press, 1999); and Meyrowitz and Campbell, "Vietnam Veterans and the War Crimes Hearings."

131. Hunt, *The Turning.*

132. Philosopher Richard Rorty, no booster of the New Left, offers this appraisal: "[T]he New Left accomplished something enormously important. It ended the Vietnam War. It may have saved our country from becoming a garrison state. Without the widespread and continued civil disobedience conducted by the New Left we might still ... be fighting in the farther reaches of Asia. For suppose that no young Americans had protested.... Can we be so sure that the war's unwinnability would have been enough to persuade our government to make peace?" *Achieving Our Country* (Harvard University Press, 1999).

133. The classic acknowledgment and detailing of this catastrophe emerged from the ranks of the professional officer corps. Colonel Robert D. Heinl, "The Collapse of the Armed Forces," *Armed Forces Journal,* June 7, 1971.

134. At its cynical substrata, this policy held that a majority of Americans would tune the war out during its final stages, including the massive bombing campaigns that, by implication if not design, targeted Vietnamese civilians, when U.S. casualties were reduced by "changing the color of the corpses."

135. My experience of the New Left collectivity steered somewhere between the "beloved community" of Martin Luther King, much evoked by Todd Gitlin in *The Sixties,* and the rather darker vision articulated by social historian David Sabean: "In community lie dangers, the more so as one is often unprepared for attack." *Power in the Blood: Popular Culture and Village Discourse in Early Modern Germany* (Cambridge University Press, 1984).

136. *The Australian,* February 17, 1971.

137. *Tribune* (Australia), February 24, 1971.

138. *Tribune,* February 24, 1971.

139. I cite here a sampling of the print media attention my speaking tour attracted in Australia and New Zealand from Feb. 17 to Mar. 13 , 1971: "Guests of the Moratorium," *The Sydney Morning Herald,* Feb. 17; *The Australian,* Feb. 18; "Have We Any Skeletons," and "Ex GI tells it like it is: My Lai logical result of war plan," *Sunday Observer* (Melbourne), Feb. 21; "Veteran: My Lais Daily Event," *Canberra News,* Feb. 24; "Former warrior now works for peace in Vietnam," *The Age* (Brisbane), Mar. 4; "US students speak up against war," *The Mercury,* (Hobart, Tasmania), Mar. 6; "Organizing GIs and Vietnam Veterans — 'in the belly of the monster': an interview with Michael Uhl," *Tribune,* Mar. 10; "Army has obsession with body count," *Christchurch Star* (New Zealand), Mar. 11; "American GI Claims Torture Is Used," *The Otago Daily Times* (Dunedin, N.Z.), Mar. 12; "Former US Officer in Vietnam Critical of America's Role," *The Evening Post* (Wellington, N.Z.), Mar. 12; "US Soldiers in Vietnam Forced to Follow a Policy of Genocide," *The Evening Post,* Mar. 13.

140. The italicized term belongs to Todd Gitlin, *The Sixties,* who wrote that "After the Chicago confrontation, Tom Hayden ... moved to Berkeley and soon became nonleader of a succession of communes, culminating ... in one called the Red Family."

141. Evidence of this is the manuscript in my possession of a very lucid presentation Hayden made before a workshop of an SDS reunion in September 1981. His talked addressed the question, "What do we want to achieve in the years ahead," and is extremely concrete in its range and focus.

142. Gitlin, *The Sixties.*

143. Personal communication.

144. Richard Rorty observes approvingly circa 1998 that "the tone in which educated men talk about women, and educated whites about blacks, is very different from what it was

before the Sixties," an outcome he correctly attributes to struggles within the New Left, many of whose adherents were stalwart participants in the antiwar and civil rights movements.

145. There was a good deal of discord and, ultimately, mutual accommodation within the diverse quarters of the movement, marking the process around which these events were organized. For the gory details see Halsted, *Out Now,* and Gitlin, *The Sixties,* for the antiwar movement as a whole, and Hunt, *The Turning,* for VVAW in particular. Also see "That's Vietnam, Jake," my review of *Home to War: A History of the Vietnam Veterans' Movement,* by Gerald Nicosia, in *The Nation,* July 9, 2001, and the exchange of letters "Vietnam Vets — Home to Roost" between the author and myself in *The Nation,* September 17–24, 2001.

146. Dewey Canyon I and II were the operational names for U.S.-backed invasions of Laos during 1969, and in February 1971. For accounts and documents concerning the U.S. secret war in Laos, see, for example, Gettleman et al., eds., *Vietnam and America* (New York: Grove Press, 1995).

147. For a lively account of this event, see Roger Daniels, *The Bonus March: An Episode of the Great Depression* (Westport, Ct.: Greenwood Publishing Co., 1971).

148. See Hunt, *The Turning,* for a detailed account of the organization of Dewey Canyon III, and of the legal maneuvering surrounding the decision to allow the encampment to occupy the mall.

149. Hunt.

150. Personal communication, May 2000.

151. In his memoir *Lying Down with The Lions: A Public Life from the Streets of Oakland to the Halls of Power,* with H. Lee Halterman (Beacon Press, 2000), Ronald V. Dellums recounts his confrontation with then House Majority Leader, Carl Albert, who, when learning of the purpose for which Dellums had reserved the Cannon Caucus Room, and unable to cancel a member's right to do so, stipulated that no media be allowed in the room. Dellums writes that, "with his [Albert's] grudging approval and now constrained by these rules, we marched forward to educate the American people about the illegality and horror being committed in their name." Perhaps Dellums had forgotten that, if Albert had indeed imposed this condition, the freshman Congressman from Oakland apparently

chose to defy him. We had good media attendance at the hearings, and pretty fair coverage.

152. John W. Finney, "Liberals Seek 'War Crimes' Inquiry," *The New York Times,* March 31, 1971.

153. A transcript of these hearings, while little cited in the literature of Vietnam, was recorded and published as an original paperback, *The Dellums Committee Hearings on War Crimes in Vietnam,* ed. Citizens' Commission of Inquiry (Vintage, 1972).

154. Ibid.

155. Ibid.

156. See, for example, "Most Feel Calley Was Scapegoat," *The New York Post,* March 30, 1971. For one front page article linking directly the prowar position of the defendant's chief counsel, George Latimer, with the antiwar perspective of Congressman Ron Dellums, see "Calley Lawyer, Congressman Agree, My Lai Verdict Is Denounced," *The Providence Journal,* March 30, 1971.

157. For the full text of Danny Notley's testimony, see *Dellums Committee Hearings.*

158. Richard Halloran, "Ex G.I. Alleges 30 Slayings Near Mylai," *The New York Times,* April 29, 1971.

159. *Dellums Committee Hearings.*

160. *Voices from the Plain of Jars: Life under an Air War* (Harper and Row, 1972). These children's drawings from Laos are the closest analogy from the Indochina War to the visual records of the disaster drawings of Jacques Callot and Francisco Goya.

161. Lynn Newerland, "Another My Lai?," *New York Post,* May 10, 1971.

162. *New York Post,* May 10, 1971.

163. Kevin Buckley, "Pacification's Deadly Price," *Newsweek,* June 19, 1972.

164. *New York Post,* May 10, 1971.

165. Michael Getler, "Notley Urges U.S. Inquiry on War Tactics," *Washington Post,* May 11, 1971.

166. "For a War Crimes Inquiry," editorial, *Newsday,* March 22, 1971. *Newsday* was then being published by Bill Moyers, at one time LBJ's press secretary, and a political observer who often speaks and writes like a genuine American radical.

167. Neil Sheehan, "Should We Have War Crimes Trials?," *New York Times Book Review,* March 28, 1971.

168. Interview with John Leonard, April 4, 1995. At the time of Sheehan's review, Leonard was the *Times Book Review* editor.

169. Leonard interview.

170. Leonard interview.

171. Sheehan, "Should We Have War Crimes Trials?"; *The New York Times* began its coverage of the Pentagon Papers, under Neil Sheehan's byline, on June 13, 1971.

172. Raphael Littauer and Normal Uphoff, eds., *Air War in Indochina* (Beacon Press, 1972).

173. While I have been unable to locate any evidence of coverage for this event, I recall quite vividly the identities of the two journalists, Erwin Knoll of the *Progressive* and Stuart Lurie of the *Cleveland Plain Dealer*.

174. As a family man, Bob Johnson had responsibilities his CCI comrades were oblivious to, so initially our parting was around such practical differences. Later Johnson's politics seemed to veer sharply rightward when he published a board game about welfare that promoted gross stereotypes of African Americans — after which contact between Bob and the rest of us ceased.

175. Sometime before May Day, I was on a platform at the University of Pittsburgh which consisted of two speakers, Rennie Davis and myself. From what I heard that day Davis was a gifted orator. We spoke indoors at a rally, standing room only; I must have been there as bait for any students registered on the G.I. Bill. And, as I have said, antiwar vets were by now getting to be crowd-pleasers in their own right.

176. Letter dated May 11, 1971, Cornell collection.

177. For one interesting take on the *Casper Hauser* myth, a child completely deprived of human contact in his formative years, procure the film of the same name by Werner Herzog.

178. Kenneth J. Campbell, "The International War Crimes Conference, Oslo, June 1971: Excerpts from the Diary of One of the Witnesses," in *Nobody Gets Off The Bus; The Vietnam Generation Big Book* (1994).

179. Lerner's initial claim to movement fame stemmed from his being a member of the Seattle Eight, "defendants in a case similar to the Chicago 'conspiracy' trial." Halsted, *Out Now.*

180. NAM, the New American Movement, eventually merged with DSOC, the Democratic Socialist Organizing Committee, renamed as DSA, Democratic Socialists of America, thus reuniting elements of the New Left with their former mentors, Michael Harrington and Irving Howe in particular. The single issue that most divided these two factions in the organization's early years was the Palestinian Question; now DSA seems to have slipped into its permanent role as a left wing caucus of the Democratic Party. For Michael Lerner's sketch of NAM's brief existence, see Mari Jo Buhle, et al., eds., *Encyclopedia of the American Left* (University of Illinois Press, 1992).

181. See, for example, Lynd's *Intellectual Origins of American Radicalism* (Vintage, 1969).

182. Tod and I would later write an "organizing chapter" for *The Red White and Blue Left* (Lyle Stuart, 1972), an anthology of essays, including one of his own, and one by Staughton Lynd, that Jeremy would assemble. Our chapter entitled "You Don't Have to Be a Weatherman to Make the Wind Blow" never made it into print, but there's one fuzzy passage in the manuscript — quite representative of New Left political evangelism — that attempts to capture CCI's emphasis on organizing among "white Middle Americans" within our "post-industrial" society: "Is there one essential social or economic class, or racial group that it is absolutely essential to mobilize before fundamental change can occur? Is this sector a numerical minority whose constituents are defined by the relationship to purely industrial production? We don't think so. For whites, traditional class lines have already blurred so thoroughly that no two radical sect-parties can agree on definitions of the 'working class,' 'middle class,' 'technical class,' etc. Ultimately, the solution for minority nations (Blacks, Puerto Ricans, Chicanos, etc.) within white America will be harmonious with that of the majority — if we are successful in winning basic social change.... Perhaps Malcolm X best understood this when he continuously articulated the necessity for socially conscious whites to focus their energies on organizing and educating people in their own communities — rather than struggling vicariously by championing the cause of Black people. Clearly only by revolutionizing the white power structure which directs the forces of oppression can the self-determination of the non-white nations within America be guaranteed." Thanks to Tod Ensign for a copy of this manuscript in draft.

183. It might be argued that this objective was later achieved when elements of NAM merged into the Democratic Socialists of America. NAM was also apparently quite vis-

ible in the larger Woman's Movement of that period (see Buhle, *Encyclopedia of the American Left*).

184. Knoll and McFadden, *War Crimes*.

185. Daniel Rapoport, "Ex-Agent Tells of Military Murders in Vietnam," *The Washington Post* (UPI), August 2, 1971.

186. Thus was the significance of our roles described by the *Washington Post's* Mary McGrory in a column, "A Policy of Death," in the *New York Post*, August 7, 1971, where McGrory was substituting for vacationing regular columnist James A. Wechsler.

187. Felix Belair Jr., "U.S. Aide Defends Pacification Program in Vietnam Despite Killings of Civilians," *The New York Times*, July 20, 1971.

188. Mary McGrory, "A Policy of Death."

189. "They all died: Agent lists atrocities by Marines," *Washington Daily News* (UPI), August 3, 1971.

190. Michael J. Uhl, Statement Before the Foreign Operations and Government Information Subcommittee, Congressional Record, August 2, 1971.

191. The next major flare up of public opposition to the war occurred with Nixon's brutal bombings of Hanoi and Haiphong during Christmas 1972. The destruction of the Bac Mai hospital in Hanoi, coupled with a campaign to raise medical aid for all Indochina's victims, became a focus of various New Left groupings in the ebbing phases of the war. Bombing hospitals is a violation of every law of warfare; clearly, concern over American conduct of the war among antiwar forces continued right to the end. For a detailed account of the organizational history of the Antiwar Movement during its final months, see Halsted, *Out Now*.

192. This point appears frequently in the literature. See, for example, James William Gibson, "Revising Vietnam, Again: A new history agues that Kennedy might have pulled us out," *Harpers Magazine*, April 2000. Gibson is the author of *The Perfect War: Technowar in Vietnam* (Atlantic Monthly Press, recently reissued).

193. Both Tod and Jeremy had established non-profit foundations to support their work; for years, I sat on both these boards.

194. "New Committee Announces Plan to Support and Defend Vietnam Veterans and Other 'Deserters' Who Will Be Returning to U.S. from Exile," press release for a press conference at the Roosevelt Hotel in New York, February 3, 1972, which generated several news accounts; "Map Test Trial of Deserters," *Daily News*, Feb. 4, 1972; "New Group Will Assist Deserters," *New York Post*, Feb. 3, 1972. Cornell Collection.

195. This work was the subject of a book by James Reston Jr., *Amnesty of John David Herndon*. The most dramatic return we sponsored involved an elaborate plan, perfectly executed, to surrender Marine Corps deserter Tommy Michaud on the floor of the July '72 Democratic Presidential Convention in Miami, prompting Walter Cronkite to interrupt his broadcast and inquire, "Roger Mudd, what's going on down there in the California delegation?" Sheila Payton, "Deserter's Surrender a Way of Opposing War: Deserter 'Surrenders' on Convention Floor," *Miami Herald*, July 15, 1972. Heavy national publicity helped win Michaud a quick administrative discharge.

196. Fox Butterfield, "War Hasn't Changed for the Men Who Stay Behind; The Americal Division Ends Role in Vietnam," *New York Times*, November 12, 1971.

197. William Beecher, "General, Ex-Aide Accused of Murdering Vietnamese," *New York Times*, June 3, 1971. News of charges being dropped against Donaldson was also reported in the *New York Times*, December 10, 1971.

198. Oxford University Press, 1978.

199. *Why We Were in Vietnam* (Simon and Schuster, 1982).

200. Meyrowitz and Campbell, "Vietnam Veterans and the War Crimes Hearings" (italics in the original), in *An American Ordeal: The Antiwar Movement of the Vietnam Era* (Syracuse University Press, 1990).

201. The quotation is borrowed from Edmund Wilson in *Patriotic Gore* (Norton, 1994). Wilson was referring expressly to the Salem Witch Trials, though he might have expanded the list — beyond the examples I enumerate above — to include the Mexican War, the Philippines, Central America, and others.

Bibliography

Books

Ali, Tariq. 1987. *Street Fighting Years*. Collins.

Allen, Douglas and Ngo Vinh Long. 1991. *Coming to Terms: Indochina, The United States, and the War in Vietnam*. Boulder, CO: Westview Press.

Appy, Christian G. 1993. *Working-Class War: American Combat Soldiers in Vietnam*. Chapel Hill: University of North Carolina Press.

Bao Ninh. 1991. *Sorrow of War*. London: Secker and Warberg.

Barry, Jan and W.D. Ehrhart, eds. 1976. *Demilitarized Zone: Veterans After Vietnam*. Perkasie, PA: East River Anthology.

Beresford, Melanie. 1988. *Vietnam: Politics, Economics and Society*. London: Pinter.

Berman, Larry. 1989. *Lyndon Johnson's War*. New York: W.W. Norton.

Bilton, Michael and Kevin Sim. 1993. *Four Hours in My Lai*. New York: Penguin.

Bourne, Peter G. 1970. *Men, Stress, and Vietnam*. Boston: Little Brown and Co.

Burchett, Wilfred. 1978. *Catapult to Freedom: The Survival of the Vietnamese People*. London: Quartet Books.

Buttinger, Joseph. 1977. *Vietnam: The Unforgettable Tragedy*. New York: Horizon.

Chanda, Nayan. 1986. *Brother Enemy: The War After the War, a History of Indochina After the Fall of Saigon*. New York: Macmillan, Collier Books.

Chomsky, Noam. 1970. *At War with Asia*. New York: Pantheon Books.

_____. 1973. *For Reasons of State*. New York: Vintage.

_____. 1987. *The Chomsky Reader*. Ed. James Peck. New York: Pantheon.

_____. 1993. *Rethinking Camelot: JFK, the Vietnam War, and US Political Culture*. Boston: South End Press.

Cortwright, David. 1975. *Soldiers in Revolt*. Garden City, New York: Doubleday.

Daly, James A. and Lee Bergman. 2000. *Black Prisoner of War: A Conscientious Objector's Vietnam Memoir*. Lawrence, Kansas: University of Kansas Press.

Dreze, Jean and Amartya Sen, eds. 1990. *The Political Economy of Hunger: Entitlement and Well Being*. London: Oxford University Press.

DSM IIIR. 1987. *Diagnostic and Statistical Manual of Mental Disorders*. American Psychiatric Association. Section 309.89 on post-traumatic stress disorder.

DSM IV. 1994. *Diagnostic and Statistical Manual of Mental Disorders*. American Psychiatric Association. Section 309.81 on post-traumatic stress disorder.

Duiker, William. 1983. *Vietnam: Nation in Revolution*. Boulder, CO: Westview Press.

_____. 1981. *The Communist Road to Power in Vietnam*. Boulder, CO: Westview Press.

_____. 1980. *Vietnam Since the Fall of Saigon*. Athens: Ohio University, Center for International Studies.

Ehrhart, W.D. 1985. *Carrying the Darkness: American Indo-China —The Poetry of the Vietnam War*. New York: Avon.

_____. 1995. *Busted: A Vietnam Veteran in Nixon's America*. Amherst, MA: University of Massachusetts Press.

Ellsberg, Daniel. 1972. *Papers on the War*. New York: Simon and Schuster.

Fforde, Adam. 1989. *The Agrarian Question in North Vietnam, 1974–1979*. New York: M.E. Sharpe.

Franklin, H. Bruce. 2000. *Vietnam and Other American Fantasies*. Amherst, MA: University of Massachusetts Press.

_____. 1993. *M.I.A. or Mythmaking in America: How and Why Belief in Live POWs Has Possessed a Nation*. New Brunswick, NJ: University of Rutgers Press.

Frey-Wouters, Ellen and Robert S. Laufer. 1986. *Legacy of a War: The American Soldier in Vietnam*. New York: Basis Books.

Gelb, Leslie H. with Richard K. Betts. 1979. *The Irony of Vietnam: The System Worked*. Washington, D.C.: The Brookings Institute.

Gerber, David A., ed. 2000. *Disabled Veterans in History*. Ann Arbor, MI: University of Michigan Press.

Gettleman, Marvin E., et al. 1995. *Vietnam and America: The Most Comprehensive Documented History of the Vietnam War*. New York: Grove Press.

Gibson, James William. 1988. *The Perfect War: The War We Couldn't Lose and How We Did*. New York: Vintage Books.

Gitlin, Todd. 1980. *The Whole World Is Watching*. Berkeley, CA: University of California Press.

_____.1993. *The Sixties: Years of Hope, Days of Rage*. New York: Bantam Books.

Graff, Henry. 1970. *The Tuesday Cabinet*. Englewood Cliffs, NJ: Prentice Hall.

Halsted, Fred. 1978. *Out Now: A Participants Account of the American Movement Against the Vietnam War*. New York: Monad Press.

Hallock, Daniel. 1998. *Hell, Healing and Resistance: Veterans Speak*. Farmington, PA: The Plough Publishing House.

Helmer, John. 1974. *Bringing the War Home: The American Soldier in Vietnam and After*. New York: Simon and Schuster.

Hendin, Herbert and Ann Pollinger Haas. 1984. *Wounds of War: The Psychological Aftermath of Combat in Vietnam*. New York: Basic Books.

Herman, Judith Lewis, M.D. 1992. *Trauma and Recovery*. New York: Basic Books.

Herring, George C. 1986. *America's Longest War: The United States and Vietnam, 1950–1975*. New York: Knopf.

_____, ed. 1983. *The Secret Diplomacy of the Vietnam War: The Negotiating Volumes of the Pentagon Papers*. Austin, TX: University of Texas Press.

Hersh, Seymour M. 1972. *Cover-Up: The Army's Secret Investigation of the Massacre at My Lai 4*. New York: Random House.

Ho Anh Thai. 1998. *Behind the Red Mist*. Chief translator: Nguyen Qui Duc. Willimantic, CT: Curbstone Press.

Hunt, Andrew Emerson. 1997. *The Turning Point: Vietnam Veterans Against the War: 1967 to the Present*. Dissertation, University of Utah. New York University Press: forthcoming.

Huynh Kim Khanh. 1986. *Vietnamese Communism 1925–1945*. Ithaca, NY: University of Cornell Press.

Jade Ngoc Quang Huynh. 1994. *South Wind Changing*. St. Paul, MN: University of Minnesota Press.

Joseph, Paul. 1981. *Cracks in the Empire*. Boston: Little Brown.

Kahin, George McT. 1986. *Intervention: How America Became Involved in Vietnam*. New York: Knopf.

Karlin, Wayne. 1998. *Prisoners*. Willimantic, CT: Curbstone Press.

_____. 1997. *Rumors and Stones*. Willimantic, CT: Curbstone Press.

Keegan, John. 1976. *The Face of Battle*. New York: Penguin Books.

Kerry, John, and Vietnam Veterans Against the War. 1971. *The New Soldier*. Ed. David Thorne and George Butler. New York: Macmillan.

Kimball, Jeffrey P. 1990. *The Reason Why: The Debate About the Causes of U.S. Involvement in the Vietnam War*. New York: McGraw Hill.

Kimura, Tetsusabureo. 1986. *Vietnam, International Relations and Economic Development*. Tokyo.

Kinnard, Douglas. 1977. *The War Managers*. Hanover, NH: University Press of New England.

Kolko, Gabriel. 1994 (Reprint). *Anatomy of a War: Vietnam, the United States and the Modern Historical Experience*. New York: The New Press.

_____. 1994. *Century of War: Politics, Conflicts, and Society Since 1914*. New York: The New Press.

Lembcke, Jerry. 1998. *The Spitting Image: Myth, Memory, and the Legacy of Vietnam*. New York: New York University Press.

Lewy, Guenther. 1978. *America in Vietnam*. New York: Oxford University Press.

Littauer, Raphael and Norman Uphoff, eds. 1972. *The Air War in Indochina*. Boston: Beacon Press.

Linton, Simi. 1998. *Claiming Disability: Knowledge and Identity*. New York: New York University Press.

Marr, David G. 1971. *Vietnamese Anti-Colonialism, 1885–1925*. Berkeley, CA: University of California Press.

_____. 1981. *Vietnamese Tradition on Trial, 1920–1945*. Berkeley, CA: University of California Press.

_____. 1995. *Vietnam 1945: The Quest for Power*. Berkeley, CA: University of California Press.

Marr, David G., and Christine P. White, eds. *Postwar Vietnam Dilemmas in Socialist Development*. Ithaca, NY: Cornell University Press.

Moser, Richard. 1996. *The New Winter Soldiers: GI and Veteran Dissent During the Vietnam Era*. New Brunswick, NJ: Rutgers University Press.

Moyar, Mark. 1997. *Phoenix and the Birds of Prey: The CIA's Secret Campaign to Destroy the Viet Cong*. Annapolis, MD: Naval Institute Press.

Mulligan, John. 1997. *Shopping Cart Soldiers*. Willimantic, CT: Curbstone Press.

Ngo Vinh Long. 1973. *Before the Revolution: The Vietnamese Peasants Under the French*. Cambridge, MA: Harvard University Press.

Ngo Vinh Long and Nguyen Hoi-Chan. 1974. *Vietnamese Women in Society and Revolution*. Cambridge, MA: Harvard University Press.

Nguyen Khac Vien. 1974. *Tradition and Revolution in Vietnam*. Berkeley, CA: University of California Press.

_____. 1978. *The Long Resistance, 1858–1975*. Hanoi: The Gioi Publishers.

Nguyen Thi Dinh. 1976. *No Other Road to Take*. Ithaca, NY: Cornell University Press.

Palmer, Gregory. 1978. *The McNamara Strategy and the Vietnam War*. Westport, CT: Praeger.

Patti, Archimedes L.A. 1980. *Why Vietnam: Prelude to America's Albatross*. Berkeley, CA: University of California Press.

The Pentagon Papers. 1971. *New York Times* edition. 1 vol. New York: Bantam Books.

The Pentagon Papers. 1971. Senator Gravel edition. 5 vol. Boston: Beacon Press.

Pike, Douglas. 1986. *PAVN: People's Army of Vietnam*. Novato, CA: Presidio.

_____. 1969. *War, Peace and the Vietcong*. Cambridge, MA: MIT Press.

Porter, Gareth. 1993. *Vietnam: The Politics of Bureaucratic Socialism*. Ithaca, NY: Cornell University Press.

_____. 1975. *A Peace Denied: The United States, Vietnam and the Paris Agreements*. Bloomington, IN: University of Indiana Press.

_____. 1975. *The Myth of the Bloodbath: North Vietnam's Land Reform Program Reconsidered.* Ithaca, NY: Cornell University Press.

Powers, Thomas. 1973. *Vietnam: The War at Home.* New York:

Quirk, Rory. 1999. *Wars and Peace: The Memoir of an American Family.* Oakland, CA: Presidio.

Race, Jeffrey. 1972. *War Comes to Long An: Revolutionary Conflict in a Vietnamese Province.* Berkeley, CA: University of California Press.

Rottmann, Larry, et al., eds. 1972. *Winning Hearts and Minds: War Poems by Vietnam Veterans.* Brooklyn, NY: First Casualty Press.

Salisbury, Harrison, ed. 1984. *Vietnam Reconsidered.* New York: Harper and Row.

Schell, Jonathan. 1988. *The Real War.* New York: Pantheon Books.

Schroeder, Eric James. 1992. *Vietnam, We've All Been There: Interviews with American Writers.* Westport, CT: Praeger.

Schultz, Ruth and Bud. 1989. *It Did Happen Here: Recollections of Political Repression in America.* Berkeley, CA: University of California Press.

Severo, Richard, and Lewis Milford. 1989. *The Wages of War: When America's Soldiers Come Home — From Valley Forge to Vietnam.* New York: Simon and Schuster.

Sheehan, Neil. 1992. *After the War Was Over.* New York: Vintage.

_____. 1989. *A Bright Shining Lie: John Paul Vann and America in Vietnam.* New York: Random House.

Skocpol, Theda. 1992. *Protecting Soldiers and Mothers: The Political Origins of Social Policy in the United States.* Cambridge, MA: The Belknap Press of Harvard University Press.

Small, Melvin and William D. Hoover, eds. 1993. *Give Peace a Chance: Exploring the Vietnam Antiwar Movement.* Syracuse, NY: Syracuse University Press.

Smith, Ralph B. 1983. *Revolution Versus Containment.* New York: Palgrave Macmillan.

Solis, Gary D. 1997. *Son Thang: An American War Crime.* Annapolis, MD: Naval Institute Press.

Stanton, Shelby L. 1985. *The Rise and Fall of an American Army: U.S. Ground Forces in Vietnam 1965–1973.* Oakland, CA: Presidio.

Starr, Paul. 1973. *The Discarded Army: The Veteran After Vietnam. The Nader Report on Vietnam Veterans and the Veterans Administration.* New York: Charterhouse.

Thompson, James Clay. 1980. *Rolling Thunder: Understanding Policy and Program Failure.* Chapel Hill, NC: University of North Carolina Press.

Tran Van Tra. 1983. *Vietnam: History of the Bulwark B-2 Theater.* Vol. 5: Concluding the 30 Years' War. Ho Chi Minh City: FBIS translation.

Trung Nhu Tang. 1986. *A Vietcong Memoir: An Inside Account of the Vietnam War.* New York: Vintage.

Turley, William S. and Mark Selden, eds. 1993. *Reinventing Vietnamese Socialism: Doi Moi in Comparative Perspective.* Boulder, CO: Westview Press.

Werner, Jane and David Hunt, eds. 1993. *The American War in Vietnam.* Ithaca, NY: Cornell University Press.

Uhl, Michael, and Tod Ensign. 1980. *G.I. Guinea Pigs: How the Pentagon Exposed Out Troops to Dangers More Deadly Than War.* New York: Playboy Press.

Wiegersman, Nancy. 1988. *Vietnam: Peasant Land, Peasant Revolution.* New York: St. Martin's Press.

Williams, Michael C. 1992. *Vietnam at the Crossroads.* London: Cambridge University Press.

Woodside, Alexander. 1976. *Community and Revolution in Modern Vietnam.* Boston: Little Brown.

van der Kolk, Bessel A., et al., eds. 1996. *Traumatic Stress: The Effects of Overwhelming Experiences on Mind, Body and Society.* New York: The Guildford Press.

Van Dyke, Jonathan. 1972. *North Vietnam's Strategy for Survival.* Palo Alto, CA: University of Stanford Press.

Veterans Administration. 1977. *"Data on Vietnam Era Veterans."* Washington, D.C. Veterans Administration.

Vietnamese Studies: 1965–1980. Various editions. Hanoi.

Young, Marilyn. 1991. *The Vietnam War: 1945–1990.* New York: Harper Perennial.

Articles

Brigham, Robert K. and Martin J. Murray. "Conflicting Interpretations of the Viet Nam War," *The Bulletin of Concerned Asian Scholars* 26, no. 1 (Jan–Mar 1994).

Brightman, Carol. "The Vet Fetish," a review of *Long Time Passing* by Myra MacPherson. *The Nation,* June 23, 1984.

Brightman, Carol, and Michael Uhl. "Bombing for the Hell of It," a review of *In Retrospect: The Tragedy and Lessons of Vietnam,* by Robert S. McNamara. *The Nation,* June 12, 1995.

Butterfield, Fox. "The New Vietnam Scholarship." *New York Times Magazine,* February 13, 1983, 26–32, 45–60.

Chen, King. "Hanoi's Three Decisions and the Escalation of the Vietnam War." *Political Science Quarterly* 90 (Summer 1975): 239–259.

Chomsky, Noam. "Visions of Righteousness." *Cultural Critique* 3 (Spring 1986): 10–43.

FBIS: Daily Report of the U.S. Foreign Broadcast Information Service: East Asia.

Hess, Gary R. "The Unending Debate: Historians and the Vietnam War." *Diplomatic History* 18 (Spring 1994): 239–264.

Kahin, George McT. "The Pentagon Papers: A Critical Evaluation." *APSR* LXIX (June 1975): 675–684.

Long, Ngo Vinh. "Reform and Rural Development: Impacts on Class, Sectoral, and Regional Inequalities," in Turley and Selden, eds. 1993.

Meyrowitz, Elliott L., and Kenneth J. Campbell. "Vietnam Veterans and War Crimes Hearings," in *An American Ordeal: The Antiwar Movement of the Vietnam Era.* Syracuse University Press, 1990.

Shay, Jonathan. "The Betrayal of 'What's Right': Vietnam Combat Veterans and Post-Traumatic Stress Disorder." *The Long Term View: A Journal of Informed Opinion* 5, no. 1, Massachusetts School of Law, 2000.

Thomson, James "How Could Vietnam Happen? An Autopsy." *Atlantic Monthly,* April 1968, 47–53.

The World Bank, East Asia and Pacific Region. *Vietnam: Transition to the Market.* Washington, September 1993.

Uhl, Michael. 1994. "Searching for Vietnam's M.I.A.s." *The Nation,* November 14, 1994.

_____. "Travels with Charlie." A review of *Dues: A Novel* and After, by Michael H. Cooper, and *Playing Basketball with the Viet Cong,* by Kevin Bowen. *The Nation,* February 27, 1995.

_____. "The God That Resigned." A review of *Anatomy of a War: Vietnam, the United States, and the Modern Historical Experience,* by Gabriel Kolko. *The Progressive,* February 1995.

_____. "How We Bombed in Laos." A review of *Back Fire: The CIA's Secret War in Laos,* by Roger Warner. *The Washington Post Book World,* Sunday September 17, 1995.

_____. "On the Lam from Vietnam." A review of *Busted: A Vietnam Veteran in Nixon's America,* by W.D. Ehrhart. *The Nation,* September 18, 1995.

_____. "Homo Vietveticus." A review of *The Things We Do to Make It Home,* by Beverly Gologorsky. Unpublished.

_____. "Obsessed by Vietnam." A book review of *Our War: What We Did in Vietnam And What It Did to Us* by David Harris. *The Dissident,* June 1997.

_____. "War and Madness." A review of *Hell Healing Resistance: Veterans Speak,* by Daniel Hallock. *Peaceworks,* December 1998/January 1999.

_____. "The Jaws of Victory: a historian argues we could have won — and nearly did — the Vietnam War." A review of *A Better War: Final Tragedy of American's Last Years in Vietnam,* by Lewis Sorely. *The Boston Sunday Globe,* August 1, 1999.

_____. "That's Vietnam, Jake." A review of *Home to War: A History of the Vietnam Veterans' Movement*, by Gerald Nicosia, in *The Nation*, July 9, 2001; and the exchange of letters "Vietnam Vets — Home to Roost" between the author and myself in *The Nation*, September 17/24, 2001.

_____. "From Heartland to Heart of Darkness." A review of *When I Was a Young Man: A Memoir*, by Bob Kerrey. *The Boston Sunday Globe*, June 16, 2002.

_____. "War and Remembrance." A review of *The Education of Lieutenant Kerrey*, by Gregory L. Vistica. *The Boston Sunday Globe*, February 16, 2003.

_____. "Warriors for Peace." *The Nation*, August 24, 2003.

_____. "Kerry and the Year of the Veteran." *Bangor Daily News*, March 18, 2004.

_____. "Vietnam's Shadow over Abu Ghraib." *AntiWar.com*, July 31, 2004.

_____. "A Skillful Chronicle of Kerry's Conflicts." A review of *Tour of Duty*, by Douglas Brinkley. *The Boston Sunday Globe*, January 5, 2005.

_____. "Combat and Reconciliation." A review of *Black Virgin Mountain: A Return to Vietnam*, by Larry Heinemann. *The Boston Sunday Globe*, June 26, 2005.

_____. "The Politics of PTDS." *The Bangor Daily News*, March 9, 2006.

Index